Love At Second Sight

ROBERTA RENK

WESTBOW
PRESS
A DIVISION OF THOMAS NELSON

WestBow Press books may be ordered through booksellers or by contacting:

WestBow Press
A Division of Thomas Nelson
1663 Liberty Drive
Bloomington, IN 47403
www.westbowpress.com
1-(866) 928-1240

ISBN: 978-1-4497-1100-9 (sc)
ISBN: 978-1-4497-1101-6 (hc)
ISBN: 978-1-4497-1099-6 (e)

Library of Congress Control Number: 2010943367

Printed in the United States of America

WestBow Press rev. date: 02/08/2011

To Bob:

You are my forever love, and I am at peace because you are totally healed.

To God:

You alone know the desires of my heart, because you placed them in me. Thank you for inspiring me to be all I am. I am so proud to be your child.

Contents

Preface

I first intended to write this book as a memoir for my husband. I also wanted it to be used as an encouragement for all those fighting cancer and for their loved ones as they stood by helplessly trying to just be supportive. It definitely was meant to be an inspiration, but that was only the motivation that started me writing. I really did not know where this story would take me, but I can tell you that I was on a real journey as I wrote about my life and poured out my heart to you. You see, at first, I had a narrow vision about this project, and my focus was on cancer. As I continued to write, I realized it was not cancer, but death that I feared. Now, I want you to understand that I feared the death of the physical body, not eternal death. As I walked in the face of death throughout my husband's battle, I chose not to look death in the face. I looked beyond death to the bright light I saw in the distance, and the closer death came, the brighter the light shone. Even when Bob died on October 11, 2008, my focus was still on that light.

Bob and I never talked about that light using these words, but we did talk about Jesus and his healing power. We also talked about heaven and eternity. We did not speak about this all the time, but our faith in heaven and eternal life was just an underlying truth. It was similar to the love we had for one another. We would say, "I love you," but that was not always spoken aloud, either. We would say it in the holding of hands or in a look we would give or maybe in a gentle touch or smile. We knew it was there as sure as we lived and breathed.

As I continued writing, the story seemed to be about my life, too, and about my walk with Jesus. Memories of my childhood with Jesus came flooding back, and I was reminded of how I prayed daily for my grandfather to be healed from his stroke. He never was healed in earthly terms, but praying for him brought me before God at an early age of maybe four or five. I can tell you that by the time I made my first communion, I prayed for my grandfather every day. I would sit at my grandfather's feet, and he would look at me and smile his crooked smile as I would recite "Mary Had a Little Lamb." Every so often, he would reach out and hold my hand and squeeze it. Even though my grandfather could not speak, I knew he loved me and I loved him, and that experience, in part, made me who I am today.

As I write this, I realize that praying for others has been a part of what God has called me to do. I have a heart to pray for those in need of a healing. My grandmother prayed several times every day, and she set an example for me about connecting to God. Even though my prayer life is different from hers, our desire to come before God in prayer has been the same. That desire is a part of my heritage from both my earthly and spiritual relatives.

I have come to appreciate how special a relationship with grandparents can be, too, and not just for the grandchild. Megan, our oldest granddaughter, is the person I can talk to about Bob the most, because she talks to me about him all of the time. She is not at all uncomfortable speaking about him, because he is in heaven, and in her mind that means he is still alive and with us. We share about our memories of him and about missing him, and we have grieved together in the past. She and I seem to have arrived at the same place now. We have joy knowing he is in heaven. We also talk about how he can see some of the happy things that are going on in our lives and about how we will be together one day when we are all in heaven. When one of her classmates lost her grandma, Megan told her, "Oh, now your grandma will be with my Poppy, and they can be friends." That is just the way her seven-year-old mind thinks, and she doesn't fear death. Megan and I are starting to memorize Bible verses together and also learning the books of the Bible. I am learning from her, too, and it is great. When I think of how special my grandmother was to me and realize that I have that relationship with my grandchildren, I know I am so blessed.

I am excited to know that Megan, her four-year-old brother Ryan, and her five-year-old cousin Sarah will all read this book one day. I told Megan about the meaning of the title, and she had the normal reaction to the love of a boy and girl that most seven-year-olds have, and that was "yuck." Then I heard her repeat the story of how Bob and I met, and her reaction was just a big smile.

You see, everyone does love a love story, which is why, I believe, I was called to write this story. It is also a love story about how much God loves me. I feel in my heart that God wants me to share this with you so that you may come to believe he loves you, too. He hears my prayers. To know that the creator of the universe hears me when I pray is more awesome than any miracle that has happened in my life. To think God is bending his ear to hear me, yes *me*, is the most wonderful, marvelous, awe inspiring, and precious knowledge that I could have. It is so simple, but to many, it is so unbelievable. I pray that after reading this book, you will understand that God is listening to you and that you will know how powerful this can be in your life. I hope with all of my heart that you will ponder that and come to have all the love, joy, peace, patience, kindness, goodness, faithfulness, gentleness, and self-control that God can give to those who know he is only a whisper away.

Acknowledgments

Thank you …

God, the greatest healer, and thank you for using the following special people along the way to accomplish your will.

Dr. Arnold Fingeret, for rechecking the liver and finding the three tumors when performing Bob's initial surgery.

Dr. Bridget McCandliss, for being an encourager in the face of death and for not giving up.

Dr. Martin Earle, for being aggressive with the chemotherapy treatments and going to bat for Bob so that he could get his liver surgery when all seemed hopeless.

Dr. Joseph Homann, for not giving up after finding five tumors in Bob's liver and for performing a great surgery.

Dr. Paul Chervenick, for treating Bob with chemotherapy, listening to Bob complain about how he hated it, and encouraging him to do just a little more.

Dr. Barthel, for being thorough in your work and having that meaningful talk with me.

Dr. Karl, for taking a vigorous approach in attempting to save Bob's life.

Dr. Chris Garrett, for seeing Bob first as a person and then as a patient and for not giving him chemotherapy when it was a time for rest.

Dr. James Schmotzer, for fighting the fight, encouraging Bob to seek radiation when the cancer went to his brain, and giving us those precious extra months.

Dr. Richard Becker, for taking care of me during Bob's illness and helping to ensure that Bob died with two perfect legs.

Dr. Christopher Willet, for intervening on Bob's behalf and being my best doctor friend when I was desperate at Duke.

Dr. Michael Miller, for being willing to do a personal favor that added almost two years to Bob's life. The third time was a charm, and God did the rest.

Ted Goldberg, our attorney friend, for looking into Bob's medical history and encouraging us to file the lawsuit.

Neil Rosen, for fighting for patients' rights, being a great lawyer when we needed one the most, and helping Bob learn the truth that he was a perfect patient.

All of the countless doctors who treated Bob at the ER and during all of the other numerous outpatient treatments. You are just too numerous to mention individually, but I thank you.

Jefferson Memorial Hospital, Pittsburgh, Pennsylvania

Western Pennsylvania Hospital, Pittsburgh, Pennsylvania

H. Lee Moffitt Hospital, Tampa, Florida

Duke University Hospital, Durham, North Carolina

Pinehurst Medical Hospital, Pinehurst, North Carolina

Aultman Hospital, Canton, Ohio

Mercy Hospital, Canton, Ohio

All of the nurses who took care of Bob in so many ways, from giving him pills and shots to taking care of his personal needs, and for just laughing with Bob along the way. Also, for being there for me and supporting me. A special thank you to the nurse at Duke who told me I was the strongest woman she had ever met when I was feeling the weakest. You helped me to go on when I was exhausted and didn't think I could make it one more day.

All of the medical personnel for your parts in giving CAT scans, X-rays, PET scans, and chemotherapy treatments, as well as for performing lab work.

All of the non-medical personnel who took care of my husband during so many hospital visits that I've lost count. Whether you prepared his meal or cleaned his room, you matter.

I know Bob had at least twenty inpatient stays and numerous ER visits, outpatient surgeries, and chemotherapy and radiation treatments. I would venture to say that over one thousand people touched my husband's life in some way during his fight with cancer. There were other doctors, too, who treated my husband over these thirteen years, and you know who you are. This is for you, too.

Bob was truly blessed to receive such excellent care through all of you.

Everybody Loves a Love Story

Everybody loves a love story, which is why I decided to share my life, or at least the best part of my life so far, with you. Where to start? It was 1976, and I was recently divorced and living in Penn Hills, a suburb of Pittsburgh, PA. Prior to that, I had been having the worst time of my life in the middle of a crumbling marriage, and I had cried out to God to give me a happy marriage. At that time, that was all I wanted for my life. Little did I know that God would one day answer my prayer.

Any of you reading this may either be divorced or know someone who is. You probably know how devastating that can be. Well, I was devastated and just wanted to pretty much crawl in a hole. My two children and I moved in with my mother, and that was a humiliating circumstance, to say the least. After having a home of my own, I once again had to depend on my widowed mother for help. Fortunately, I had a wonderful mother who never threw my failure in my face. That was the way I viewed myself, as a failure. So here I was, twenty-eight years old, divorced with two children, feeling fat and frumpy and all alone. I felt hopeless that no one would ever want me again. So how did I go from that to being sixty-one, recently widowed, and feeling alive, full of hope, and loved?

Life is stranger than fiction. I've heard that before, and I really believe it. You never know what will happen along the way, and just the slightest possibility that something wonderful and unexplainable could happen keeps us going. We may not tell anyone or even admit it to ourselves, but somewhere deep inside us, we are longing for something more. Some of you may have already found it, and others may have no clue what I am talking about, but I believe we all have a desire to be loved. Maybe the head-over-heels kind of love that sweeps us off our feet is the kind of love people will admit to wanting, but I am talking about that love-me-truly-no-matter-how-strange-I-may-seem-to-you kind of love—the kind of love that lasts a lifetime, through good and bad, no matter what. It is our hearts' desire to be loved for who we are. We need self-love, too, but maybe we need help to get there by being really loved by someone else first. So, with this in mind, let me begin my love story.

We met over the phone. I belonged to PWP, Parents Without Partners, which is a story in itself. A friend of my cousin's went to a coffee house in Oakland, Pennsylvania, which is where the University of Pittsburgh is located. My cousin thought I might be interested in going there for my debut "get myself out there" night. She made arrangements for me to meet her "experienced divorced" friend. Okay, so I drove there thinking, *What am I doing?* I just remember that and being so scared. I parked the car, went into the coffeehouse, and was engulfed in a scene of people of all ages who were trying to get out there in life, too. I met my cousin's friend, and she and I didn't seem to click well. She gave me a few pointers and that was that.

I can hardly remember that night, but I did meet another woman, Sue, who invited me to PWP. Sue was a very energetic woman who had been divorced for quite some time. She was ten years my senior, but she looked and acted more my age than I did. She and I became very close friends over the years, and I even ended up being the maid of honor at her wedding.

The friendship that Sue and I shared was life-changing for me. She was just the friend I needed at that time, and she was the person who nicknamed me "Bobbie." We shared more than a common desire to find a mate, because we truly had a wonderful, honest, and caring friendship. We could tell each other anything. We also had fun together, and Sue helped me to come out of my shell and be comfortable in social situations. I remember one winter when Sue would call me and say, "Let's go out! Maybe we'll meet someone tonight." She was always looking to meet that special someone. I would drag myself out and go to these dances and wait for someone to ask me to dance. It was so depressing, and I wanted to give up because I wasn't having any fun at all. I just couldn't see anyone I was remotely interested in, and I was very nervous to even ask someone to dance. One night, Sue said, "Let's go to this dance that is being held at some hotel in New Kensington." It turned out to be ballroom dancing, but I didn't know it at the time. I finally agreed after much convincing on her part. We walked in, and there were only a handful of people—mostly older men. These men were in their late seventies or eighties. I danced with them, and it was fun because they just wanted to dance. I think it helped me to relax and not be afraid of dancing with strangers. I have a tendency to lead when I dance, but these gentlemen knew how to take the lead. I was actually able to follow them because they were such good dancers. So, it turned out to be a great experience for me.

After I had been a member of PWP for about six months, I had the opportunity to be on the amigo, or welcoming, committee. Part of that position requires you to call the new guests and members to invite them to different PWP activities besides the bimonthly dance that was held in downtown Pittsburgh. Members would host discussion groups, game nights, and sometimes have a party that would be open to new people. If you wanted to invite the new members to your activity, you could announce it in the newsletter, and the callers from the amigo committee would extend an invitation to the new guests or members as part of their phone calls. The purpose was to encourage new people to come to these more intimate gatherings so that they could meet people more easily than they would at a dance, which usually had around two hundred or so people. That could be rather intimidating to a newly divorced or widowed person and to anyone new, for that matter. Sue had convinced me to be on the amigo committee, and her selling pitch was that we would get first crack at the new guys. I am comfortable talking with people I don't know, especially on the phone, so I thought this was something I could easily do. In fact, I did enjoy talking to both the men and women I called. I guess you could say I am a people person.

So, as I said, we met over the phone. The first time I heard his voice, I was attracted to it and to his laugh. We talked on the phone for almost three hours. He said he never had talked on the phone that long with anyone. In fact, he told me he hated talking on the phone because at his job, he had to be on the phone a good part of his day. Bob told me he worked for U. S. Steel in the billing department, and part of his job required him to talk to the salesmen in order to confirm the pricing discounts given to individual customers. I told him I was a stay-at-home mom and that I loved having adult phone conversations. I think he sensed that I liked to talk. We talked about our children and about each having a son with the same name, Robby and Robbie. We also laughed because his name was Bob and mine was Bobbie. I told him about the "whoever talks first looses game" my family and I had just played that night at dinner and how it ended up that everyone in my family talked except for my brother-in-law Jim and me. Jim and I are the biggest talkers, actually, but we had gone about an hour past everyone else and were both determined not to lose. Earlier, Jim had tricked my mother into talking by pretending he was going to pull down her slacks and, of course, my mother yelled at him. He tried it with me, but I already had the wooden spoon in my hand to fend him off. So, he went in the living room to watch TV. We had the kind of phone with which you could dial your own phone number and it would ring back. So, I motioned to my accomplice, my mother, as I dialed my phone number, and she caught on. When the phone rang back, my mom answered it, called Jim, and told him he was wanted on the phone. He didn't want to answer, so my mom said she didn't know who it was, but the person on the phone had said it was important. Of course, Jim had no choice but to answer the phone. I stayed calm and cool, and Jim got on the phone. When no one was really there, he knew we had tricked him. It was so funny, and it was sweet revenge. I told this story to Bob and he just couldn't stop laughing. I think at that point, he really thought I was clever and that I had a fun family. In time, Bob and Jim became best of friends, once Jim got over Bob's long hippie hair. At the end of our long phone call, I got around to the purpose of the call, which was to invite Bob to a discussion group that PWP was having on Sunday, and he said he would think about going.

I went to the discussion group with my friend Sue. I met up with a guy I had been casually dating, Art, with whom I had plans to go out to the Holiday Inn to dance and socialize after the meeting. I saw Bob, and I was immediately attracted to him. What I first noticed was his beautiful smile and his perfectly straight white teeth. His soft brown eyes drew me in, and I remember thinking how peaceful his eyes seemed. He was wearing a forest green collared shirt, which showed off his fair skin. He made a comment about how I was talking with my hands, and I said I was 100 percent Italian, which was probably why I used my hands when I talked. He replied that he was 100 percent German. I was with my friends, but Bob picked up on the fact that Art and I were dating. Art and I were not in a committed relationship, but Bob didn't realize that, and eventually Bob admitted to me that he had been disappointed that first night when he found out I was dating someone. I wanted to see Bob again, so I asked him to come to an "Ungame" night I was hosting for PWP. The Ungame is a board game in which participants pick a card and have to answer the question on the card. For example, it might ask if you would kiss on the first date or if would you tell a friend that you don't like her new haircut if she asked. It's a fun game, and it helps people get acquainted. Bob agreed to come, so I wrote the directions to my house in a circle around the outside edge of a paper plate and told him to put it on his steering wheel so he could read it while he drove. And, of course, I used my hands to demonstrate it. He had the biggest smile, and I just knew he was special.

On Friday, August 13, 1976, which is a date I now love, Bob came to the group activity I was hosting. We sat together and played the Ungame, and we had such a great time. At one point, someone said to Bob, "The way you are looking at her is like you are wanting to buy a horse. You better check out her teeth." I opened my mouth, and he looked at my teeth and said they looked great to him. Years later, when we were married and I had so much trouble with my beautiful teeth, I would remind him that he couldn't complain about the cost because he had checked them out. We would fondly remember that Friday the thirteenth and would relive those feelings we both experienced that night as we talked and opened up about our lives.

Bob met my children that first night he came to my home. My son Robby was being a typical three-year-old and wouldn't go to bed. Bob said, "Don't worry. I'll go up and tuck him in and read him a story. You stay with everyone down here." I think he saw I was torn between hosting this house full of people, some of whom I had just met, and trying to put my son back to bed. It just seemed perfectly natural to me for him to do that, even though I had just met this man. Remember, this took place in 1976, and things were different then. This was before the time when sexual abuse became a regular occurrence on the news. Today I would not be comfortable trusting someone I didn't know to tuck my children into bed. Things have certainly changed, and it makes me sad to think that that era of innocence is over, especially for single moms. A few minutes later,

Bob came down and said Robby had fallen asleep. I remember thinking that he really had a way with Robby and that it was so great of him to be so helpful to me.

We remembered that night often, and as I write about it, it seems like yesterday. As all the other guests were leaving, I asked Bob to stay and talk. We stayed up and talked the entire night. We shared things about our marriages that we had in common. We both blamed ourselves for somehow not being able to make our spouses happy, and as we spoke about the details, we realized that we had our shame and embarrassment over our failed marriages in common, too. He said I was so easy to talk to, and he was surprised that he was able to tell me things he had never told another person.

We continued to talk, and he revealed more details about his marriage. One thing I noticed was that as he talked, he didn't seem to have the usual anger or bitterness that so many people have when getting divorced. Looking back, I think it was a common thread in his attitude that he blamed himself instead of other people when there was a problem. Bob also accepted people and didn't try to change them, as I did. I remember that my response to all of this was how much we both valued marriage and had done our best. We also realized it was humiliating that we had allowed our spouses to treat us in ways that we really didn't deserve. We realized that we had tried to change our values to save our marriages, but in the process, we had lost part of ourselves. I knew he was totally able to understand how I ended up with a mental breakdown right before my divorce, because he felt that he had almost had that happen to him, too. It was wonderful to connect with each other on that level and for the first time honestly believe that we deserved to be loved in the way that we thought love should be in a marriage.

I remember we kissed, and I think this was when he asked me if I believed in love at first sight. I said no, and he smiled and said, "I don't, either, but this is the second time I've seen you." Now I know you are probably thinking, *What a line!* You'd have to know Bob to know it wasn't. It was the most romantic thing I had ever heard. It seemed perfectly natural, because I felt the same way. We were so authentic with each other that looking back, I know God was with us. He was helping us heal from all our past hurts. We just felt such a connection from the first moment we spoke.

When Bob was leaving early Saturday morning, he asked when he could see me again. We knew we both had dates that night, so we made plans to see each other on Sunday. We agreed we would keep our previous commitments, and we would tell our dates we had met someone else. It is unbelievable to me that two people would do this so soon, but it seemed so natural. The fact that we both had the same thought reinforced that it was the right thing for us to do. So, on Saturday night I went to the circus with Art and his family, and Bob took his date to dinner. I recall that Bob called me earlier on Saturday afternoon, before our dates, and we talked some more. We had planned to see each other the next day for dinner, as I had plans to go to church Sunday morning. Bob said, "I would really like to go to church with you." He hadn't been to church for a while, and he really wanted to get back to going again.

So, I guess our first date was when Bob and I went to church together. He stayed with me all day, and I cooked dinner as I had originally planned. I wanted everything to be perfect. As we were sitting at the dinner table, the kids started acting overly silly as kids do sometimes when they are having fun. I was getting uptight because I wanted to make a great impression, and Bob sensed it. He put his hand on mine and said, "Stop worrying. They are just kids, and I really am enjoying them." That was the moment I was totally hooked, and I remember it so clearly. I know some people can remember where they were during the 9/11 attacks or when President Kennedy was shot. Some people remember the exact moment they accepted Jesus. Well, this was one of those moments for me. It would mark the beginning of Bob showing so much care and love for me. And it was also the moment I believed I could trust this man with my heart.

After that Sunday, Bob and I continued to go to PWP; we would spend most of our time there with each other, but we also mingled with the other members. When we weren't seeing each other at the

PWP functions, we would go out on dates, or he would just come to my house and visit. When we weren't together, we would spend a good part of the evening talking on the phone.

The following Sunday, we picked my mom up at the airport. She was coming back from her annual two-week vacation in California. Now, I think this is a funny little story, too. You see, when I took my mom to the airport before her trip, Art was flying back from seeing his son. I met him at the airport that day for lunch, and my mom knew of those plans. Then, two weeks later, I picked my mom up at the airport with Bob. She got in the car, and we started talking. She asked, "What's new?" I pointed to Bob and said, "He is," and all three of us just started laughing so hard. It was another bonding moment. My mother fell in love with Bob so easily, too. It was great to know that my friends and family really liked him. I think that is a measure that is important, and sometimes we don't value the opinions of our friends and family in matters of the heart. I have learned to listen to them, because when my first marriage ended, so many people came forward and said they had not liked my first husband from the start, but they never shared that with me before I married him. They said their dislike was based on a feeling they had, but they didn't feel it was their place to judge. So, you can understand why it was so important to me that others really liked Bob and thought that he was a great guy.

Bob and I had dated a few weeks before I met his son. Even though we were seeing each other frequently, on the days when he had visitations with Rob, he preferred to spend alone time with his son, and he was not ready to introduce us yet. I think he was being cautious, and I know he was also preparing him to meet all of us. So, the third weekend we dated, Robbie came over with Bob. My children were home that day, as they only visited their dad every other Sunday. I think Bob had his son on Wednesdays and part of every weekend at that time. The kids seemed to connect with each other just as much as Bob and I had. I don't remember everything we did that day, but I do know that Bob and the kids did some wrestling around on the floor, and there was lots of laughing. We all started going places together on weekends, but Bob still saw his son by himself on Wednesdays.

We found out we were both praying to God to send us someone special, and we truly felt he did. We bonded in such a way that we never questioned or doubted that we were meant to be together. The only hesitation Bob had was that he worried about the effect that getting a divorce would have on his son. He had a legal separation at the time, and most of the issues they agreed on centered on their son. Bob definitely had his son's best interest in mind. Later, he said he regretted not fighting for custody of his son, but at the time of his separation, he never thought that was an option that would have been available to him. As he shared his feelings, he said he just couldn't stay in that marriage anymore, which is why he moved in with his dad. We continued to see each other almost every day, and we had a wonderful courtship.

The hard part with three children was that sometimes one would feel left out. It seemed it was always either my son or daughter, because they both wanted to do things with Big Rob, as Bob's son affectionately came to be called. In a way, their wanting to do more with Bob's son was a good thing. The kids also went through the tattling stage, which was hard to deal with at the time. Every few minutes, one of the kids would come and tell on the other. We finally set a rule that if it wasn't dangerous or life-threatening, the kids had to work it out themselves or the tattler would have a timeout. That seemed to help a little. I also remember that Bob and I were very affectionate with each other, and we were kissing each other often. The kids would watch us and say "yuck," but their smiles said everything. What child doesn't want to see a loving relationship? It got to the point that the kids would say something like, "Aren't you two going to kiss?" We had fun as a family, and it is surprising now to think that this blended family worked so well. I think the children liked that we kept the focus on the family unit, and they were included in almost everything Bob and I did except for our outings with our friends for an evening here or there. We did so many fun things together, and for the most part, we all got along with each other. This was a huge change for my children, who had witnessed so much hate, anger, and even physical abuse in my first marriage. I think it restored their belief in a loving God.

Bob and I were married a little over a year later on November 5, 1977. The day of the wedding, Big Rob, my daughter Tracy, Little Robby, my mom, Bob, and I all went out to an early dinner. It was a bright, sunny, beautiful fall day, and I think it was around seventy degrees, which is outstanding weather for a time of year that is normally cool and cloudy in Pittsburgh. We all went back to our house to get changed for the wedding ceremony. It was an intimate wedding and was only attended by our extended families and a few of our closest friends. We had the reception at the church, and the women of the church made little tea sandwiches. It was the best wedding ever. During our vows, my son, Robby, who was three-and-a-half at the time, came up to me and tapped me on my leg and said, "Mommy, can I stay with you?" Of course, everyone laughed and thought he was adorable. Tracy, my daughter, wore a pretty white lace jumpsuit, and I wore a peach floor-length, long sleeved evening gown. My friend Sue was my maid of honor, and she wore a darker peach lace dress. She had already had her dress, and it was amazing that it went so well with mine. We each carried flowers and later used them as a centerpiece on the table.

Bob had a big surprise for me on our wedding day. He shaved his mustache off, and I had never seen him without it. He said he wanted me to see what I was getting. His smile was even bigger then. I teased him and said, "I changed my mind." Then we just laughed. I think Bob got more attention than I did that day because everyone was commenting on his new look, and I was just so proud he was my husband. I was pleasantly surprised, because he was even more handsome without his mustache. He was so happy that day that he wanted a picture of himself holding our marriage license. What more could a bride ask for? I had everything I always prayed for, and it was a wonderful day.

We had our struggles that come with having a blended family, and blended families were a minority at that time. It was not as common to have a stepfather in 1978 as it is in 2010. In my daughter's quest to have a "normal" family, she asked if she could call Bob "Daddy." He answered her by saying that that wasn't necessary, and she could just continue to call him Bob. Her reply was, "Okay, Daddy." He never mentioned that she should call him Bob again. He truly was her daddy. Even though this was a small thing, it was amazing. God had brought us all together as a true family, and the love we all had for each other was special. We still share one thing: we love and miss Bob.

Our life was typical of most people our age. We had our financial struggles and our normal problems raising children. We had our ups and downs, but through it all, things seemed to always work out for us. Bob and I were always open about our past relationships, and neither one of us ever put our ex-spouses into our relationship as a weapon. We stood firm and united in our marriage. This is hard to do, but if we hadn't, we never would have made it.

Sometimes when you are happily remarried, an ex-spouse unknowingly can cause problems, and we had our share of problems that go with divorce. When an ex-spouse's hurts haven't healed, it can cause such disharmony in new families. It might be too hard for ex-spouses to see what could have been had they been willing to be honest, make changes, and really stay firm in hope. Maybe it is hard for an ex-spouse to have to rethink the fantasy that his marriage's failure was completely the other person's fault. When you witness your ex-spouse in a loving relationship and see the peace in that person, I imagine it can be unnerving if you are still unhappy and struggling.

For us, there were many issues around visitations, for example, that caused friction. One time when we were planning our first vacation to Florida, at the last minute we found out that Big Rob wasn't allowed to come. We were all so disappointed. Tracy and Little Rob loved when he was with them. He was their big brother, and they looked up to him. I know Bob was sad, and I was just plain angry. We did the trip again the following year, and that time Rob came. I think Bob had learned how to become assertive that year. He just said to his ex-wife, "Robbie is coming to Florida this time."

That was that. It was a fact. So that was something good that came out of it.

We had trouble from the other camp, too. My ex-husband wanted the children every other Sunday, but then he would say he had to work or he would have some other excuse, and so that was a constant irritation for all of us. I was torn about rescheduling, because if he didn't get them the following week, it would be a whole month without seeing them. I was trying to help my ex-husband build a relationship with his children. After a while, however, Tracy and Robby complained a lot because their father's cancellations messed with their plans. I finally just said to Jack, my ex-husband, "You missed the visit, so we are sticking to the schedule." This would lead to fighting, and he would threaten to go to court. Over time, Tracy and Robby complained so much that I finally went before the judge and brought the children so that they could speak for themselves about their dad. The judge removed the court order that the children had to visit their father, but she told Jack that he still needed to build a relationship with them. She told him to invite the children out for pizza and work on a relationship with them. She was a very wise judge. Unfortunately for Jack, he only made one attempt to see the children after that. They said they wanted time to think it over, and he never called them again. He missed out. He had beautiful children, and it was his loss. For the rest of us, it was all gain. The game playing came to an end, which was a blessing. I am sure this is why to Tracy and Robby, Bob is their dad. I thank God for giving Bob to all of us. He was a truly wonderful father to all three of his children.

Even though this was a marriage made in heaven, let's be real here. There were times Bob and I didn't get along. We still were two people with individual personality traits, and we had different work habits and ideas of the way things should be done. We usually had the same goal in mind, so that wasn't the source of our problems. Having three children brings another set of tensions, especially since spouses rarely have identical parenting ideas. And old habits and hurts have a way of returning when you are tired or stressed, or even when life gets boring. However, Bob and I were blessed to be very sensitive not to make each other insecure. I think we remembered our pain from our previous marriages just enough to try not to create situations that could have similar results. There were times when we weren't getting along and I would talk openly about how I was feeling similar to how I felt in my first marriage. Bob was always sensitive to that and would work very hard to reassure me he didn't want me to feel that way or that he understood that when I was overreacting to something he did, it was most likely because it reminded me of my previous marriage. Sometimes misplaced anger from the past came into our marriage, but if I told Bob a certain behavior felt threatening to me and made me feel scared or insecure, we would work it out.

Now, I am not saying this just flowed perfectly. We would fight and have words, but once we were honest about how we felt and talked it out, our talking seemed to help heal the past. We just had to remember to be extra patient and understanding with each other. I think we were actually keeping each other's hurts in mind and were trying to treat each other better to bring healing. We knew each other's pasts and were extra careful not to open up old wounds. Bob knew I feared him drinking, so he didn't go out drinking with the guys and was careful not to drink too much. I knew there were issues in his marriage that would make him feel threatened, so I was sensitive to his feelings and always reassured him of my love for him. I know second marriages don't always work out, but ours was the greatest. I don't know if I ever would have been able to handle the battle we were about to face if I hadn't healed from the terrible hurts from my past and if I hadn't found such a strong foundation in my new marriage. It's hard to see that sometimes in the middle of my storms, but when the rain dries and the sun shines, I am able to look at the struggles and see just how much I have learned in those troubled times and that God was there through it all.

As I said, in every way, ours was the marriage I had prayed for years earlier. We went on family vacations to Disney World and the beach, took day trips to amusement parks, went to church on Sundays, loved our church work, went on family picnics, spent time with extended family and close friends, and lived life the way you would expect life was meant to be.

At that time, we were members of St. Mark's Lutheran Church in Pittsburgh, which was like our second home. We spent a great deal of time there, and our children grew up in that church. Bob and I were youth group leaders when our children attended youth group. We went on many fun trips and outings with our children as leaders. We eventually led the senior high group, and we took the kids to Niagara Falls, Canada, for a regional youth group convention. It was great. At that time, Tracy and Big Rob were in that group. I think I enjoyed the trip as much as the teenagers, and I felt young when I was there with them. We just had a great time, and I have many fond memories of those days. At another youth activity, we went camping, and I was awakened in the middle of the night to girls screaming. I thought the boys had pulled a prank on the girls, but it turned out there were bats in the cabin. Fortunately for me, they were on the other side of my sleeping area. We had to go get the men and boys to come help us. I think they got brooms and chased the bats out. The kids in the youth group laughed about that many times over the years.

Bob and I were helpmates to each other, and we seemed to function in one accord. Bob would help me with the house and cooking, and I helped him in his garden and with the yard work.

We had the kind of marriage in which we preferred to be together all the time. It wasn't a trust issue; we just enjoyed each other, and it seemed there was never enough time to be with each other. When he would go to work, we talked on the phone three to four times a day during work hours. We just loved to be with each other, and we looked forward to weekends and planned everything with that end in mind. We were each other's best friends, and there was nothing that could take the place of us just being together. We never were tired of that, and it motivated all of our hopes and dreams. This was quite the contrast from my first marriage.

The Breakdown and the Breakup

My first marriage had been volatile, and my husband ended up becoming physically abusive, which led, in part, to the breakdown and the breakup. Our marriage was like a bomb just waiting to explode. We couldn't even talk to one another toward the end of it. Where did it go wrong? It went wrong from the start. You see, my first husband was married when I met him. Also, I was in no condition at that time to choose a spouse.

I met and began dating Jack the summer of my junior year of high school. I was seventeen years old, and he was twenty-two. He was managing a gas station at the time. We dated for several months before I found out that he was married but separated. I broke up with him, but he convinced me that his marriage was over—which, I guess, it pretty much was. He said how much he loved me and that he wanted to marry me. At that time, that just sounded so tempting, so we began to see each other again. He then found out his wife was pregnant. It happened right before they were separated, so I guess their marriage hadn't been as over as he'd said. He decided to go through with the divorce. His wife actually was dating someone, too, and ended up marrying him right after the divorce.

I'd like to blame my involvement with all of that mess on being young and also on the fact that my dad was so sick. At the time, my dad was facing open-heart surgery. Today, valve replacement surgery is very commonplace, but in 1965, it was a new frontier. In fact, because it was so new, the surgeon put off my dad's surgery for five years. Added to this was the fact that my dad kept getting unexplainable high fevers after his heart catheterizations. So, you can understand why the doctors were apprehensive and postponed the surgery for as long as possible. For about two years prior to the surgery, my dad's family doctor gave him a monthly shot of penicillin as a preventative drug. Penicillin would never be used that way today, but around the time of my dad's open-heart surgery, the doctors did not know any of the information we do now about overexposure to antibiotics.

After the open-heart surgery, my dad continued to get really sick and was hospitalized. The doctors did not know what was wrong, because the strep did not show up in his blood work. After testing his bone marrow, however, the doctors discovered that the strep was in his bones. By the time they realized this, the penicillin would not kill the strep. The doctors finally concluded that that was why my dad always got so sick after each heart catheterizations. We were told the strep had been dormant in my dad's heart since he had had rheumatic fever when he was a teenager. I think the strep may have become penicillin-resistant, too, or the penicillin was just not strong enough to kill the strep that was in his heart around the valve. I will never know or understand the exact details, but the medical explanation the doctors gave me was that my dad died from a strep infection. He was only forty-six years old. The medical world has come so far in less than fifty years.

Jack was there for me when my dad died, and I think I confused this caring with love. Jack was very upset because he had come to really care for my dad, and my dad was fond of Jack, too. Jack even went to the hospital to see my dad right before he died because he wanted to talk to my dad and get his blessing to marry me. My dad had been moved to intensive care, so Jack never did get to have that talk. I know he was sincere, and he cried when my dad died. My father died less than two months before I graduated high school. Two months prior to this, my grandfather, the one who had had the stroke, died, and shortly after that, my dad's father had a heart attack. He was eighty years old at the time, and he survived.

I know with everything going on in the family, my mom was very overwhelmed. Jack and I spent time with our friends, and my mom spent time with her friends and family. I don't think anyone in the family noticed Jack's drinking at the time, because he only drank occasionally. What I began to notice was on the occasions that he drank, he had a hard time staying sober.

Jack and I dated for over three years before we were married. It seemed the closer the wedding was getting, the more I was having second thoughts about it. To me, he didn't seem that interested in getting married. He actually suggested changing the date so he could go to Indiana for an auto race with his identical twin brother. Eventually, he did choose our original wedding date over his brother's tempting offer, but I don't think I realized at the time just how much his brother was trying to interfere with our relationship. Later, his brother would cause many arguments in our marriage. His brother would guilt-trip Jack into putting him first over me, and I don't think I realized that his brother was jealous. Their mother would also talk about Jack's brother being his other half. I thought she meant me because I was Jack's wife, but as I listened to her conversations, I realized she meant Walt, his brother. I should have suspected there was something odd about that, but I was very naïve.

Later, after we were married a few years, I came to understand that I was way down on the list, because it seemed his entire family came before me. Add to this the fact that he started drinking heavily, and you may understand how complicated the situation became over time. Because of my insecurities, I became very demanding and explosive, and Jack did, too. We got to the point when we couldn't even speak to one another, and all we did was fight.

Eventually, Jack ended up having an extramarital affair. I saw that coming, but I was pregnant at the time with my second child, so I was very passive and denied the signs. I actually went to Florida with my daughter, my sister, and my brother-in-law on Jack's urging. Because I was suspicious at the time, maybe I should not have gone, but I am not blaming myself. They still would have found a way to be together. I just made it easy.

This young woman, who I thought was my friend, came to my house the morning I returned home. I had to go to the grocery store, and I surprised myself when I made a comment to them that they should change the sheets when they were done. I guess something inside me just knew. If I was surprised at my words, imagine their shock. I later confirmed my suspicions, and Jack finally admitted to the affair. Because I was pregnant, I ended up trying to work it out. I forgave him, but the emotional abuse only got worse, and so did the drinking.

After Robby was born, I was very depressed, and I finally went for some therapy. Jack was really threatened by that and demanded that I not go back. I lied and told him that I wouldn't, but he could tell I was lying. That is when he hit me. He had been very emotionally abusive prior to this, but the physical abuse is what led to the breakdown and the breakup. Even though Jack never hit me again because I pressed charges, I don't think I got over the physical abuse. It just changed everything. I think something inside me died when that happened. I could forgive the infidelity, but the physical abuse was just too much for me to endure. I really did fear for my life when that happened, and I don't think I recovered from the shock of it all.

My pastor convinced me to drop the charges. The pastor used the seven times seventy verse from the Bible that refers to how often we need to forgive, and he guilt-tripped me into dropping the charges. Fortunately, the fact that I went to the police and pressed charges did accomplish something, because Jack was afraid to hit me after that. I told him that the next time he did, he would go to jail. He knew I meant it.

This domestic violence all happened in 1974 before many professionals knew how to deal with it. I remember the policeman told me to just go on a shopping spree. Can you believe that was the advice I was given? I also was told by a neighbor to lie about why I had a cut lip and a black-and-blue face. I was out in the open about all of it, even at the hospital, but no one offered me any help. I think that was what really led to my breakdown. I had no support from the police, the clergy, or the neighbors, and my dad was not around to protect me, either. My mom and sister stood up for me, but Jack wasn't respectful of them.

On top of all of this, I told Jack's sister what happened, and then his mother called and yelled at me for upsetting his sister. When I went to his parents' house shortly after this incident occurred, his mother told me not to speak to her unless I was spoken to, and she wouldn't allow my children to have lunch with them. Everyone was eating hot dogs for lunch, and I tried to take some out of the pot to feed the kids. Jack's mother came and actually took them away from me. His sister and her family were visiting from out of town, and his entire family ignored me. I was treated as though Jack hitting me were somehow my fault.

When I write about all of this now, I realize just how abused I was by all of them. It is no wonder I had a breakdown. I remember that day so well because it was Father's Day, and I was still mourning my dad. I had driven to my in-laws' in my own car after church, so I ended up leaving with the children. I just remember going home and reading the Bible. I looked for the passages that spoke about God taking care of my enemies. That gave me comfort and helped me to not want to take revenge. I think I read the verse that said something like, "Revenge is mine, says the Lord." I trusted that God would handle everything for me.

I accepted Jesus as my personal Savior while watching *The 700 Club*. I called in for prayer about my situation, and I also remember praying that Jack and his family would be saved. I figured that either way, God would handle the situation. If they were saved, great, as then they would stop treating me so badly. If they didn't accept Jesus, then God could take his revenge on them since they were my enemies. That was my thought process at the time. I wasn't going to use the seven times seventy rule on them. It was enough trying to use it with Jack.

I think it was only a few weeks later that I ended up in the psych ward. That is when my pastor, who had been counseling me, came to visit and made a comment about God being with me even in the hospital. I knew God was, but I also resented that this pastor had let Jack off the hook. We were to do couples counseling as part of the agreement for my dropping the charges against him, and I was angry that the pastor didn't hold Jack to the agreement and instead was just counseling me. I remember one positive thing from his visit, though. He used an illustration about leaning on God as one would lean on a chair, and he leaned on a chair nearby. It is a good thing that I knew Jesus from when I was little and had that childlike trust in him, which is what got me through all of this. I knew in my heart from a little child that the Jesus I loved would be there for me. Maybe that is why I could relate to the pastor's illustration about the chair and still remember it thirty-six years later. I think that was all my mind could handle at that time.

I believe our childlike faith is there for us in our deepest times of need. I needed Jesus, and he was my friend and wouldn't let me down. That helped me recover from my breakdown, as did my stubbornness and determination to get well again, which were two of my most useful God-given traits. I often wonder if I had post-traumatic stress disorder, because at the time Jack hit me, I really feared for my life. I was able to get away and run to the neighbors' house to call the police. I haven't thought about any of this for years, and it almost seems as though none of this was a part of my life at all. I have included this information from my past just to let you see how far I have come with God's help.

I had been consumed by guilt, and having a complete breakdown really set me free. It was like starting over. Jack started to come to my therapy sessions, and we tried making some compromises. I remember he wanted to sell my car, and I wanted him to go with the kids and me to the zoo. So, the agreement was that he could sell my car in exchange for going to the zoo.

Now as I write this, I am thinking, *What?* What therapist would even think these two issues would be related and that this would be a compromise? I see how insane and ridiculous that was now, and I wonder what school that therapist graduated from. We also went to a marriage counselor after I was released from the hospital, but when I mentioned the affair, the counselor said I was turning the knife in Jack's stomach. *So much for that discussion*, I thought. In my mind, it was the good old boys' network, and I just felt abused all over again. We didn't continue with the counseling after a few sessions because Jack didn't want to, and at that point, I saw no need to go alone. I just became even more depressed.

I liked it much better when I had been in the hospital and living in my pretend but mixed-up world. It had been a break from the insanity that was my life. I did eventually go to Al-Anon, but even that was confusing to me because I was so overwhelmed I couldn't process the twelve-step program at that time. So, I continued to become more and more suicidal in my thoughts because I saw no way out. I felt so trapped. I don't know if the medical profession has come any further with treating mental illness, but I believe that having Jack's alcoholism to deal with was never addressed. Many issues led to my misdiagnosis and mistreatment.

I really believe God healed me, because I can clearly see that no one else did. Others' lack of understanding only added to what I was going through at the time. I always considered my healing the first miracle God would perform in my life. That I was taken off all of my medication after my divorce speaks volumes of what God did for me. God kept me in his care, which was the start of my healing and of my seeing God's work in my life. All of the people who knew me saw the old Roberta again—or so they thought. I was becoming a new person in Christ. I was still struggling with getting that divorce, but God was showing me he could forgive that, too.

Over the years, I forgave my ex-husband. I also asked him to forgive me for all the anger I had toward him. He said he did, and he told me he divorced me because he thought it would be best for me. In the end, I would say that was a wise choice.

So why am I sharing all of this with you? It could be risky, because some of you may think I am still crazy. I like to think I am a little crazy, too, but the fun kind of crazy that loves life and is not afraid to be myself and laugh at myself. That breakdown, as hard as it was to go through, prepared me for life. It probably prepared me for death, too. I know it taught me total dependence on God. The reason I am sharing this now is to give hope to all of you who read this story. That is my purpose for writing my life story and baring my soul, so to speak—to give hope to the hopeless.

Some of you may feel like you're about to lose it, too. With the struggling economy, some of you have lost money in the market—me, too. Some of you may have even lost your jobs. And some of you are either divorced or in a marriage that is not what God intended. Your partner, your other half, may be the source of your struggles, rather than the helpmate God intended our spouses to be. I just know that if I am going to write a story of hope, I need to take that risk and tell my entire story. That is the only way I can truly be an example of hope in a world that sometimes seems so hopeless. Just keep walking. Put one foot in front of the other. Walk in the path God has set before you. I know it sometimes seems hard to find that path, but I believe there is One who will light our way. I am not saying life is easy. I still struggle with things even now, but I have to stay hopeful and keep my eye on the future. I pray that my sharing of this story will bring hope to you. What brought me through the worst of times was the knowledge that my struggle would not last forever, but that my time with God would. Even in the psychiatric ward, when I was pretty much out of touch with reality, I clung to the words that God was with me. Immanuel. It is rather telling that I am writing this story a few weeks before Christmas. Consider it my gift to you.

I know from experience that emotional and mental health is a topic few people are willing to discuss. Although it seems that people are more accepting these days of taking anxiety or depression medication, mental health issues still carry a stigma. All I can say is when I had these problems in the early seventies, few people were willing to talk about them.

I remember going to see Elvis Presley with Jack, my sister Norma, and her husband Jim, and the comedian who opened the show made a joke about how one out of four people would go crazy. So, of course, we all looked at each other and laughed. I remember thinking Jack was the crazy one because he had been drinking and acting so different. Little did I realize his drinking would drive *me* crazy.

If I hadn't come to Christ, I don't know if I would have been healed of my mental health issues. For a while, I had such feelings of hopelessness. I worried that I would never be back to my normal self. In time, I became mentally well again, and I was changed. I was slowly becoming a new person in Christ, and I was beginning to feel worthwhile and loved by God.

So, with this background, now you can go on to read about my life with Bob and my dream come true. To think how my life has transformed into one of such blessings and such happiness is truly unbelievable. It is wonderful to think that God may be able to use my struggles to reach you, no matter where you are at this time. Maybe you have never had problems of this magnitude; hopefully you haven't and never will. I just want you to see how God was and still is in my life. I pray that this story will inspire you to trust God in all things, and I pray that I will forever remain faithful to God, too.

Post Script

Today I received a note from the legal department that was reviewing the book. They said that there could be some issues with my speaking about my ex-husband Jack's affair and domestic abuse in this chapter—unless he was deceased. I let them know that that was indeed the case. I would not have felt free to write about my ex-husband in this chapter if he were still living, because I would not have wanted to cause him any pain or trouble by bringing this up. I knew that he had died, which was why I believed I could write the story without causing any harm. When I originally wrote this chapter, I had learned about Jack's death, but I deliberately chose not to include that information because I did not understand why things happened the way they did. I have obviously had second thoughts and have decided to share the rest of the story with you. Maybe I was wrong not to want to tell this part of the story, and maybe writing about it will help me understand it a little clearer myself.

It was in the spring of 2002 when I learned of Jack's death. That very day I had been working on making a new address book, so I went on the Internet to update some of my family members' addresses. For some reason, I tried to see if I could find Jack's address. I told Bob that it would be funny if I could find Jack on the Internet when the court hadn't been able to find him in 1997 when I had gone for my last hearing to try to get the issue of back owed child support resolved. At that time, I was making one last attempt because I thought any money I received I would give to the children to help them pay down their student loans. In fact, the Family Court of Allegheny County had actually issued a warrant for Jack's arrest because he failed to show for a previous child support hearing a month earlier. Since nothing came of either hearing, I decided that I had done all I could and that this would be a closed chapter.

I had not thought about Jack or the family court in years prior to this day. About an hour or so after I attempted to find Jack's address, Bob went outside to get the mail. When he came back inside, he handed me an envelope and said, "Bobbie, you are psychic." Now, I don't like to be called psychic because I don't think of myself that way and I also don't think that term represents the Holy Spirit, but I can say I have good intuition. Still, this was strange, even to me. As I read the envelope, I saw it was sent from the Family Court of Allegheny County, and I was shocked. I was also a little puzzled, but when I opened the envelope and read the letter, I was astounded by what had just transpired. I am not sure whether that was what is called a "word of knowledge" or not, but I think that for some reason, the Holy Spirit was revealing something to me. I realized that in 1997, the court had issued a warrant for a dead man. Now the court was informing me that after attempting to purge the files that were over five years old, they discovered through the Social Security office that Jack had died on December 15, 1995. As I began to process this information, I was shocked that Jack had died at the age of fifty-two, three days before Bob's liver surgery. That part really had me shook up for some reason. It had taken seven years for me to learn that fact. After the news finally hit me, I was thankful that Jack and I had forgiven each other for all of the hurt we caused one another when we were married. I have never heard any more about Jack and have no idea what caused his death.

I think God had gone before me to prepare me for the news when I, for no apparent reason, decided to look Jack up that day. I know Bob looked at it that way, too. Maybe this was a gift of the Holy Spirit, but I am not quite sure what to do with it except to give glory to God that he goes before me to prepare my path. I can summarize this by saying it was yet one more time when God made his presence known to me. He wants me to know he is personally involved with every aspect of my life.

The Battle Begins

It was July 1995, and Bob was having some trouble with rectal bleeding. He had mentioned this fact to his primary care doctor quite a while ago, but the bleeding seemed to increase. The doctor said it was just internal hemorrhoids and to use Preparation H. So, that is what Bob did. A few months later, he had a physical at work, followed by a routine sigmoidoscopy. It turned out that he had a rectal tumor. The next week, he had surgery. The surgeon told us it was cancer and had spread to Bob's liver. Dr. Arnold Fingeret cried with my son as he told us the news. He apologized and said he wasn't acting professional because he had just lost his own father. You know things are bad when your doctor cries with your family. This was in September of 1995.

I will never forget what it felt like to hear the words, "Your husband has cancer, and I'm so sorry, it has spread to his liver." Then the doctor said, "Please don't say anything to Bob yet. I want to wait until tomorrow when he is stronger to give him this news." I was afraid to tell any of our friends or family, because I didn't want anyone else to have to carry that burden of keeping quiet. I was so afraid Bob would notice it in our voices or that someone might accidentally say something to Bob before the doctor spoke to him.

The next day, when I went to see Bob, it was so strange. I kept waiting for him to say something, but he didn't. He was just distant and mean, which was so unlike him. I wasn't sure if the doctor had talked to him about the cancer, and I was at a loss about what to do. Looking back, I should have realized that he knew. The entire day went by without either of us speaking of it. I remember being out in the hall crying, and a nurse came to talk to me. She said that Bob knew and to give him time. He never brought up the subject about his cancer, and when visiting hours were over, I went home. The next day, when I came back to the hospital, I finally brought up the subject. It seems Bob didn't even know that I knew, and it was all a misunderstanding. He had been trying to find the words to tell me, but he could hardly accept the news himself. He had known before the surgery that he had the cancer in his colon, but learning that it had spread to his liver was devastating. After we began talking, Bob told me he felt so alone when he heard the news, and I was so thankful that I had trusted my intuition and approached the subject instead of taking the nurse's advice to wait for Bob to do it. I was so sad that Bob had to go through what had to be one of the most traumatic experiences of his life alone. I wish I would have insisted that I be there when Dr. Fingeret talked to Bob, but my passionate insistence was what later drove me to be with Bob as much as I could during his hospital stays and to always accompany him to his doctor visits and treatments. I was blessed to be able to do that. I was in God's care, and he kept me healthy, strong, and sane during what would be a thirteen-year battle with cancer.

Bob and I managed to get through that first hospital stay. Before Bob was released from the hospital to recuperate from his colon resection, Dr. Fingeret talked with both of us. He told Bob to get out of bed every day, take a shower, and get dressed because it would make him feel better. He also said, "You never know. I could die before you, so enjoy your life as best you can." These words gave us hope, as we felt that it was God indirectly saying to us, "I am in charge." I know Bob took Dr. Fingeret's simple but wise advice, because Bob did get out of bed every day and just kept going without giving up. This shows my husband's resilient character and his will to live.

I believe that this desire to live is a gift from God, and it comes in the form of hope. I just know hope was what kept us going in the midst of our trauma, and we needed to encourage one another to keep that spirit alive. Bob seemed to have hope in the inner part of his fiber.

I remember so clearly our first oncology visit with Dr. Martin Earle. He went over the five-year survival rates of those with fourth stage colon cancer who were helped by the different treatments, such as chemotherapy, radiation, and surgery. When he was finished explaining it all, he told us that my husband had around a 25 percent chance of surviving five years with this advanced colon cancer if the chemotherapy worked and if he had the liver surgery. He didn't say it exactly that way, but when you did the math, that was what it came down to—and my husband was a math person. I was devastated hearing those statistics, but I was amazed at my husband's response. He said, "Well, someone has to be in that percent; why not me?" Looking back, this definitely was a Spirit-filled moment. I believe that the Holy Spirit was giving us a word of knowledge. Those were not just empty words, but Bob's proclamation of hope. It was from those words that I took my resolve to live alongside Bob in that spirit of hope. That is when I became his cheerleader.

Bob and I had the same reaction after intensely anticipating that first visit at the oncologist. We had put all our focus and hope on it, and when the appointment came and went, we both proclaimed that we would never live from one doctor's appointment to the next, as if those appointments were what gave us hope and gave our lives meaning. We promised each other that our day-to-day lives would be our focus, not the doctors' appointments. This resolve helped us to get our priorities back in perspective.

Bob soon had to begin his regiment of chemotherapy, and we were blessed with a nurse who helped us by saying, "Live your life, and even if you need to change your chemotherapy because you have something important to do, remember there is no magic to this chemotherapy. One week later isn't going to change the final outcome." She was giving us permission to live our lives with cancer, but not have cancer rule our lives. She was honest about the chemotherapy, too, and said if it was going to work, it would. She took the pressure off so that we didn't feel the need to be perfect and so that we wouldn't feel responsible if the chemo didn't work. I remember thinking how right she was and that it was really all up to God.

That was the attitude we kept throughout the entire course of Bob's treatments. I'm not saying we weren't compliant, but we weren't rigid, and we always told the doctors when things would be convenient for us. We took back some of the control over our lives and planned to do things. In the beginning, we never made plans more than a few months in advance, as that was scary. We eventually found our comfort level and would plan for up to six months in advance. I believe that making these plans helped Bob to go on, and it gave us both something to look forward to. By making plans, we were saying we believed Bob would still be alive and healthy.

I think some cancer patients stop making plans altogether. They live their lives around their treatments instead of scheduling their treatments around their lives. I encourage people to make plans and have as much control as possible so that they don't just become cancer patients. Doctors won't say to you, "Is this schedule convenient to you?" However, we began to notice that if the doctor was going to be away, he didn't follow the routine 100 percent. We believed it was reasonable to plan trips in between chemo treatments, but if the routine was altered because of a poor blood count, for example, and our plans weren't going to work with the chemo schedule, we chose our plans over that schedule. We didn't allow cancer to rob us of everything. We continued to live this way and made plans with the idea that we would "go with the flow." I had started using that motto before Bob got sick. I used to quote it to my mom, and it was good to hear her say it back to me when our plans didn't go as expected.

Someone once told me that we make plans, and God laughs. For those of you who are planners, and especially if being inflexible is a part of your personalities, having cancer or any sickness can be even harder to accept. Once the shock of having to live with Bob's terminal illness was over, I began to realize we were never really fully in control of our lives anyway, and I started to learn to live in the here and now.

In October of 1995, Bob returned home to recover from his first surgery. We took walks around our neighborhood together, which helped Bob regain his strength. That year we had an Indian summer, and the warm, sunny days were perfect for walking and watching the leaves change colors. It is ironic that Bob both started chemotherapy and would die in the month of October, the heart of my favorite season, when the leaves are most brilliant. I still love the fall, and the fact that I can still say that gives me hope.

Bob's first course of treatment was by far the scariest. We just had no idea what to expect, and the stress combined with the chemo made the process a living nightmare at first. Bob had several weeks of chemotherapy, and he experienced many of the side effects, such as mouth sores and diarrhea. He used mouth spray, took Imodium A-D, and managed to finish his course, only to find out that his CEA (carcinoembryonic antigen) level had continued to rise. Doctors use the CEA test as one way to track whether chemotherapy is successful; if the CEA level goes down, chemo is probably working. The oncologist said, "Unless we get those tumors out of your liver, I don't think this chemo has any chance of working. There's too much cancer in your liver, but Health America doesn't want to allow the surgery unless they think the chemo is reducing the CEA level."

What a catch-22. So, in my infinite wisdom, I said, "Well, would it be helpful if my attorney writes a letter to our HMO?"

Our doctor immediately said, "No, don't do that. I'll see what I can do." It wasn't long after that visit that we were given permission to have the liver surgery. I'll never know if the doctor passed on my comment to Health America or not, but I'd like to think those little words gave Dr. Earle an added tool when he went to bat for us. I never did ask him if that was true.

The only requirement Health America stipulated for Bob to become a candidate for liver surgery was that he could not have more than three tumors in his liver. They wanted the doctor to perform some scans to identify and count the tumors. So, off we went to get those scans. The doctor confirmed that he only had three tumors on his right lobe, and we were told that we could have the surgery at either Western Pennsylvania Hospital in Pittsburgh or the Cleveland Clinic in Ohio. We wanted to go to UPMC, University of Pittsburgh Medical Center, because of its world-renowned reputation for organ transplants. We knew it was the best hospital, by far, for any type of liver surgery. That wasn't to be, however, because Health America was no longer contracted with UPMC. My husband wanted the surgery to be performed close to home, because he was worried about me and wanted me to have family around to support me, so he chose Western Pennsylvania Hospital.

I think Bob's concern for me and the insurance company's limitations took our focus off the actual surgery. I remember interviewing Dr. Homann and asking him how many of these surgeries he had performed. He said, "Nine or ten." I said, "A month?" He said, "No, all together. There aren't many patients like your husband who meet the criteria to even have this surgery."

Years later, I found out from a UPMC nurse that doctors there did around nine or ten liver surgeries a week, although not all of these were necessarily for malignant tumors. Still, let me tell you that God was in charge. During the surgery, two more tumors were discovered in the left lobe, and Dr. Homann resected them and removed Bob's entire right lobe. I am convinced to this day that first of all, God hid the other two tumors on the MRI, and second, that God meant for us to be with this less experienced surgeon. Maybe another doctor with more experience might have seen the five tumors and just closed my husband back up again. I truly believe God had my husband right where he needed to be.

While I waited in the hospital for Bob to have that surgery, it was as if time were standing still. I saw so many people come and go out of the waiting room. By the time the doctor came to see me, there were only a handful of people left in the room. I don't remember getting any updates during the procedure, as hospitals often give today; I know that it took around ten to twelve hours, and after the doctor spoke to me, I was told that I would have to wait for Bob to go from the recovery room to the intensive care unit before I could see him. My sister and her husband had had spent part of the day with me, and later my son came to be with me. At one point, someone came and asked my son and me to go into the recovery area to see Bob. This is very unusual. The nurse said, "Let him know you are here. Call out his name and talk to him."

When Rob and I went back, I was surprised to see Bob on a respirator. I didn't remember at first that he would be on one, but seeing him jogged my memory. Dr. Homann had explained that he would be cutting through the muscles of the diaphragm in order to get to Bob's liver, so in order to help Bob breathe, he would have a respirator. Even though I remembered Dr. Homann's explanation, it didn't alleviate the fear I felt upon seeing Bob and knowing he was in such critical condition. This was the moment I realized how serious this surgery was, and the possibility that Bob might not pull through crossed my mind. I remember I was trembling, and my son Rob looked so concerned, too. All I could do was just keep praying to God to keep Bob alive.

Bob and I had accepted the surgery with such confidence that we just did not worry about it. It is hard to believe that we were in that place, but I guess it was one of those moments when there was only one set of footprints in the sand. If you are familiar with that poem, you'll understand my meaning. The poem, by Mary Stevenson, is titled "Footprints in the Sand," and it is about the times of trouble in our lives when the two sets of footprints become one—not because Jesus leaves us, but because he carries us. I have no other explanation for the confidence Bob and I shared about deciding to go forth with the liver surgery. We looked at it as our best hope for more time together. Little did I know that Bob would live so much longer than either of us could really hope for or dream would be humanly possible, but with God, all things are possible. I think Bob and I went into the surgery just focusing on extending Bob's life, and we skipped over all of the worries about the surgery. I am honestly glad we did, because it would have been too scary to consider all the complications that could have happened. I remember when I went into the recovery room and called out to Bob, he opened his eyes, and I thought he knew we were there. When I spoke to him later about it, he didn't remember that, but he said he remembered dreaming about me. I believe we had one very smart nurse, because I think my husband was near death that day. He had lost a tremendous amount of blood and had been given nine units of blood during surgery. Now, this may be expected during that type of surgery; I honestly have no idea. I never inquired about it. I just know that this nurse knew Bob needed to have a reason to hold on, and she sensed that I was his reason.

When I think about those days following the surgery, I don't know how I managed to get through them. I spent my days and nights waiting in the room provided for those with family members in intensive care. It had a TV and comfy burgundy sectional couches that seemed to fill the entire room. It was very quiet and cozy. We were given pillows and blankets, and we sort of found our spots and camped out. I remember there were many tearful relatives doing the same thing, just waiting for time to pass. All I lived for were those few brief minutes every few hours when I was allowed to go into the intensive care unit and hold Bob's hand. It all seems like a blur. He was still on the respirator and had so many tubes and wires. There was so much going on at the time that it was more than I could cope with. I just spent time in prayer. After being in intensive care for several days, Bob finally went to a regular room for a few days and then was released from the hospital. He'd had his surgery on December 18 and came home two days before Christmas. It hardly seems possible that he could have been released that soon.

Prior to Bob's liver surgery, we made a few anticipatory preparations. One thing I remember was going to buy Bob a recliner. I thought a recliner would be much more comfortable than our couch and easier to get in and out of than our waterbed. I also thought maybe Bob could take naps in it, and if he needed to, he could sleep there at night. I had had my gall bladder removed eight years earlier, and I had not been able to move in our waterbed after that abdominal surgery, in which doctors made a large incision to get to the gall bladder. I knew Bob would have that problem, too.

We went to the furniture store with my sister and her husband, who bought a chair, too. The sale was two for one, so we split the costs. We had a good time trying the recliners. There were even some that vibrated or lifted you up, so we all took turns on the different chairs. My favorite was an off-white leather one because it fit me perfectly. I am short, and this one was easy for me to open and close and was just my size. I think I was getting silly and talking about the story of the three bears and how I was Goldilocks. You see, this is how I was able to cope with life. I was learning to live in the moment. Bob found his perfect chair, and when he came home from the hospital, he used that recliner quite a bit. I still can visualize him in that chair. Just as Bob was the centerpiece of the living room, he was the center of my life, and I could not bear the thought of him dying. I was not going to think that way, and I truly believed he was going to beat that cancer.

We were so excited that he was released from the hospital in time to be home for Christmas. We all were together as a family, and I planned a Christmas service at our home on Christmas Eve. We all took turns reading parts of the Christmas story out of our Bible and giving glory to God, and we had Christmas music just like the music at church. I know we sang "Silent Night" and had candles. The following day, our extended family came to spend part of Christmas with us.

That Christmas epitomized our decision to live in spite of cancer. Looking back, I am amazed that we were even able to do these things. I guess we were truly living the meaning of Christmas. Peace, hope, and joy were God's gifts to us. I remember my husband bought me a tennis bracelet that year. I cried because I knew he had bought it before his surgery, thinking he might not be there. I was so happy that he lived to give me that gift. I never gave a thought to the possibility that he wouldn't be around for that Christmas, but when he started getting sick shortly after the holidays, I had to wonder if that would be our last Christmas together.

Bob was readmitted to the hospital on December 28 because he was retaining fluid. He was given IV Lasix and released the next day.

He was again readmitted on January 3 because he was having more complications. It turned out that when the surgeon performed the surgery on the liver, he accidentally nicked the bile duct, and Bob was getting very sick. A different doctor, Dr. Robert Kania, had to implant a stent to keep the bile duct open. During that hospital stay, my husband ended up with acute pancreatitis and was in the most severe pain I'd ever witness during the entire time he battled this cancer. Thankfully, it eventually cleared up. We didn't know at the time that that was a common risk of that procedure. The doctors managed to get his pain under control, but I learned I needed to speak up and fight for him all the more.

I learned a lesson that January night, as I should have dealt with the problem a lot sooner on my husband's behalf. It took them way too long to get his pain under control. We had to be seen by the house doctor on call because the order for the pain medication needed to be changed, and then there was a mix-up because a doctor from Health America came to see Bob, too, and apparently neither doctor wrote a new order for the pain medication. The tears Robby shed when he visited his dad and watched him suffer were what drove me to finally insist that Bob be given something for pain *immediately*. It's unfortunate, but the "squeaky wheel gets oiled" theory applies to health care sometimes, too. Over the years, I never hesitated to get my butt over to the nurses' station with a request. With God's help, I always remained polite, professional, and assertive. With my emotional Italian background, you know that was a gift from God.

After Bob had the stent inserted to keep the bile duct open, he remained in the hospital for a few more days. All that bile that should have been leaving my husband's body ended up leaking into his peritoneal cavity, which had made him very ill. He had lost a lot of weight, and his energy level was very low. However, Colleen, Rob's girlfriend at the time, had bought Bob a pair of huge shark slippers, and Bob and I would slowly walk the halls with him wearing them. Looking back, I know that with each step we took, we were giving encouragement to the nurses. They would comment about Bob being so sick and yet still walking the halls, while they couldn't get their less sick patients out of bed.

It's those little things that I remember now that take on entirely new meanings. Whenever Bob would be in the hospital, I would think about how important it was for him to keep on walking. After Tracy graduated high school, I went back to college and eventually entered a registered nursing program, where I learned the importance of walking to build strength again after surgery. I also learned a great deal of information that would help Bob in his battle against cancer. The Bible often speaks of the importance of perseverance, so I combined the two to come up with the commitments of "don't give up" and "just keep walking." Bob and I were determined to just put one foot in front of the other and walk. There were times when Bob and I would actually count the number of steps, and we would set our goal to take ten more steps the next time we would walk. Amazingly, this motivated him and built up his physical strength and my inner strength. Bob was finally discharged from the hospital, but again, he had to return in less than two weeks, if I recall properly.

It was the middle of January 1996, and Bob was getting much sicker. He couldn't eat, and he was getting weak. He was also getting so skinny, but his weight was actually going up. That may sound like a crazy statement to you, but it was water retention, not fat. I called Dr. Homann and told him how much weight Bob had gained over the previous few days and that his legs were swollen. I said that Bob normally had very skinny legs. He said that it was impossible to gain that much weight, and we had a discussion about how I had weighed him. Well, believe me, even with the little nurse's training I had, I knew how and when to weigh a patient. I told him that I used the same scale at the same time each day and that my husband was in his undies, so all of those ideas he had about what could have accounted for the weight gain didn't hold water, so to speak. My husband was filling up with fluid; I knew that much. I would call our exchange over the phone our first fight. I called our new primary doctor from Health America and said I wanted her to see Bob. I also told her I couldn't speak to Dr. Homann, and she agreed to be our advocate.

We went to our appointment with Dr. Bridget McCandliss. She was the first and only doctor who asked us to call her by her first name. Bob was so thin that you could see all of his bones. He was greenish yellow and looked like death. I really hadn't noticed, because I just saw him through the eyes of a loving wife—a wife who may have also been in denial. To me, he looked the same. When we entered the waiting room of the doctor's office, I saw the looks and stares of the other people when they saw Bob. It was only then that I realized how bad Bob really looked. We finally went into Bridget's office, and I remember her telling us to get our affairs in order. She asked if Bob had a living will. Then she said, "I have not been a doctor very long, but I've been a doctor long enough to know that some people I think will die end up living and some people I think will live end up dying." Those words were music to my soul, as I really didn't think Bob was going to die. Bob's blood work showed that his levels of bilirubin and liver enzymes were elevated. Bilirubin is a pigment that gives bile its yellow-orange color, and it was what was causing the change in Bob's skin tone. Also, his sodium and potassium levels were off the chart, which, she said, indicated he was near death. I vaguely recall her telling me this. She said he needed to be readmitted and that she would speak to Dr. Homann to make the arrangements.

Bob was readmitted to the hospital that very day, and I never did get any of our affairs in order. I didn't have time, and my energy was spent on helping Bob to live. I wasn't thinking about him dying. Because he was so sick, I don't think Bob even knew the seriousness of all of this. He lost every ounce of fat on his body, and all of his bones were showing. His appearance reminded me of pictures I had seen of inmates in the German death camps of World War II.

I was getting very frustrated at the hospital because Bob's bilirubin levels were continuing to climb. When the doctors first put the stent in, the bilirubin levels were the topic of discussion and seemed to be what all the doctors were focusing on. Within a few days, those levels dropped to the low teens, but then they went back up to twenty-one. This is pretty high, as one is a normal reading. I confronted Dr. Homann about this, and his reply was my husband had only had eleven months to live when we came to see him, and even if the surgery had been a complete success, he would only have a twenty-two month life expectancy. I guess that's when I started to feel like he was planning his defense instead of trying to treat my husband. I later learned that Dr. Homann was planning on discharging my husband. That is when I left the hospital and went to my son's house to take a breather.

I went to my son's apartment in Oakland and just tried to relax, but I couldn't. I decided to call Dr. Homann's office, and I was able to speak to him on the phone, which is when we had our second fight. I told Dr. Homann I didn't want my husband going home. His reply was, "I could make arrangements for a nursing home if you don't want to take care of him."

I said, "That is not what I'm talking about. I don't want my husband going home like this."

He then made a comment about how I questioned him all the time. I said, "Let's get one thing straight. I am just trying to understand and help you in any way I can."

"What do you want me to do, guarantee the life of my firstborn son?" he asked.

Well, I said, "Don't change the subject. This is about Bob, not you or your son, and I do not want Bob going to a nursing home. I want my husband better, and I am trying to help you by giving you information about my husband. Also, I am asking questions so I can understand the situation. I am not planning on suing you, so please don't think that I am." I don't know whether he was worried about that or not, but I just felt I needed to clear the air. "I know this was a delicate surgery, and I understand that there were risks."

That was the end of that conversation. I really had no idea what to do next at the time.

After resting at my son's apartment for a little while, I decided to return to the hospital. Dr. Homann eventually visited Bob and said that Dr. Kania was going to perform another ERCP (endoscopic retrograde cholangiopancreatography), a procedure that would enable him to look at the stent and change it if it was clogged.

On January 19, Dr. Kania performed the procedure while I waited, as instructed, in Bob's hospital room. Dr. Homann came to see me immediately afterward and said, "I wanted to tell you myself, and I didn't want you to wait one minute longer to hear this good news." Dr. Kania had discovered the stent was indeed clogged, so he removed it. Amazingly, Bob's liver was working, and the nick in his bile duct had healed.

Dr. Homann's news and visit meant the world to me. I knew he had been there, observing the procedure. I think the doctors may have thought my husband was experiencing liver failure. All of the bile that his liver had been producing hadn't been able to move through the liver, so it had been backing up into the bile duct system and the bloodstream. I am sure there is a better medical explanation for this, but in layman's terms, that's about what was happening. To them, Bob had been dying. I can only imagine their delight when they saw Bob's liver was producing bile and that the nick in his bile duct had healed. They knew this because when they took out the clogged stent, the bile began to flow the way it was intended, and I think they were able to see that the nick was no longer there. The doctors did not need to reinsert another stent.

The original plan was for Bob to have this stent for about six to eight weeks, but I think he only had it for around two weeks. Bob's nicked bile duct had healed in that remarkably short amount of time. I remember one of the interns explaining the process to me during Bob's previous hospital stay. The intern said that the stent would keep the flap to the bile duct open so it would take pressure off the bile duct and allow it time to heal. He even drew a picture for me and explained it as being similar to the mechanism of a toilet. That part I couldn't relate to, but I did understand that rather than have the bile duct fill up and then open when under pressure to release the fluid, the stent would keep the bile duct open so that the fluid continually dripped out and would not put pressure on the bile duct.

I felt a little better having some head knowledge about things I had no control over.

After this situation with Bob, whenever we would go to any new doctor, I would explain what made me feel comfortable and that I was one of those people who asked many questions. I would just ask doctors to please understand that about me. I learned to be open and honest with doctors and tried my best to form good lines of communication with them. In 1996, maybe this was unusual, but today we are encouraged to be involved in our health care by any doctor who is worth his weight.

When I had spoken to the intern, I also found out that the doctors were debating whether to use that stent or to operate again to stitch up the nick in Bob's bile duct. The majority agreed that he was in no condition to survive another abdominal surgery. During the ERCP, a scope is inserted down the throat to the esophagus, and then through the stomach and the duodenum (the first part of the small intestines), until it reaches the bile duct. This procedure enables doctors to see inside these areas for diagnostic purposes and even perform a few procedures, such as inserting a stent. The knowledge we now have about the intricate body God has so miraculously designed is amazing. It is hard to study anatomy and physiology and not marvel at God's creation. There is no big bang theory going on in my mind; I definitely believe in intelligent design. Oh, God, how marvelous are your works! You made all things.

Looking back, I remember the day Dr. Homann finished Bob's initial liver surgery. It was a very long day, and he looked exhausted when he came out to speak to me in the waiting area. I told Dr. Homann that I had been praying for him. He had a shocked look on his face, so I know he heard me. I guess God was working on my relationship with Dr. Homann, because I know God used him to save Bob's life and that God knew about our upcoming fights. When Bob had all those complications after his surgery, I vented to one of the nurses about the problems I had been having with Dr. Homann. She was shocked and said that it didn't sound like the doctor she knew. She told me she thought that Dr. Homann had been a military doctor and that nothing ever seemed to rattle him and that he was such a caring doctor. Apparently, he was rattled, and even Dr. Kania made a joke to me that he was going to throw cold water on Dr. Homann to cool him off.

I believe Dr. Homann had become emotionally involved, and I think he really liked my husband and didn't want to be the one who robbed Bob of the few months of life he had left to live. When the intern explained the stent procedure, he implied that Dr. Homann was afraid Bob was going to die. That intern was the only one besides Bridget who had even mentioned that scenario. I knew it was a possibility, but I just didn't believe Bob would die from the surgery. We had prayed about it, and I had such peace about Bob having that surgery. If I hadn't, I never would have considered Bob having it in the first place. Some could call this blind faith, others might call it denial, but I had a confidence in my spirit that is hard to put into words.

When Bob became sick right before I took him to the hospital to be readmitted for that second procedure, Tracy, Robby, and I were hugging Bob, and we were all crying. Then I had an out-of-body experience, as if I were watching the scene while floating up above everyone, and at that moment, I just did not believe it was Bob's time to die. Through the remainder of his life, through all of his further complications, I still had a hope that sprang from something inside me that I could only call my spirit. This is not to say I wasn't emotional and at times afraid and overwhelmed, but I just trusted God for my strength. As Dr. Homann had reminded me during our first phone argument, Bob's prognosis only went from eleven months to twenty-two months with this liver surgery. We weren't buying a whole lot of time here. Little did any of us know that God had other plans. It was becoming quite clear that God was saying, "I determine when you will live and when you will die. I am a God of miracles." Because of the numerous complications Bob had, some of our family members used to joke that the doctors tried their hardest to kill Bob, but God had other ideas. I liked to say God wanted to make sure he received all the credit. Looking back, there was no doubt that he was the one keeping Bob alive.

Bob was supposed to have that stent in for several more weeks, but because the nicked liver was healed and the stent wasn't necessary anymore, we were free to take a vacation. What were we thinking? I needed to get away and wanted so badly to be in the sun and warmer weather, so I planned a trip through RCI vacations. Bob wasn't really that excited about taking the trip, but he did it for me. I thought it would do him good, too, but I honestly needed that escape. RCI called the week we wanted to travel "President's Week" because President's Day took place during it. Someone at RCI told me that we would have a difficult time finding a time-share at such a last minute, but I put in a request. We were blessed to find a time-share in Hilton Head. We were to spend a week there and then head to Florida for a few weeks.

Prior to leaving for this trip, we had one last follow-up visit with Dr. Homann. At that visit, he reminded us that the battle wasn't over. He explained that Bob needed to get his strength back because he had more treatments ahead of him, including chemotherapy and radiation. Since Bob had been through a great deal, the doctor agreed the trip would be a good time of healing and strengthening for Bob. To me, it was going to be like an oasis in the desert.

One thing I won't forget was at that last appointment, Dr. Homann said to me, "You were right. Your husband does have very skinny legs." When Dr. Homann said that about Bob's legs, it meant so much to me. It was his way of making amends, but I had already forgiven him. Bob and I liked Dr. Homann from the moment we first met him, and we still felt that way on our last visit. We just had some bumpy roads to travel in the middle of our journey.

Right before we left for this trip to Hilton Head, Bob had a doctor's appointment with Bridget. She ordered some blood work to check his bilirubin and liver enzyme levels, as well as the all-feared CEA level, the marker used to track the colon cancer and evaluate whether treatments were working. The level should be around one to five. I think Bob's was forty-nine at the time of his colon surgery, and I don't recall how high it had climbed prior to the liver surgery.

Bob had the blood work done before we left, but we told Bridget we didn't want the results until we returned from our trip.

When we arrived at the time-share at Sea Pines Plantation in Hilton Head, we discovered that the unit that had been assigned to us had a water leak, so we were placed in a brand new unit. It was a two-story, two-bedroom villa with a beautiful kitchen, living room, dining room, full laundry room, sensational bathroom, and a shed with, surprisingly, two brand new his-and-her bikes for our use that week. We would take little spins around the complex, and by the end of the week, we were both riding pretty far. Although we weren't setting any speed records, we were going farther every day. I remember Bob would complain about being tired, and I could keep up with him, though just barely. He had so much more energy normally. I kept encouraging him, but I really don't think he ever realized the magnitude of what he had just endured. If so, he would have marveled at his progress. We would cook dinner together, eat in the beautiful formal dining room, and then clean up the kitchen. Then we would go up to our bedroom early in the evening and play cards in bed. Of course, Bob would win the majority of the time, and I hated losing. We were both competitive when it came to playing cards. It was unseasonably warm and very sunny. I could not believe that only two months before, Bob had had that liver surgery and that only one month before, he had almost died. To go from that critical surgery, with all its complications, to riding bikes in Hilton Head was what I'd like to call miraculous.

While we were in Hilton Head having fun, I honestly put everything out of my mind. One day, we received a call from Bridget. She had our cell phone number and decided to call us. She said that she knew we wanted to wait until we got home to get the results of Bob's CEA level, but she said that she was so excited about the good news that she just couldn't wait any longer to talk to us. Bob's CEA level was one—*normal*. Now remember, Bridget was the doctor who told us that one never knows who will live and who will die. Imagine her amazement. We were all on cloud nine. Only a few weeks prior, the greenish yellow Bob had been near death in her office. How could this be?

Later, when we returned to Pittsburgh, we went back to see Dr. Earle. He made arrangements for Bob to get a pump so that he could have a twenty-four-hour infusion of the chemotherapy that he would be receiving along with his radiations over the next six weeks. He also made arrangements for Bob to see the radiation doctor. I remember telling Dr. Earle on that visit that maybe all that poison that was in Bob's body killed the cancer cells, too, and because Bob had been so sick, maybe more cancer cells couldn't grow, either. He just shrugged his shoulders as if to say, "Who knows?"

I replied that God answers prayer. I said, "Who knows what good God can make out of something bad?" It's as if God wanted everyone to know Bob had so many complications and still lived. I would tell the doctors God used them to help heal my husband, and I commended them for never giving up or taking our hope away. I always felt it was part of our mission to give hope to our doctors, too. Later, we moved to Florida, and when we returned to Pittsburgh to visit our family, we would stop by to see Dr. Earle to let him know Bob was still around. Dr. Earle would always say, "How many tumors did you have in your liver? Wasn't it five?" We'd say yes, and he would shrug his shoulders in disbelief. Then we'd say that we just stopped by to thank him and give him some hope for his other patients.

As I sit here writing this story and know what more there is to follow, I am in awe that this was my life. If I were just reading this, I probably wouldn't believe it. And this was just the beginning of our journey. My husband used to ask, "Why is God keeping me alive? What is it he wants me to do?"

First I'd say, "He's keeping you alive for me, and you are to make me happy." I was teasing him, and we'd laugh. Then I said, "Look at how many people are praying for you. You're bringing them before God, and they're seeing an answer to prayer." I thought to myself maybe that was the reason God was keeping him alive. I am sure it was part of it, but now I know there was so much more. It is very surreal to truly believe and see God's hand in your life. I know people mention God and say he helps them, but to actually be able to write this story knowing there is an explanation for all of this unexplainable healing has given Bob's life a bigger purpose.

Please, if you have not experienced physical healing in your life, do not make the false conclusion that God doesn't love you. I just believe that for whatever reason, Bob and I were chosen to have this happen to us because we were to share this story of love, hope, and faith with others. I am sure my story is not unique, and I have heard countless other people tell me that their loved ones lived much longer than expected with cancer. It does happen. I have also been told stories about how fast a loved one died after a cancer diagnosis. I don't have answers for all of this, and I am learning not to question God, because he is God. I have learned to believe he loves us and wants us to trust him in all things.

When Bob and I returned from our winter vacation, he was feeling much stronger and ready for battle. He had to have six weeks of radiation and a continuous twenty-four-hour infusion of chemotherapy called 5-FU and leucovorin. That was the way they aggressively treated his colon cancer at the time. We were feeling pretty good because his CEA level was still low. However, many of his liver enzymes were still elevated. Dr. Earle had no explanation as to why these were so high. Bob's GGTP (gamma-glutamyl transpeptidase) level, which gives doctors information about the liver's functioning, was in the twelve-hundred range at one time, and it only went down to around nine hundred. The normal range is around sixty.

Our oncologist referred us back to consult with Dr. Kania. If you recall, he was the doctor who had put the stent in. Dr. Earle wanted to make sure everything was okay with the healing of Bob's liver, as he was concerned about prescribing more chemotherapy with such high liver counts. So, Bob and I went to Dr. Kania in August of 1996. He had no explanation for why Bob's liver enzymes were so high, but he said that Bob could continue with the chemotherapy. I asked if Bob would have a normal life expectancy with that high of a liver count. His reply was, "No, not really." I remember being so worried and praying to God about all of this. It wasn't long before the oncologist noticed that Bob's liver count began to slowly lower. When we went to see Dr. Earle in July of 1997, he reported that the blood work revealed that Bob's liver functions had somewhat improved. His GGTP was still elevated at 201, but this was quite an improvement from the one-time high of 1,200.

At the time, I was still thinking that maybe Bob would beat his cancer. It seemed to me that each problem Bob had with his health issues was somehow miraculously resolved. My faith that God really was behind all of this was growing, and I would repeat the stories to Bob's doctors. I think I had some doubts, but when the doctors had no medical explanation for Bob's repeatedly miraculous healing, I gained more courage to say to the doctors, "We believe that God is healing Bob and that he is teaming up with you."

Most doctors didn't seem to be offended by this conclusion, and since they had no scientific rebuttal, I felt more and more confident to tell the story to all the health care providers we saw. I would add that I felt God wanted them to have hope and that I was being used to pass it on to them. If the doctors doubted, no one ever said anything to me. As the years passed and Bob's medical records thickened, I can tell you he was an inspiration to so many doctors, if nothing else. It was amazing that Bob seemed to not only be healing from the liver surgery, but also there were no signs that the cancer was growing. I am sure no one expected Bob to live another twelve years with fourth stage colon cancer. I must have had hope, or I wouldn't have asked Dr. Kania if Bob could live a normal life expectancy with his elevated liver readings. What was I thinking? I still believed Bob was not going to die from cancer any time soon. And yes, eventually all of Bob's liver enzymes returned to normal.

All of this was so amazing, and I'm sure the doctors were even more shocked than we were. It was as if Bob began to heal before our eyes. Now, livers are known to regenerate, and that was what was happening, too. Even though Bob had only one lobe of his liver, over time it returned to a normal size and was functioning like a totally healthy liver. Considering all the chemotherapy he was receiving at the time, this is remarkable. As time passed, I don't know if any one doctor could fully grasp the true miracle that was taking place. I just know that countless times I was told Bob wasn't even on the bell curve. He far outlived his life expectancy. Doctors had no precedent that would suggest he could live as long as he did.

The next Christmas, Bob and I bought a used motor home. We wanted to go to Florida again after the holidays, and we thought that would be a good chance to test it out. It was to be our practice run for the trip across the country we were planning to take in May. What a difference a year makes. Now, keep in mind that Bob had an eleven-month prognosis at the time he was first diagnosed with fourth stage colon cancer. We had beaten those odds and were planning trips to Florida and out west.

So, off we went on our first adventure in a motor home that neither one of us had any idea how to operate. I guess all we'd been through somehow made us fearless. We stayed a few weeks at an RV park, which was good because we had several problems with the motor home. One night nothing would work in the kitchen, and we were clueless. I said, "Let's walk around and see if we can find another motor home that looks like ours." We did, and we stopped to tell the owners about our problem. They told us exactly what was wrong, and it was such an easy fix to what seemed like an insurmountable problem. Imagine that. After all we'd been through, how could we let something like this get us so unnerved? It was all new territory to us. We survived, and after many such incidents, we decided a motor home was not in our distant future. We weren't as worried about Bob's liver or his sudden demise as we were about all of the electrical problems we kept encountering in this motor home.

We managed to enjoy our trip to Florida, and we stayed for several months. It was during this trip that Bob said he wished he could live in Florida. I said, "Well, let's do it." We did some research and met with a realtor to get some ideas of what the houses cost. We returned to Pittsburgh and started to give the idea of moving to Florida some serious thought. We spent the next few months getting our house ready to put on the market. We listed it with a realtor and then off we headed for our cross-country trip to Arizona and then California. I wanted to put my toes in the Pacific Ocean.

There was only one glitch in our plans. Every three months, Bob was getting scans of his liver, and he had a scan several days before we were to leave. The day before we were to take off, our primary doctor told us that the scan didn't look good. We were crying and so disappointed and afraid. Bob said, "You know what? I still want to go on this trip."

I called the oncologist and told him our plans to go on vacation, and he said, "Go ahead, and I'll call you once I look at the scan."

We got the call a few days later, but our phone kept cutting out. I ended up calling the doctor back on a pay phone. He asked, "Where are you?" I said, "Albuquerque," and he responded, "*New Mexico*?" I said, "Yes, we told you we were going out west."

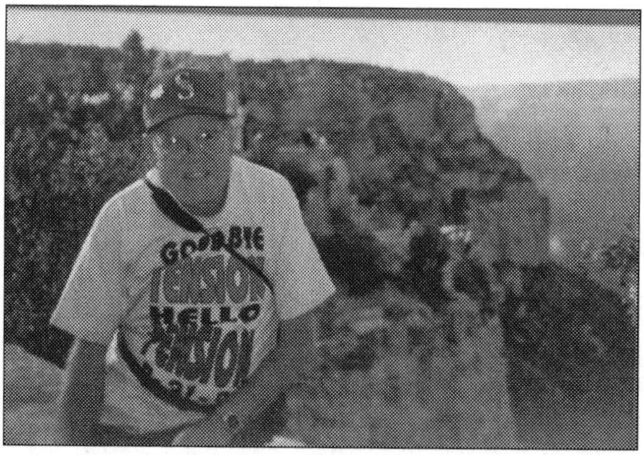

I don't think he had quite understood that when he gave us his blessings to go on the trip. But, thankfully, he said there was nothing wrong with the scan, and the problem the first doctor had seen had turned out to be a shadow. So, we continued with our trip to Phoenix, Flagstaff, the Grand Canyon, Las Vegas, and San Diego. I put my toes in the Pacific Ocean, as did Bob. And this was only the half of it. While we were on our trip, our house sold, so we changed our plans and headed to Florida to house hunt. Bob said he could have cancer in Florida the same as anywhere, and I wanted him to live his dream. Our actions showed just how much hope we had, or we never would have done these things. I don't think either of us expected that he would live as long as he did, but we were willing to take the chance to live our lives and continue to trust God to be there with us. We thought God had kept Bob alive through impossible odds, which meant there must have been a good reason. We wanted to see just what that reason might be.

We arrived in Florida to find that our favorite house from our brief house hunting in Florida a few months back was still on the market and had, in fact, been reduced by ten thousand dollars. We made an offer, it was accepted, and our move to Florida became official. If our oncologist was surprised about our trip across country, the news of our decision to move to Florida was, I'm sure, even more shocking. He answered us in a calm voice and said, "I understand," but his wide-eyed expression said otherwise. His final remark was, "Make sure you go to a university hospital down there because with your condition, that is where you need to be seen."

He connected us to H. Lee Moffitt Hospital in Florida and to a specific oncologist who practiced there. That doctor wasn't able to see us and referred us to Dr. Paul Chervenick, who happened to be originally from none other than our hometown of Pittsburgh. We found this out on our very first visit with him. It was comforting to have that Pittsburgh connection. It also turned out that his son knew our good friend Ted Goldberg. Ted was the attorney I had had in mind when I had spoken to Dr. Earle about having my attorney send a letter to Health America when they were debating about the liver surgery. Coincidence? I don't believe so. There is a lot more to this story, too. You will hear more about Dr. Chervenick later.

It was hard to believe that my husband not only survived this disease and all its complications, but he was even feeling good enough to paint our house, unpack, and do all the things that go along with moving. It was September 1997, and we were living in Florida. Who would believe this story? We continued to go to Moffitt in Tampa and regularly made the two-hour journey to see the oncologist.

Eventually, Bob had an elevated CEA level again and had to have exploratory liver surgery. Both of our sons came down to be with us for that surgery. We stayed in a hotel in Tampa for a few days while Bob had some scans and underwent final preparations for the surgery. The surgeon, Dr. Karl, later apologized because he found no trace of cancer in Bob's liver or anywhere else that he could see in Bob's body. He did find a tremendous amount of scar tissue and junk, however, that probably came from the bile leakage. So, Dr. Karl cleaned Bob up on the inside, so to speak.

Prior to that surgery, we had visited a church that wasn't our home church. Bob had been anointed with oil and was prayed over for a healing. We had no idea that that church even did that, and it only came about because in casual conversation after the service, we mentioned to one of the members that Bob was going to be having surgery. That person asked us if we would like some of the members to pray for Bob. Of course, we said we would. We were seeking prayer, and we were grateful for the opportunity to be prayed for by other believers. God was filling us up with more hope. We kept seeking and trusting him, as well as the great doctors he provided for Bob's treatment.

Our oncologist, Dr. Chervenick, followed up the surgery with a new type of chemotherapy called irinotecan, but Bob was beginning to get depressed. He hated the chemotherapy and much preferred surgery, because with surgery he could see himself improving day by day. With chemotherapy, he felt worse as time went on, but he was a very cooperative patient. He underwent this chemo for sixteen rounds. He had it once a week for four weeks and then took one week off. That much I remember, along with the long drive to Tampa from Punta Gorda, Florida. Bob and I were both so happy when we had a week off. That chemotherapy kept his CEA level under control, and the doctors continued to scan him to look for any sign of the cancer. Nothing showed up.

Our oncologist recommended that we seek a second opinion with another doctor who had just arrived at Moffitt and who specialized in colon cancer. That was when we met Dr. Christopher Garrett. If any new trials for colon cancer became available, he would be the doctor to get Bob into the study. We decided with Dr. Chervenick's blessing to go to Dr. Garrett from that time on. It worked out well, because when Dr. Garrett would order Bob's scans, we were able to get the results that very day. For some reason, when we went to the clinic where Dr. Chervenick worked, it didn't work that way. It was a small blessing to have results the very same day, even though it made for a long day at Moffitt. Also, Dr. Garrett was comfortable with not keeping Bob on chemotherapy. He said that if Bob could live with the idea of doing nothing, he would just monitor him until we either saw some evidence of the cancer on the MRI or Bob had some physical symptoms. This meant a break from chemotherapy, which made Bob extremely happy.

About six months later, Bob noticed a very small amount of blood in his stool. We immediately called Dr. Garrett. He sent Bob to Dr. Barthel, who had been doing all of Bob's routine colonoscopy follow-ups since Bob started being seen at Moffitt. I had been in the habit of getting copies of all of Bob's reports and reading them to stay acquainted with the latest findings, so I read while we waited in the recovery room and found Dr. Barthel's note on a previous colonoscopy that stated there was no evidence of hemorrhoids. I quickly spoke to the nurse and asked if I could talk to Dr. Barthel. She replied, "Sure he's right across the hall."

So, I walked over to his little cubbyhole of an office and said, "Excuse me. Can I ask you a question about Bob's colonoscopy report?"

He said, "Sure. What would you like to know?"

I showed him the report and asked him, "Are you sure my husband doesn't have hemorrhoids?"

"Yes, I'm sure."

"Could he have had them before and now they're gone?"

"No. Not unless they were surgically removed," he answered.

I said, "No, he never had that surgery. Are you sure he doesn't have hemorrhoids?"

"I am sure your husband doesn't have them now, and he never did."

He then asked me why I wanted to know. I explained that his primary care doctor in Pittsburgh had been treating Bob for hemorrhoids prior to finding Bob's colon cancer. Dr. Barthel said once again, "I can say for a fact your husband never had them." Then we had a discussion on the importance of screening for colon cancer, and I could tell by his voice that he had such a passion about early detection. I'm sure that knowing Bob's case as he did, he knew what it had cost Bob to not have had the screening done. Later you will see how this bit of information helped to change our lives.

About a few days after this colonoscopy, Dr. Barthel called us at home to let us know the biopsy results from the lab. He said the spot he saw on Bob's colon was cancerous and that the cancer had actually grown outside the colon. We went to see Dr. Karl as Dr. Barthel recommended, and we learned that Bob had to have more surgery.

Dr. Karl was pretty confident that Bob would not need a colostomy because the site of the small spot of cancer was far enough up from the anus that Dr. Karl thought there would be no problem with reconnecting his colon. He even had another doctor come to Bob's hospital room, perform a rectal exam, and take a measurement prior to the surgery. I know this doctor also felt confident that Bob would not need the colostomy. There really wasn't much of a discussion about the colostomy, although the possibility of it was mentioned. The focus was more on the fact that there was enough distance from the anus to reconnect the colon again. I knew about colostomies from my nursing school experience, and I think I actually talked to Bob a little about this because he didn't know a thing about them. I had actually had a patient who had had one. When you have a patient with a specific medical condition when you are a nursing student, you need to do individual research.

After the surgery, Dr. Karl came and told me they had had to do the colostomy after all, because the tissue in the colon had been too damaged from the radiation treatments to be reconnected. Dr. Karl worked very hard to reconnect the colon, but in the end, he decided it was too risky. I know Dr. Karl was very upset about this, and he explained that he just wasn't willing to take a chance. Bob had had so much radiation in that area that even though the anastomosis site was far enough away from the anus to reconnect it, the staples were not holding. He feared that even when he did get them to hold, they might not stay connected. That is when he wisely decided to go with the colostomy. If the colon separated, Bob could die. However, this procedure meant that Bob would no longer have use of his anus and would have to wear a bag.

Bob had to wait over a week for his bile sounds to return, which is an unusually long time. I was getting very worried because I knew if they didn't return, he would die. Though I had gone back to school for nursing in 1990, I ended up getting my degree in health information management instead. My very first patient as a nursing student had colon cancer, and he died because his bowel sounds never returned. I also had a different patient later on that year who had a colostomy. I had one who had a bowel blockage, one on a respirator, one with a nasal gastric tube, one with problems with venous circulation and swollen testicles, and many others too numerous to mention. All of these patients helped prepare me to be the best private nurse for Bob that he could have hoped for. My education in the medical field prepared me to ask good questions and to know when things were serious. I guess it also prepared me to write this book. All I know is that I would just pray and pray for all Bob's needs.

I know other people were praying for Bob, too. Bob would say that he had friends from all different religions praying, and he would jokingly say that no matter what religion God is I have it covered. I know Bob felt in his spirit that he was being lifted up to God in prayer. He would say he trusted Jesus for his healing. We would try to spread this message to other people who had cancer, but we mostly wanted to give hope to the doctors. We felt strongly that they needed to believe in miracles, too.

The entire time Bob was waiting for his bowel sounds to return, all he thought about was being able to eat. I think that was a good thing, and it kept him alive. Maybe it was mind over matter. I don't think Bob understood the possibility that he could have died. The doctors never mentioned it to Bob, and I didn't either. Sometimes ignorance is bliss.

When Bob's bowel sounds returned, that meant his colon was working and that he finally was able to start eating. Dr. Karl asked if anything sounded good to Bob. He said, "I have been watching the trays go by with that chocolate cake on it, and I would like a piece."

Dr. Karl said, "Sure, I can order you chocolate cake."

When Bob's tray came, it only had chicken broth, Jell-O, and tea. Well, if you knew how much that combination sickened Bob after all the times he'd had to eat it in preparation for a colonoscopy and after his surgeries, you could understand why he was so upset. He had his heart set on that chocolate cake. He rang for the nurse and said, "Where is my chocolate cake that Dr. Karl ordered?"

"You've got to be mistaken Mr. Renk," she replied.

Bob said, "Oh, no I'm not."

This was pretty funny to me because this was the same guy who wouldn't speak up for pain medication because he didn't want to bother the nurses, so I would run down the halls to request it for him. But after not eating for so long, it was a miracle in itself that he even wanted to eat. And consider that this man also had a colostomy to deal with, and you'll understand my husband's love for chocolate. Well, the nurse checked, and Dr. Karl had indeed ordered the chocolate cake. So, Bob had a piece at lunch with his clear soup, tea, and Jell-O. Then at dinner his tray again came with chocolate cake. I said, "You aren't going to eat that now, are you?"

"You just watch me," he said, and he ate every tiny morsel. He even licked the plate to be silly. And it was good chocolate cake, with chocolate icing between several layers and chocolate chips on top.

Years later, this nurse took care of me when I was at Moffitt having a benign lump removed from my breast. She kept saying we looked familiar. We started to talk, and as we spoke about Bob's cancer and his treatments, we mentioned the story of the chocolate cake because we loved to tell it. It was fun to watch people's reactions to our cute little story, which we had woven into the fabric of what could have been a more devastating tale about Bob's colostomy. Then the nurse remembered us and told us she had been Bob's nurse at that time. We got the full story. She told us that she had called Dr. Karl and had refused to let Bob eat chocolate cake. She said, "I told Dr. Karl that you hadn't eaten solid food for more than a week and reminded him you were a diabetic." The nurse told us that Dr. Karl said, "Give him the chocolate cake." Her reply to Dr. Karl was, "I'll give it to him under one condition; when he throws up, you get up here and clean it up." I assumed he agreed. Can you imagine this conversation between the surgeon and this nurse? Well, Bob never did throw up that cake, and it was so wonderful to hear the rest of the story. The nurse also told us that that story spread like wildfire all over Moffitt hospital. What a fun story, and what a privilege to share it with you.

And if this is not enough proof that there is a God, the first Sunday I was back at my North Carolina church after Bob died, my pastor went off on a tangent during his sermon and talked about how there had to be chocolate cake in heaven. He had no idea that my husband had even died while we were at our summer home in Canton, Ohio, and he surely did not know my husband's love for chocolate cake. He probably is learning about this now as he reads my book. I love it. Pastor Randy said, "Could you imagine heaven without chocolate cake?" I knew for sure God had placed that message on my pastor's heart so I could live in hope. And when I say "hope," I am talking about the real hope of eternal life. God is real, and he is wonderful. Isn't it neat to see when something fits into God's plan of hope for all of us? The following Sunday, Pastor Randy once again started talking about heaven in his sermon. This time he mentioned that there must be apple pie there. Then he described how it would be made. When he recited the recipe, I started to cry.

Apple pie was Bob's favorite dessert when he was growing up, and he used to tell me how his mother made it. It was the same recipe Pastor Randy just quoted. I pictured Bob in heaven along with his mother. Could this really just be coincidence, or is it a message of hope given by the Holy Spirit through Pastor Randy to me and now to you? Someday we will all know the answer. I believe it is tangible proof that God wants us to know he is intimately involved in our lives. "And even the very hairs of your head are all numbered" (Matthew 10:30). Knowing this makes it so easy to believe God could know about the chocolate cake and the apple pie.

There is another cute story about this hospital—my all-time favorite story. After Bob's bowel sounds returned and he had enjoyed his chocolate cake, I told him this joke I am about to tell you. Bob really laughed when I told him it, and I had his blessing to tell the joke to Dr. Karl. When Dr. Karl came in to check on Bob, I decided to change my joke into a question so that I could pull the doctor in on it. I very seriously said to Dr. Karl that I had a question I needed to ask him. He said, "Ask me anything. What do you want to know?"

"I just wanted to know, since you preformed this surgery, does this mean I can no longer call my husband an a**hole?" (Not that I really did, but at times I did call him stupid!)

Dr. Karl looked at me rather shocked because my delivery was so serious, and I think it took him a moment to process this. His face turned all red. Then, he started to laugh, and Bob and I joined in. Bob made some remark like, "That's my wife," and Dr. Karl said, "You two are going to be just fine." That was my way of helping Dr. Karl, because I knew how hard it was for him to make that decision. His diagnosis that we were going to be all right was 100 percent correct. Later, when you read about our trial, you will see how the seriousness of Bob's colostomy turned out to bless us even more.

So, my husband was coping with having had a colostomy. One of the teachers at my nursing school orientation had said, "Some of you won't finish, but what you learn here will be invaluable to the lives of your family members." That just stayed in my mind. I dropped out of nursing school my last year and switched to health information management because I was so uncomfortable in a hospital environment and could not function under the pressure. Imagine that. I have to be honest here and tell you that while I was a nursing student doing my clinical rotations, I complained all the time because I always seemed to get the sickest and most complicated patients. And now I know why. Each time Bob was in the hospital for one thing or another, I couldn't help but feel God had gone before me and prepared my path. You'll understand more as I tell you the next part of this amazing love story.

The only problem Bob had with his colostomy was it leaked. Because the doctor had worked so hard to try to get the staples to hold, Bob's stoma was more an "inny" than an "outty," which meant the stool sometimes would go under the appliance rather than into the bag. When this happened, it could end up very messy—as you can imagine. Sorry to be so graphic, but this is what my husband had to deal with, and we never knew where or when he would have an accident. He had so much trouble with his appliance because of this leakage, and if it would totally let go, he could have stool all over him. Sometimes it would go down his leg, which was just horrible. Most times we were at home, but I can think of several times he had a terrible mess when we were out. It was such a source of anxiety for me that I was beginning not to want to go anywhere. When we did go out, I would get such anxiety every time Bob went to the men's room, wondering if he had a problem. If he was in there too long, I would stand close to the men's room thinking that if he didn't come out soon, I would ask a man who happened to go in to check on him. Fortunately, I never had to do this, but you can understand how anxious I was.

I finally convinced Bob to wear one of those zippered purses that buckle around his waist to carry his appliance and all the things he needed in order to change his appliance in the men's room if it started to leak. I must say, he got quite good at it. We also carried extra clothes in the car, just in case. I was constantly trying to see if I could detect any odor, and if I did, I would tell him it was getting time to change the appliance. I felt like a dog that's trained to sniff out drugs. My husband had learned to deal with it in some ways better than I had. I was afraid to travel anywhere by plane because an accident there would have been the worse thing ever. I think Bob feared that also, and that may be the reason it didn't take that much convincing to get Bob to agree to have his stoma surgically repaired.

We made an appointment with Dr. Karl to talk about the problems Bob was having. Dr. Karl said for Bob to just change his appliance every day. He did not want to operate on Bob again. He didn't think it was worth the risk. If you can imagine wearing a band-aid over a certain area of your skin every day and then taking it off and placing another one there you can understand how dangerous skin breakdown can be. You see, the appliance has a part called a wafer, which adheres to your skin. The bag attaches to the wafer and seals much like Tupperware. The entire thing is known as an ostomy appliance. These appliances have come a long way today toward becoming as convenient and sanitary as possible. There are many types of appliances, but my husband wore what was called a two-piece system, so he was able to empty the bag from the bottom or change the bag completely without having to change the wafer. If the wafer has a good fit, it should last a week or more. So the idea of changing a wafer every day is ludicrous, and any ostomy or wound care nurse would agree that you never do that. If you developed total breakdown of the skin, you could not even wear your appliance. The area can get very sore when stool gets on it, too, because the stool is very harsh on skin, especially if it is allowed to sit there for any length of time. All you parents understand about diaper rash and how important it is to protect the skin. The problem with having an ostomy is you cannot put anything on to protect the skin, or the wafer will not adhere. My husband could not use Dove soap, for example, because the cream in it would cause the wafer not to stick, and he couldn't use deodorant soaps because they were too harsh on his delicate skin. He really could only use Ivory.

Eventually, Bob did have the repair done. When we made our annual trip to Pittsburgh for the summer, we consulted with one of Dr. Fingeret's partners. Dr. Fingeret was the surgeon who did Bob's original colon surgery, and his partner, Dr. Quinlin, performed the repair on Bob's stoma in June of 1999.

Looking back, this was the best decision, especially because Bob lived nine more years after this surgery. We never would have been able to travel to Greece, the Mediterranean, Mexican Baja, the Caribbean, Aruba, back to Arizona, or down the entire cost of California if he'd still had an undependable leaky stoma. Would you ever consider getting on an airplane or a boat if you thought that at any minute you could have stool all over your clothes?

I know you may find this entire subject repulsive and wonder why in the world I am including this in my love story. Well, it was an act of love that Rob nagged my husband and I to take care of this problem. After Dr. Karl refused to do the surgery to repair Bob's stoma, Rob suggested we get a second opinion, and he kept bringing the subject up to Bob and me. It was because of Rob's persistence that we made the appointment to see another doctor. It was also another one of those messages of hope, as we hoped he would live long enough to make the surgery worthwhile. And boy, was it worthwhile. Bob was truly given a second chance in every way to live a happy life.

Right after Bob had the surgery, he told Dr. Quinlin that he did a great job. The doctor said, "How do you know?" Bob said that he had looked at it. He had come a long way in less than a year from the time when he couldn't bear to look at it and I had to take care of it for him. I was able to help my husband learn to take care of his colostomy himself because that was the goal I had set for my patient so many years ago when I had gone to nursing school. I knew that in order to feel whole and independent, you needed to be able to take care of your colostomy yourself. I remembered my goal for the day was to get my patient to at least look at his stoma in the mirror. He never did meet that goal for me. It simply amazed me to hear Bob tell the doctor he had already looked at it. I'm sure the doctor was surprised, too, because that is not a typical response. I think for a moment the doctor had forgotten that my husband had already had this colostomy for almost a year, or maybe Dr. Quinlin was surprised that my husband peeked under the bandage and looked at it first. Bob was so excited to see it look so pink and healthy and to see an "outty." He knew all the problems he had with it were now in the past.

When we went back for our follow-up appointment, Dr. Quinlin was on vacation, so we had to see one of his partners. He looked at my husband's incision and could not believe he had just had that surgery. It had healed so fast. That was the fifth time my husband had been cut open there, and the doctor was telling us that it was impossible to have healed that quickly. He looked at the chart and said, "You're right, it has only been a week," and he shock his head in disbelief.

As I write this, I am having a similar reaction. I have lived this story and have spoken of various events over the years, but I have never told this much of this story in such a sort span of time. Even I am amazed as I think about all of this and see God's remarkable miracle unfold.

I was always cheering my husband on, and Bob and I participated in the annual cancer survival walks when we lived in Punta Gorda, Florida. We also belonged to an ostomy support group. When Bob went to his first ostomy meeting, he told them about going to Nags Head three weeks after his surgery. None of the members could believe it. I wasn't at that first meeting, but when I learned spouses were encouraged to come, I went with him from then on. At that first meeting, Bob said he told them, "My wife just said, 'Let's go to the beach and take walks.'" Even I didn't realize at the time how important it was to get back out there, but I just wanted Bob to be somewhere he loved. Even though we lived in Florida, Nags Head held special memories for us. We used to go there to celebrate our anniversary every September, although our actual anniversary was in November. We felt it was too cold to go anywhere for a few days in November within a day's drive of Pittsburgh, so that was how that tradition started. Somehow it seemed healing to return there again. We had a time-share there, and we'd had to cancel our previous trip there when Bob first found out he had the tumor in his colon.

So, in a small way, it was a victory vacation. We had survived four years, and this cancer wasn't going to stop our plans that time. It was bittersweet.

Love and Puppy Love

Before you read this chapter, I want to explain why I have included it in this love story. I believe this chapter reveals a great deal about Bob and my relationship and how we interacted as a couple. It also shows how we continued to have dreams and lived life to the fullest in spite of cancer.

I wanted a dog. I was feeling very sad because we were living in Florida; I missed my children, and my grandbabies weren't born yet. I finally said to Bob, "I want—no, I need—a dog."

"Bobbie, what are you thinking?" Bob said. "We can't get a dog because we travel too much, and we never know when we will need to go to Tampa for treatment."

I am sure he was thinking, as I reflect on this, *What if I get really sick? Bobbie, do you really need to be taking care of a puppy?* Well, when I get my mind set on something, I am determined, and there is no stopping me. However, I would not go out and get a dog without my husband's blessings. Though I would not manipulate or guilt him into giving me what I wanted, I would relentlessly try to persuade him to my way of thinking, and I would pray about it. I put my heart's desire aside for a while, but then it kept returning to me. Well, if I couldn't have a dog, I reasoned that I could still dream about a dog. So, Bob gladly came to the pet store with me, where there was an endless supply of puppies to hold and pet and laugh at.

It was next to our grocery store, so we started to go there often. We would stop in for ten to fifteen minutes before we shopped. When Bob would put the groceries in the car, he would say, "Okay, Bobbie, you can go look at the puppies one more time." I had back trouble at the time, so I wasn't lifting the bags and helping pack the trunk. Off I would go back to visit my favorite puppy of the day.

Now, most days there were cute ones or sweet ones, but only on occasion did I find puppy love. And, when I did, Bob knew it. He sensed it. He'd recognize the look, and then the battle would start. I didn't even have to say a word, and Bob would start with, "We're not getting a puppy."

"I know; I didn't even ask you, did I?" I would say.

He'd say, "I know you, and I saw you with that puppy." Somehow he'd know the one that had won its way into my heart. There were times I saw it happen to him, too, but my puppy love and his didn't usually match. Some people like big dogs even if they are hairy and will shed. They don't think about all the mess that a big dog makes. I pretty much stayed away from what I knew wasn't my kind of dog and focused on what I liked. I had the image already. When I found a puppy I had puppy love feelings for, I would name the dog. Then I would actually sneak back to visit the puppy in the store.

One time when my son came to visit us in Florida, Robby and I fell in love with a tiny white Westie. The dog was in a cage and was on display by the window. He was at the same level as our face, and he was so cute. He would sit up and beg, and when my son blew on him, the dog fell over. Robby and I laughed. Well, the dog came back for more, and when Robby softly blew on him again, the puppy fell over again. Now, I can't tell you how many times this happened. It seemed endless. The puppy kept sitting up and begging, and every time Robby softly blew on the puppy, he would fall over. I was sure he was trying to win us over. I remember Bob came in, and Robby said, "Dad, look at this." Robby blew on the puppy, and the puppy fell over. Well, to this day, Robby and I remember that moment, and we still share the happiness we felt. Robby had come to visit his dad not knowing if he would ever see his dad alive again after Robby returned to Ohio. But that was not how my family lived. We learned to live in the moment. Sure, there were doubts. Bob's condition was real to us, but hope ruled.

So, on and on this puppy fantasy of mine continued. I am not sure when the turning point was. I guess it was when the fantasy could no longer satisfy my hunger for a puppy. I needed the real thing, and I was on a quest. I knew my husband wasn't going to spend five hundred dollars on a puppy he really didn't have a desire to have, and I would never expect that, either. I was a very practical person so, of course, I shopped for discounts. I had my nose in all the newspapers looking for *the* puppy. I made a few phone calls here and there, but to no avail. Then, to my amazement, I found not one but two puppies. And they were my dream puppies. They were shih tzus in the colors I had hoped for, and they were potty trained—or so I was told. On and on, my desire for the puppies increased. Well, my husband saw my joy, and he was not about to deny me that. Fortunately or not, he halfheartedly agreed to drive to see the puppies. On the way to Siesta Key Beach, however, I was given the "Daddy" lecture. Bob said, "Now, Bobbie, we are only getting one puppy." The woman who owned the puppies wanted them sold as a package deal, but I promised Bob I would only get one as a compromise.

When we finally arrived, Roxie and her sister Georgia came to greet us. When Roxie peed upon seeing us, I should have known something wasn't right. The owner snapped Georgia away, indicating that I was not allowed to pick whichever puppy I wanted. Georgia went off into another room to be with the golden retriever, and the woman invited us to sit on the couch and discuss Roxie. Roxie sat on her owner's lap for a while, and then the woman asked if I would like to hold Roxie. Of course I said, "Yes, I'd like to hold her." Well, instant bond. Roxie was kissing and cuddling with me, and it was great. Little did I know the woman was probably holding her breath because she was about to pawn off a psycho dog on us. Then came test number two, which is what I term the "hand off." Bob attempted to hold the dog, and no way was Roxie going for this.

Well, dogs loved Bob, and I should have known this was another sign something wasn't right. Instead, I was thinking this was great.

You see, on the drive up to get the dog, Bob and I had the talk about how he was not to steal this dog's heart from me. This was my dog. All animals preferred Bob to me. Bob had stolen my cats' hearts, but cats are different. They are independent. Now, I was willing to share them, but this was to fulfill my grandbaby desire. I told Bob he was not to feed the dog or she would not bond with me. I was very serious. I wanted a dog, my dog—a dog that would come to me and bond with me. I didn't want Bob to steal her heart, which I knew he could do so naturally. I honestly did not realize just how much Roxie would favor me. When Roxie sat on Bob's lap, she turned her head to me and wouldn't even look at him. She was having none of him.

The owner proceeded to tell us that her husband traveled a lot and that Roxie was just used to being with one woman. She also mentioned that her son, a special needs child, kept hitting the dogs with his toys, which was why she needed to sell the two dogs. I think this was the moment we again asked to see Georgia. The owner said, "No, if you are only taking one dog, Roxie will be the best choice because she will be able to be without Georgia. Besides, Roxie is the best suited to be with your two cats." *Okay,* I thought, *that makes sense. She knows her dogs' personalities.*

Now, when we arrived back home, the first thing Roxie did was run away. She ran into the empty cleared lot across the street. I felt panic because I was thinking that I might never see her again. There were so many thickly vegetated lots surrounding us. If you know Florida like I do, you understand that we were not talking pine forests or Pennsylvania woods here; we were talking jungle. If you went into one of those empty lots, you might never come back out again. Now, I am exaggerating here, but I was scared to death of those palmettos, which we call roaches up North. I couldn't believe kids in Florida actually went into those swamps to play. How very brave. There were snakes in there, too, so how was I ever going to be brave enough to get this dog if she went in there? And forget

Bob; Roxie wouldn't even look at him, so he would never be able to catch her. Well, Roxie was a tease with me. She started to run up toward me, and then she ran away, and she did this little dance of hers as she ran circles around me. Every time I went to get her, she ran away. I started to cry. You see, my fear overtook me, and I was not having fun anymore. I didn't even know this dog, and she was teasing me. I was not sure if she loved me or had even bonded with me. I think she sensed I was upset, so she came to me and allowed me to put the leash on her. Then we crossed the street and went back to our house.

Once inside, Bob gave me the look and simply said, "She's your dog."

"Yes she is," I said. I hope you are getting the spirit of these remarks; they were said with love and a huge dose of sarcasm.

Then Roxie went under the couch, and hell arrived. The dog was not potty trained. She would not come out from under the furniture, but I didn't care. I was more determined than ever to have my special dog. She was special, all right. That night after Bob went to bed, Roxie came out to play. And boy did we play. We ran around the house. We played chase. She ran endless circles around the dining room table and ran so fast that she sounded like a train. We played with toys, and she chased the cats and stole Nicky's favorite ball. He sat on the couch and swatted at her every time she tried to get close to him. I was in heaven. My dream came true. I had my grandbaby. I wasn't feeling old, however. I was feeling like a child. My God knew exactly what I needed, and he supplied. Roxie helped me get through the homesickness I felt at times, even though I loved being with Bob in Florida.

I finally went to bed around 3 a.m., and before I knew it, day two arrived. Roxie kept peeing on the tile floor, and when we would go out to potty, it took her literally half an hour to relax enough to go. I finally determined that she had a bashful bladder. This dog was so mixed up that she was not like a dog. She didn't even want to be outside. She was afraid of every noise and everything she saw. She was so jumpy outside I couldn't believe it. Then when we returned home and she saw Bob, under the couch she would go. Bob was getting a little frustrated because Roxie wouldn't even look at him. I was so happy, and I told him how much fun Roxie and I had had the previous night. He just looked at me sort of puzzled. Well, this went on for many days and nights. I finally got the video camera out so Bob could enjoy seeing my Roxie's other side. That was a mistake because Bob saw all the fun Roxie and I were having and he felt even more rejected by her.

Things started to get really tense, and Bob said, "Call that woman and see just what is up with that dog." I called and the husband answered, and he said that his wife wasn't home. I told him how Roxie was behaving, and he said, "I'll have my wife call you when she comes back home." She never returned the call. That was how I concluded that she had pawned off the dog on us.

About a week after we took Roxie home with us, Bob and I went out for the day. We put her in her great big crate, and when we returned home, she was nowhere to be seen. She disappeared, and I couldn't find her. At that same time, the doorbell rang. It was my neighbor, who was also conveniently a doctor. She was my little security blanket. Remember, I never knew if Bob was going to get sick, and I was in Florida without any family. Rosa was from the Dominican Republic and had been educated in New York City. She was married, and her husband was a stay-at-home dad who used to be a paramedic in New York City. Isn't that amazing? Rosa was the woman who had the black and white shih tzu that started my desire for Roxie.

Rosa said, "While you were out, I came to peek at the dog. She was in her cage, and the next thing I saw, she was escaping." Rosa continued to tell us that she couldn't believe Roxie got out of the crate and that she didn't know how Roxie did it. We called Roxie Houdini for a while, and eventually we got a different crate. After Rosa's visit, we knew the dog was in the house. Off we went searching for her, and we found her under the bed. After some coaxing, I got her close enough to grab her tail and gently pulled her out.

Still to this day, if Roxie is sleeping under the bed or couch and just doesn't feel like getting up, I grab her by the tail. That dog has never once even growled at me. I have plucked the hairs from her ears, shoved pills down her throat when she was too sick to swallow, force fed her after a surgery when she refused to eat, yanked knots from her hair, brushed her teeth, and my dog endured it all because she loved me.

Roxie eventually accepted Bob, but it took some time. When Roxie did not want anything to do with Bob, he started to get angry. He once said, "I will not have a dog living with me that doesn't listen or come to me. You are getting rid of that dog." I started to cry. I was shocked. At the time, I had lived with this man for over twenty years and had never seen him act that way to me. Bob could be grumpy and sarcastic at times, but never was he mean-spirited. I can be that way sometimes; I'll admit to that. I know when I am wrong and can easily say I am sorry, but Bob had a hard time with the phrase "I'm sorry." I knew there was more to this situation with Roxie than what he was saying. I don't even think he realized it himself, or he would have told me. Bob could not stand to see that dog hide from him. It was breaking his heart. He couldn't tell me that, but I knew. So I said to him, "Please don't make me get rid of the dog. I love her." I said something like, "Maybe we could get a trainer."

I made a call to a trainer I found in the yellow pages, and he told me how much the training lessons would be. Bob was agreeable to this idea, so I scheduled the first appointment. After everything, I can tell you that we did end up having a five-hundred-dollar dog in Roxie. That bargain dog was more than we had bargained for when we bought her. Anyway, the dog training was more like marriage counseling for Bob and Roxie, and my husband gladly went for me.

Now would you believe, the very first thing the trainer asked my husband was, "Did you even want this dog to begin with?"

Bob said, "No, not really." I didn't tell any of this to the trainer, and I was laughing inside when he asked Bob this. It definitely wasn't the time to laugh out loud.

The very wise trainer said, "Well that's the problem right there. That dog knows you don't want her. You need to get down on the floor and play with her and feed her and walk her."

I think this is when Bob interjected that I wanted to be the one to feed and walk her. The trainer told me, "Let him have time with her. Let them be alone."

Maybe this was marriage counseling for Bob and me after all? I decided that if that was all there was to it, "Go, Bob!"

Roxie and I still had our special time together, but now the three of us could take long walks together, too. Bob also walked Roxie alone, but as Roxie left the house, she would longingly look back at me. My heart would melt, but I was not jealous. Bob always told me how Roxie was so happy once they were close to home, and he had a hard time controlling her when she would start pulling him toward the house. Bob understood that I wanted that dog to be mine, too, and that I was so happy to hear how much she wanted me.

I initially theorized that Roxie was like a baby that had her days and nights mixed up, but I was wrong. That dog was guarding the house. I didn't know it until Ed, Rosa's husband, told us that sometimes he didn't sleep well at night and would hear Roxie barking. He'd look out and see an armadillo. He said when he would walk his dog early in the morning, Roxie would go nuts barking. Neither Bob nor I heard her because we were sound asleep. For years, even when Roxie slept in the day, she slept with her eyes open. Bob would sit and rub her belly, and if Roxie would relax and close her eyes to sleep, Bob would say, "Look, she even has her eyes closed. She feels safe with me now." I know that dog was meant to be ours.

Roxie has brought so much fun and joy into our lives. For example, once I wanted to surprise my mother, sister, and brother-in-law Jim with the dog. I think I had had Roxie several weeks by then. I never told anyone up North about the dog. Bob was so surprised that I didn't tell, but he knew why and went along with me. Roxie was the cutest puppy. She had a pretty, long coat, and everyone who saw her when we first brought her home wanted to pet her—although, of course, she wouldn't let anyone close to her. I knew, however, that she would be okay with my sister. I was wrong. The three of them arrived from the airport in a taxi. I was so excited to bring out the surprise. I was carrying Roxie in my arms, and when she saw them, she peed all over me. Well, I did the hand off to Bob and ran in to get changed. As I looked back, poor Roxie became so upset that she lost her bowels. When I returned, Bob handed Roxie back to me so that he could clean up the mess. That was my hubby. What a great guy. Now, this was very funny, but it was also so sad to think a dog would be that afraid. But don't despair, because my dog goes to almost everyone now. She comes out to greet people, wags her tail, and barks. She even goes up to some complete strangers. It took years, and I am very serious when I say *years*, for her to come this far. I think a big part of her becoming healed is that we got Rocky. Of course, you have to know by now that there is another story on its way.

Once Roxie was well over her fear of Bob, I still thought she seemed sad. Our cat, Nicky, had died, and I believe that our beloved Crissy, our other cat who was inseparable from Bob, had gotten cancer. She had surgery, but I don't think she was doing very well, and I remember thinking that Roxie needed a mate. Now, I have to be honest here and tell you that I always wanted two dogs. So, when Bob finally agreed that we could get a second dog in a few months once we had returned from our annual trip to Pittsburgh, the little kid in me hurried up and started making some phone calls in response to ads in the newspaper.

I finally reached a woman who lived in Englewood Beach. She had just moved to Florida from New York City, and she said she had a very cute puppy. The woman explained that her husband was a truck driver and that the dog was going to travel with him in the truck, but it wasn't working out. She had two other dogs and four small children, and a puppy wasn't on her agenda right then. I told her my plans to find a breeder because I wanted a male dog that looked similar to Roxie.

She said, "I am not going to be breeding any dogs, and I only have the one puppy." She described the dog, and he was the exact coloring I wanted. She said, "He is just adorable, and my husband already named him."

I asked what the dog's name was. When she responded, "Rocky," I was in shock, because that was what I was planning on naming the dog. I told her I had to talk to my husband and tell him about Rocky.

I was also feeling as if this was confirmation from God that he had heard my prayers and we were meant to get this dog. I told Bob about finding Rocky, and he agreed to drive to Englewood Beach to see the puppy. We entered the house, and there was a lot of commotion with the children. I was standing at the door, and I saw Rocky sitting off in the distance in the kitchen. The owner suggested that I call him because he knew his name. So I stooped down and said, "Here Rocky," and this little ball of fur came running right to me. As I reached to scoop him up, he jumped into my arms just like a scene in the movies. What can I say? It was puppy love! He was so adorable. Bob held him and "bingo." That was that.

The woman said, "Rocky needs a bath, and we would like to keep him for one more night. Could you come back for him tomorrow?"

We agreed and gave her a small deposit on the dog. Then Bob and I left and took a drive to the beach and talked about Puppy Love as we walked on the beach. We decided that Puppy Love would be his nickname, you see. I was so excited and so was Bob. We went out to eat, and while we were walking back to our car, my cell phone rang. It was the dog's owner.

"If you'd like to come back today and get Rocky," she said, "he is ready, although he still is a little wet. I saw how excited you were to have him, and I didn't want you to have to wait until tomorrow to get him."

"We haven't even left Englewood yet," I said. I don't think she was surprised.

We drove back to her house and picked up our partially dry puppy. He was all wrapped up in a towel, and I carried him to the car.

The woman walked out with us. "I just wanted you to know many people have called me inquiring about this dog, and you were the only person I would even let come to see him." Those were her parting words to us.

Now, when we brought Puppy Love home, Roxie just went nuts. It was love at first sight. She kissed him and played with him, and there was none of that slow adjustment. They got so wild that I had to yell at both of them to settle down. They were mouthing each other, and I was afraid they were going to get their mouths stuck together. I called that kind of play the shih tzu frenzy. I said, "You two are crazy." They were in crazy love.

Now, I must admit that as much as I liked Rocky, I really hadn't quite fallen in love with him the way I had with Roxie. I felt a little sad, but I knew he was okay. He had Bob and Roxie. One day, however, he and I were sitting together on the couch. We looked at each other, and in that moment, I loved him every bit as much as Roxie. And I will tell you, that dog is so special, and every one who meets him thinks he is special, too. They are so attracted to him, and many people have said they wished I could clone him. I would never do that, because I don't believe in it, but I understood their meaning.

I believe we were meant to have Rocky. He was good for Bob and for Roxie, too. You see, the dog trainer I had for Roxie said that we would never break Roxie of her fears because once a dog became afraid after not being properly socialized, it was almost impossible for the dog to get over not trusting strangers. He explained that we just didn't want Roxie's submissiveness to turn into aggressive behavior. Well, our trainer hadn't met Rocky. That dog had the biggest and happiest heart, and when Roxie watched him fearlessly go up to people, she saw that it was okay. I watched her, and I could see she wanted to be fearless like Rocky. She became braver by the day. Even though Roxie is the alpha dog, Rocky set an example for her to follow. She trusted Rocky, and little by little, she changed. It is amazing what love can do, even in the dog world.

The Trial

It was cancer awareness week at Jefferson Hospital when my husband had his first colon surgery there. There was a table by the elevator with literature from the American Cancer Society, if I correctly recall. I remember picking up the booklet on colon cancer, which, of course, would catch my eye because we were living that nightmare. Anyway, I read the booklet and learned about the screening for colon cancer and I was angry—very, very angry that Bob had never had that screening. Our HMO at the time promised preventative medicine. I was so livid. How could this be? At times, I looked for someone to blame, and I sure wasn't about to blame God. He had been so good to me in my past, which you've read about by now. And God had answered my prayers and given me Bob. I didn't think he was the cause for Bob's cancer then, and I am still certain of it now. I had nowhere to put my anger, however, because Bob was my focus. He was just starting to deal with the shock of having colon cancer, and frankly so was I. That is why I think I buried my anger.

Then we came home from the hospital, and there were the doctors' appointments, the chemotherapy, and the fact that we were just trying to recover from the initial colon resection and adjusting to the idea of Bob having fourth stage colon cancer. I read up on everything I could get my hands on about colon cancer, and we even requested the physician's reference that was available, I think, through the American Cancer Society, which is how we learned the prognosis of around eleven months. No doctor ever said that to us in those terms except for Dr. Homann when we discussed the liver surgery. Bob's oncologist had only given us statistics of survival rates.

Before Bob even knew he would have to end up with liver surgery, our friend Ted Goldberg, who is an attorney, asked if we would like him to take a look at Bob's medical record. Boy, I was all over that idea. At first, when I tried to approach Bob with the idea of a lawsuit, he wanted no part of it. I never once heard Bob blame the doctor. In fact, Bob respected all doctors for their profession as healers. When he understood the lawsuit as a way of settling a dispute between him and Health America for not offering him preventive care and as an opportunity to get to the truth, he was more supportive of the idea.

I came to realize that Bob was blaming himself. Well, I am like a lot of other wives, and I wouldn't let it go. I said, "Bob, let's just have Ted get the records and see what really did happen. Maybe we don't even have a case." I was starting to accept that idea myself. Maybe it was no one's fault. Then Bob had his liver surgery with all its complications, so the lawsuit idea wasn't discussed anymore. I was just dealing with Bob's health issues, and so was he.

One day, after Bob was doing much better, Ted called me and asked again about looking into Bob's medical records. He said we needed to make a decision, as we only had a two-year window within which we could file a suit. So, I brought up the subject to Bob, and this time he agreed that it was okay to just look into it. Bob signed the necessary papers so that Ted could get access to Bob's medical records. This was probably at least one year after Bob's original surgery, because we were still living in South Park, Pennsylvania. Ted's law firm requested all of the medical records up to that point. After reviewing the records, the lawyers determined that they thought we had a case. They filed the lawsuit right before the two-year limit would expire. This was late in the summer of

1997. The next step was that the judge had to make a ruling as to whether or not our case had merit before we could proceed any further. The ruling was in our favor.

If I understand this correctly, the case was going to be based on the fact that we had a contractual agreement with our health maintenance organization to be provided with preventive health care. We were suing because Bob wasn't given the preventive screening for colorectal cancer. I don't remember if that was actually stated in the suit or how that was legally presented. All I know for sure was the suit was filed against Health America, Penn Group, and Bob's primary care doctor.

Ted was not really expecting to go to trial. He said we might be able to get some of the money Bob lost through early retirement through arbitration. Ted also said, "I know you could use the money, and they may be willing to settle." Whenever I would mention the attorney fee, he would say that we would talk about that later. We were working mostly with Tony D'Amico, who was one of the associates at Ted's office. I remember a part of me was hoping this would come to trial, because I was hoping to learn what really happened and have an answer to the "why." The other part of me had a dream that some good would come out of the trial to spread the truth about colon cancer and preventive screening.

Health America, Penn Group, and the doctor were not going to arbitrate. At that time, I didn't know the full details; I just knew this was going to trial. So, Ted asked if he could turn our case over to Neil Rosen, who specialized in malpractice. That was also when Ted asked us to sign our contract with him for his legal fees. I was fine with being assigned a different law firm, and I appreciated that Tony would come over from Ted's office to help Neil with the case. I trusted Ted to do what was best, and I remember Ted brought up the fact that he didn't want the trial to jeopardize our friendship. I totally agreed with his thoughts about that, and I thought he had made a wise decision. It proved to be a great decision.

The trial began in May of 2000. We were living in Florida at the time, but since the incident occurred in Allegheny County in

Pittsburgh, Pennsylvania, that is where the trial would take place. It would be a trial by jury of our peers and, I suppose, the doctor's peers, as well.

Well, we finally met Neil, and I remember that meeting very clearly. Neil is very handsome and captivating. I thought this was a good start. The jury would like him. He was very striking. We began to talk, and as I was talking away as usual, Neil turned to me and said something like, "Let's get one thing straight. I am in charge of this trial, not you."

Well, I was taken back and caught off guard, but I heard myself say to him, "Well, let's get something else straight here, too." I remember having an edge in my voice. I surprised myself because being assertive was a struggle for me, and I thought I came off rather aggressive, at least in my tone. So I continued to say to Neil, "I am the kind of person who likes to be involved. I'll tell you what I think and what I know about Bob's history with this cancer, and I hope you will listen." I felt myself starting to calm a bit, so I added, "But of course you will have the final say, because you're the expert."

I was thinking, *I've been involved in all aspects of my husband's health care and I'm going to continue to speak my mind with these legal matters, too. But I'm not that stupid. I know I don't know the first thing about being a lawyer, so I will most likely follow your advice once I understand the rationale. That's why we are paying you.* Fortunately, I kept these thoughts to myself. This was pretty much the gist of the beginning of our first conversation.

Then we started to go over my husband's medical records, which is where I shine. I knew that medical record inside and out, and Neil picked up on that. He asked me questions about Bob's medical history and used my memory as a resource, and I know I gained his respect, which meant the world to me. I mentioned the issue with the hemorrhoids and how no evidence of hemorrhoids had been seen on one of the colonoscopy reports. I told him how I had questioned Dr. Barthel about this fact. I think that may have made an impression, because I was very detailed about everything concerning Bob's medical condition.

In some small way, Neil became a big part of Bob's healing and of mine, too. We need total healing, not just healing of our bodies. As I continue my story, I am certain that this will all make sense.

We had days of jury selection, petitions to the judge, pretrial arguments, and trial rulings that would dramatically affect the case. I am not an attorney, so I can only give you my perspective on the things I was privy to as one of the plaintiffs. I remember the defense had a doctor who had testified before in Neil's cases. Neil was upset with this doctor, to say the least, because the doctor had published a complicated theory with some mathematical formula that could determine when the cancer first occurred in the body and when it spread, for example, to the liver or some other distant organ. Therefore, it didn't matter if you found the cancer or not, because the patient had already had the cancer and the injury had already been done. Hope you're following me here.

A copy of this theory was mailed to us in Florida before the trial started. I read it, and frankly, I thought it was baseless nonsense. I was irate at that theory, too, because it seemed to ask, why screen for cancer? What a terrible philosophy. And in the world we live in, let's face it: lawsuits have influence. Agree or not. You can look at it any way you like. They can be seen as good or evil. I know things aren't black or white here, but in this day of high medical costs and all of the talk of health care reform, the dollar is the most powerful tool on either side of the debate.

All I know is my perspective, and I thought his theory was absurd. We needed to find cancer as soon as possible, treat it, and hopefully cure it. And we could not let doctors off the hook by saying, "Well, this person really had these cancer cells X number of years ago, so it wouldn't have made any difference." That is basically what his theory was in my eyes, just a smoke screen.

I said to Neil, "Well, the defense just accused our doctor of testifying for money; why not do the same thing?" I truly believe Neil was so blinded by his outrage toward that doctor that it only took a simple remark on my part to open his eyes to some legal tactics he could use to put an end to this kind of trickery.

And by the way, our doctor usually testified for the defense, but he felt passionate about our case and the need for colon screening, so he agreed to testify for the plaintiff this time. It turned out that when the doctor with the absurd theory was ordered to disclose his tax statements showing his income from testifying in court, he refused. So, the judge ruled that this doctor wasn't allowed to testify unless he agreed to cooperate, and I think we can all come to the proper conclusion. It was all about the money, and he would have no clout once the jurors had those facts available to them. I love this part. See, good does happen sometimes. Truth can prevail, and if that doesn't give you a good dose of hope, I don't know what will.

Now colon cancer, when detected early, is curable. Find a polyp before it turns to cancer, get it out, and you have intervened. You have prevented it from becoming cancerous. Not all cancers work this way, but colon cancer does. Health America knew that, which is why they recommend a sigmoidoscopy at age fifty. Many insurance companies will pay for a sigmoidoscopy or, better yet, a colonoscopy because they have learned it's a lot cheaper to pay for testing than the cost of treating full-blown cancer. Doctors typically agree, especially now that they can be sued. It doesn't take a brain surgeon to get on board here.

I don't know if it is cheaper for HMOs to treat a few cancer patients than it is to fund numerous colonoscopies, but if they can be sued and the legal awards are large enough, prevention costs might be cheaper in the long run for them, too. I shouldn't say that preventing lawsuits is the motive behind HMOs providing coverage, but money does factor into the decisions made by HMOs, their doctors, and even the hospitals they use to provide services within their health care plans. Welcome to the world of managed health care.

I know doctors are aware that it is essential to perform a sigmoidoscopy or colonoscopy and also a fecal stool test, so these practices are becoming standard now. Between Katie Couric's on-TV colonoscopy and maybe our trial, which was conducted in a city known for its medical facilities, such as UPMC, word got around.

Another interesting part of our trial, I think, was the fact that Health America sent publications that were meant to be educational and informative to their subscribers, and at least one of these mailings had talked about screening for colon cancer. I'm not sure of the details, but I know that they tried to use this as a weapon against my husband by saying that since Bob had this information, he was somewhat responsible for making sure he had a sigmoidoscopy. The judge ruled that there was no way my husband was going to share that responsibility. There are situations in which the injured party can share a percentage of the liability. That was not to be the case here, and the judge said that there was no way Health America could prove that Bob had even read those mailings. I can tell you he didn't. It was my job to sort through the junk mail at home, and with our busy life, I may have browsed through a few of these mailings, but then I'd throw them away. I knew Bob had no interest in reading about medical things. Like I said before, he came from the old school, in which medicine was the doctor's responsibility and you just trusted your doctor to provide the care and information you needed.

What was ironic about this story was how many times either the doctor's attorney or Health America's attorney would try to use this literature. Then they would be called up to the judge for a side bar, or a private conference. Each time, the judge would rule that they could not cite anything from the mailings they'd sent us. I guess their defense was going to be that Bob should have demanded that his doctor talk to him about this information and insisted on preventive screening. They tried to use the literature in their defense so often that it was comical to Bob and me. After the trial, Neil told the jurors they could speak to him and ask any questions they had about the case. Several of them came up to Neil and wanted to know what had been going on when the judge asked the attorneys to approach the bench so many times during the trial. It had aroused their curiosity. Then some of the other jurors admitted that they also were wondering what had been going on when that happened. What I think was so great was that Health America could not use these mailings against us, but we were able to paddle Health America with them. These mailings allowed us to demonstrate what their recommended screenings were for colon cancer, because they outlined what screenings were to be used and at what age the screenings should begin. These mailings included what Health America considered to be their guidelines for colon cancer screening. Our lawyer was able to make the connection that those guidelines were what Health America considered to be the standard of care and that Health America offered them as part of their preventive care to their subscribers. My husband and I had to keep from laughing during the trial because we found it funny that they would not give up on this idea for their defense. I even think at this point God might have been calling them *stupid*, which is his pet name for me when I am slow to learn a life lesson.

It is not my intention to replay the entire proceedings of the trial to you. I will try to summarize it as best I can. I know that we, the plaintiffs, had doctors testify about how colon cancer begins, spreads, and also how it can be detected and even prevented. The doctors also testified about Bob's specific medical history and his diagnosis, treatment, and prognosis.

The trial brought to everyone's attention that Bob's cancer was discovered at his workplace when he participated in a physical and sigmoidoscopy that was being offered to all employees for the first time at U. S. Steel. Prior to this, it had only been offered to the top management, but because of a change in the law, U. S. Steel had to offer it to all of its employees. Bob thought it was a good idea and took advantage of the physical they offered, along with the cancer screening. He even encouraged his coworkers to go for the screening, too. Two top level managers from U. S. Steel actually came and testified that this was indeed true; the year Bob had his sigmoidoscopy at work was the first year this testing was offered to all non-management personnel. The defense tried to paint a picture that Bob could have had it previous years and had refused it.

Neil dotted every "i" and crossed every "t" so that no false statements made against Bob went undefended. That is the kind of attorney Neil is. He is very detailed, which contributed to his winning Super Lawyers' Top 50 Pittsburgh Lawyers award in 2004, 2005, and 2006. His peers recognized and honored him with a "Best Lawyers in America" award in 2009 and 2010, according to his website (caringlawyers.com). He also earned a 2006 Shalom Award from the Kollel for giving back to the community. We believed Neil was a great attorney at the time of our trial in 2000, and the fact that he received these awards demonstrates that others agree. I'll borrow my brother-in-law Jim's favorite saying: "Isn't it great when a plan comes together!" We had a great attorney when we needed one the most, and I believe it was a God thing!

Neil knew it would be bittersweet to win the lawsuit, so he said, "Bob, wouldn't it be great if you won and lived to be eighty?" Bob did live eight more years, and I believe Neil's prayer was answered. God understood the spirit in which it was said.

The trial also brought to everyone's attention that Bob had indeed mentioned his concern for rectal bleeding to his primary care doctor and had not been offered diagnostic testing. Bob was merely treated for hemorrhoids that he did not even have. Neil proved that Bob had never been educated about colon cancer, but most importantly, he proved that Bob had not been given a colorectal cancer screening at age fifty, which was the age set in Health America's own standard of care.

Neil further proved that Bob's doctor, who was an employee of Penn Group, did not implement Health America's standard of care. Penn Group was employed by Health America, so that was the order of responsibility. Health America was on top, and with authority comes responsibility. I learned that a long time ago in one of my business management classes. Can't have one without the other. Remember this! That is why three parties were named in the lawsuit. The irony of all of this is that Penn Group was dissolved by the time we went to trial, but their insurance company was still liable to pay. If Penn Group had still been in existence, they might have insisted on their own attorney, too. That would have been some three-ring circus to behold.

We did not have to divide and conquer. In my opinion, Health America and our doctor did a great job by themselves. During the trial, much of their defense was to blame each other. It was like watching a bad marriage. How cool was that? We just sat back and watched. Sometimes when you are falsely accused, that is the best defense. They shot themselves in the you know what, and I don't mean the foot. I am sorry, but I cannot resist these jokes.

We had several doctors testify about colon cancer, and one specialized in performing colonoscopies. He explained the process and the necessity of early screening. He discussed the statistics of survival rates within each of the four stages of colon cancer, and he discussed my husband's prognosis. By then, Bob had had his reoccurrence and his colostomy, and things weren't looking the brightest. If I recall, Bob wasn't looking so great at the time. He didn't look like death, but he looked a little frail.

When the doctor testified that Bob's prognosis was about one year, Bob and I began to cry maybe more than a little. The doctor apologized to us after his testimony and said, "I thought you knew." He was surprised, I guess, about how those words brought tears to our eyes. Well, it's hard to hear under oath that you probably aren't going to live more than a year. It almost makes it true. But this doctor didn't know that Bob and I didn't live like he was going to die. We didn't plan or speak of it because when you believe God is healing you and keeping you alive, to talk like that or give into that is not trusting him.

Now, that doesn't mean that we didn't have a doubt. Every time Bob was in the hospital, I would give the facts to our family and friends. I hated to do that, but the facts were what were real. I hated it even more because people would give pep talks or ask questions I had no answers for, and I guess I was thinking, *Do I seem negative or scared, or are they seeing something I'm not? I'm just living this day by day, and I can't go there. I can't go into the future, because I am having a hard time just with the here and now. I am in a fight here, and I am dealing with doctors and medical staff. Bob and I only have God to help us with this.* I knew God was helping, but I didn't want to share my beliefs because I didn't want it to seem like I was lecturing or that I was being unrealistic about Bob's health concerns. I just kept my thoughts to myself. Another reason was I honestly didn't have the energy to try to explain myself. It was exhausting to talk to everyone and give updates about all that was medically going on with Bob, and at times, I guess I was feeling resentful. I just wanted to state the facts and be done with the conversation. God helped me to see that that was their way of trying to support me. Then and only then was I able to be more patient and more understanding. I almost could anticipate who would act which way, and I began to see that it was all out of love for Bob and me, so I started not to be as agitated. I cannot explain it, except that God, Bob, and I did it together. Even now, as I write this, I have no words to fully tell you how Bob and I did this. But I can tell you that Bob and I understood it together. We had hope and we basked ourselves in it, but sometimes we wondered whether others saw our hope. I know some did and that in their ways, they tried to be encouragers. But I knew the prayer warriors we had were there. So for all of you who truly pray for others, carry on. I believe someday we will fully know the extents to which those prayers have reached.

If you recall, our oncologist in Florida was Dr. Chervenick from Pittsburgh. Well, since he was Bob's current oncologist, he would be the doctor to testify about Bob's medical condition and explain Bob's treatments and diagnosis. I guess you could say it was through his testimony that Bob's past and current medical condition would be explained to the jury. Our attorneys along with the two attorneys for the defense flew to Tampa, Florida, to take Dr. Chervenick's testimony, which was filmed and later presented to the jury. Neil informed me that the woman attorney from Health America would not pay for her trip, so he had to pay for her expenses. He told her not to worry because when he won the case, she could reimburse him. Now this was rather funny to us.

I have to admit that I really did not like that attorney. She seemed heartless, but now I see it was only because she represented Health America. At the time of the trial, I resented Health America for not making sure Bob had his colorectal screening. My feelings toward the attorney were not based on anything she did as the defense attorney. She acted very professional, and her conduct was above reproach. She did not try to use any nasty tactics. But I will be honest and say that I delighted in the fact that after we won our case, Neil was able to remind the Health America attorney that she needed to reimburse him for her trip to Florida.

The trial was very emotional, especially because we had to recall things I didn't want to relive. I was also worried about Bob having to testify, and I was afraid he wasn't going to be able to do it. He wasn't good at speaking in front of a lot of people and was somewhat shy. So, I was scared for him. But let me tell you, God showed up for Bob's testimony. Bob testified with such ease, and he spoke to the jury as if he were just talking to his best friend.

Bob testified on his own behalf, and he did a great job. He even demonstrated how to take care of his colostomy and educated the jury about how to change his appliance. I remember the doctor's attorney tried to trick Bob by asking him to read the back of the tube of Preparation H. It read to discontinue use if you are bleeding. The attorney asked Bob, "Why would you use this if you say you had blood?"

"I told the doctor I was bleeding, and he told me to use the Preparation H," Bob replied. "It says right on the tube to consult your doctor. I had just been there, so I did what the doctor recommended."

You see, it was simply the truth, and sometimes when people think they are so smart and clever, the truth comes back to bite them. I think Bob would find this joke of mine to be very fitting.

For me, the highlight of the trial was when I was called to testify. I was able to talk to the jury and be unemotional. God was definitely with me as I looked at all the jurors and testified about how much I loved my husband and that his colostomy did not change the love I had for him. I also said, "I love his stoma, because it kept him alive." When I said Bob was still a whole man to me in every sense of the word, the judge had to reach over and take one of the tissues she had put close to me. Then I looked at her and saw she was crying. When

I looked back over to the jury, many of them were crying also, and not just the women. It was a wonderful moment because I knew everyone in that room understood the love I had for Bob. To me, that was the most important truth I came to testify about that day.

I also testified about our move to Florida and that I wanted Bob to live his dream, but that it was hard to leave my children. However, I said that I also thought it would be good for them not to have to deal with Bob's cancer all of the time. I wanted my children to be free to live their own lives. I knew firsthand what it was like to live with a sick father. I also testified that we prayed about that move to Florida, and when every door was so easily opened, I believed God was answering us and saying he gave us his blessings over it. I think that gave the jury enough insight as to why we did what others might think was so strange under the circumstances.

More importantly, the jury was able to understand firsthand what Bob had to endure while living with his cancer. And let me say, if this story is not a motivator to do the prep and get a colonoscopy, I don't know what else I can say. So for all you readers over fifty years old, get your butt to the doctor and get tested. It could save your life. Tell all of your friends and family to do it, too. If you feel the least bit of empathy for what Bob and I have been through, then do it for us. Fair enough?

Before the trial, I had prayed to ask God to help me forgive the doctor. By then we had so many good doctors, and Bob seemed as though he might actually beat his cancer, which helped me have faith.

One thing I recall very vividly was the moment I realized I had truly forgiven the doctor for not taking better care of my husband's health. I remember being outside and walking with my neighbor Ellen and talking about the upcoming lawsuit. She and I walked about three to four miles every day together. I remember telling Ellen about how I was so at peace about the lawsuit. I realized in my heart of hearts that I had forgiven the doctor because Bob was pretty healthy, we were living in paradise, and God had turned something bad into something good. How could I be angry anymore? I said to

Ellen, "No matter what happens during this trial, I am at peace and leaving it up to God." I was just in that mindset, and I didn't want the trial to stir old resentment.

I knew one thing for sure in my past: living with bitterness, hurt, anger, and resentment hurts me more than the other person (or in this case, corporation). I had learned that firsthand in my first marriage. So, I honestly was willing to forgive partly out of the selfish motive that it was good for me. I truly believe God knows that, too, which is one of the reasons why he tells us to forgive others. "It's good for you, stupid." I like to think God talks to me that way sometimes. We have a sense of humor in our relationship. He is a mighty, awesome God who knows everything about me, so why pull any punches here? I reason that he is the God of creation who made everything, so he is pretty smart. I will never get one over on him. When I think I will, I am being stupid. I believe forgiving others is an act of obedience to God, and he will honor that by equipping me with the ability to forgive. I only need to ask him, as it is his will for me to forgive.

When I said earlier that the trial was healing, it eventually helped me to forgive Health America, but I can tell you that it didn't help me get over my fear of losing Bob. When the verdict came in, I was starting to consider that maybe Health America wasn't the villain I had made it out to be. My heart was softening even more when Neil told me that Health America had considered arbitration, but it was the doctor who had refused. He wanted to fight to the bitter end. I wasn't mad at the doctor anymore, but I did think he was stupid for not wanting to arbitrate—especially considering the outcome of our trial for him. Even though the jury did not find Health America guilty, I still wasn't sure I agreed. I still had some doubts that they had really intended to give Bob a colon cancer screening. In time, as God continued to soften my heart, I came to see my unforgiving heart was doing my thinking. When I realized this, I was finally able to believe Health America really intended and planned to offer preventive screening to its customers. Accepting this idea helped in my forgiveness process. What an awesome God I serve!

At first I hesitated to write about the trial, but I love this part of my life. I don't love it because of the financial outcome, although it is a blessing, and certainly not because of the emotional toll the trial had on everyone, but because of the healing and yes, the drama. I'll admit to that. It was drama. It was real life drama—the kind that makes for good movies. In fact, when we had the trial, I would joke about this becoming a movie and that Sidney Poitier, one of my favorite actors, who I thought was humble like Bob, would play my husband. Oprah would play me because someone once told me that I resemble her, probably because we talk similarly. And, of course, Will Smith would play our oldest son. Bob and I would joke about how Big Rob looked similar to Will Smith because of his buzzed haircut and his expressions when talking, but mostly because his personality resembled the one Will Smith portrayed on his TV show, *The Fresh Prince of Bel Air*. That was the clincher. Even though our family is white, I imagined these actors would portray us in my make-believe movie.

The trial was very stressful, and I ended up with a terrible cold. I remember coughing so much at times that I had to go out into the hallway to get a drink of water. I hated sitting there with an annoying, uncontrollable cough, and I was trying so hard not to blow my nose during the testimonies. The stress was beginning to show on me, and I was exhausted. And as if there weren't enough stress between the trial and my awful cold, would you believe I had to have a breast biopsy during the preparation for the trial? I was worried about it interfering with our preparation time with Neil, but somehow I was able to get it scheduled without it being a conflict. The doctor's office scheduled me to learn the results of my biopsy and meet with the doctor on the same day that the jury came in with its verdict. It was rather ironic that the trial would end that very day. I wanted to reschedule my appointment, but Bob insisted I keep it. As I reflect on this now, I realize that he was probably more worried than I was about my results. I honestly don't remember feeling worried. I was more anxious about getting out of the doctor's on time to get back to court. It's funny that all worked out perfectly, too. I was only a few minutes late to court that morning, and thankfully, I can say that the results of that biopsy were negative for cancer.

I don't know if this is the time or place to discuss colon cancer further or even the rest of the trial's events. I don't think that is my purpose except to say that this trial and its outcome had a far-reaching influence. I know articles where written in the Pittsburgh papers, and I learned that our case was somewhat of a test case. Our case ending up being the first time a doctor was held responsible for not meeting the standard of care set up by the HMO. Usually doctors are limited by what insurance companies will approve. Later, when we were talking with a woman at the American Cancer Society in Florida, she cited our case, though not by name, stating that doctors could be liable if they didn't recommend colon cancer screening. We had a somewhat brief discussion and she said that the cancer society was going to report that to the local doctors. I eventually found out from Rosa, our neighbor across the street, that this information was indeed passed on to local doctors. The doctors' group that Rosa worked for educated all the doctors in the group about the legal implication of not screening for colon cancer. So, without any hard facts to back this up, let's just say that I believe Bob and I, by means of our trial, accomplished part of what we hoped for in terms of screening and colon cancer awareness.

We truly hoped that our trial and our experience would spread awareness about colon cancer and maybe save other lives. We would often talk to others and promote getting a colonoscopy. We participated in a cancer survival walk in Port Charlotte, Florida, to spread awareness, and I remember how happy I was to be walking around the football stadium holding Bob's hand. It was bittersweet because we lit candles for Bob's brother, Ralph, who died of testicular cancer when he was twenty-eight. That cancer is now usually curable when detected early.

One year, I think around 2000, we participated in another cancer walk that was to start at the harbor in Punta Gorda. I remember it rained. While we were standing under the shelter, waiting for the rain to stop, a reporter went around and talked with some of us.

When he learned that Bob was a five-year cancer survivor of fourth stage colon cancer, he wrote an article about it for the *Charlotte Sun Herald*. I came across the article in my memorabilia box not too long ago when I was looking through the stack of cards Bob sent me over the years. It was so special to go down memory lane one last time.

This trial turned out to be big, and we thought that maybe it would get some attention. I don't know that we ever really believed it would, but we had hope. To this day, I am not sure how far-reaching the trial's results were, but I am sure now that Bob is in heaven and he is seeing some of the fruits of his suffering.

That word, "suffering," brings me back to my emotions about the lawsuit. I know seeing Bob's pain and the fear of losing him sparked my anger in the beginning. I also know that seeing Bob suffer and watching him in pain healed me of that anger, too. I loved Bob, and his pain and suffering were all I could endure. I had no room in my heart for anything more. His pain was all encompassing for me, which I carried in my heart but could not show to him. My heart eventually had no room left for bitterness, hate, anger, or resentment. My life became just about Bob and his well-being. I focused on practical things, such as making sure the doctors had all the information about Bob's medical history so that Bob didn't have to relive it each time we saw a new doctor. He hated the questions, so I would answer them instead of him. Bob was always a very compliant and responsible patient who took an active role in the process, however, which came out in the trial, too.

When the defense attorneys tried to imply that my husband was in any way responsible for this cancer, Neil was able to prove using the facts in the Bob's medical record that Bob was the most responsible of patients. As Neil questioned the various witnesses, he proved that Bob kept every appointment and every follow-up, and the medical record was a testimony to that truth. So why is this so important? You would have to know Bob. He was such a responsible, hard working, honest person, and he blamed himself for his cancer. I know he did. He never blamed God or the doctor or Health America. He blamed himself. I think he thought he should have been more of a spitfire, as I was. But I believe that Bob's humility was why the doctors went the extra mile. Or, maybe our love for each other, which was apparent, was the reason. When we had this trial, the truth came out, and Bob was set free from the lie that his cancer was in any way his fault. He finally learned the truth. He'd had a bad doctor when he'd needed a good one the most, as Tony and Neil would so often repeat to him. Bob was not the type to question a doctor. He trusted and respected doctors, and he did as he was told.

Today, I think we are expected to be more active participants in our health care. Also, when certain things are so commonplace that they are common knowledge, such as getting a mammogram or a pap smear, I don't think you can get away with having zero responsibility for not asking your doctor for these tests. Back in 1992, when Bob should have had his first sigmoidoscopy, getting colorectal cancer screenings was not common knowledge. So, at some point, we are responsible for our own care. I say this not because I believe that doctors are shrugging off their responsibilities, but because there is a lot of good information out there. It's our lives and our bodies, so we must take as much responsibility as we can to partner with our doctors about our health care. Everything needs to be put in perspective. This trial took place in 2000, and it is now 2010. Today the world is changing, and thanks to technology, there is a lot of good information available to us. Read up on your health issues and concerns on the Internet and use this information to ask questions to your doctor. A good doctor will confirm whether the information is true and relevant to your particular health concerns and will not be threatened by your desire for information.

The trial was also educational, and I believe we had the perfect jury. I say that because some of the jurors knew about colon cancer screening because they had good doctors who had educated them about it. These jurors were able to confirm a great deal of the testimony to be true. Some older jurors had experienced first hand how their doctor did not educated them about screening for colon cancer and they could relate to Bob's situation with his doctor. Talking to the jurors after the trial was enlightening to us, too.

Now, this trial became about more than just the money, but the day the verdict came in, it was all about the money. It was kind of fun because at the last minute, while the jury was still out, phones were ringing, and there was all kinds of activity going on out in the hall. I think what prompted the flurry was that the defense knew the jury had reached its verdict.

Before that flurry, earlier that day, the jury had called for a question. We received that call while sitting in Neil's office waiting for the jury to deliberate. I said to Neil, "What's the question?"

"The jury wants to know if Health America is still financially responsible even if they are not found guilty," he said.

When he said that, I thought, *I have to write a book.* You see, I had read a few of John Grisham's books, such as *The Client* and *The Runaway Jury*, and I was thinking that our trial was as good as it gets. I felt sure we were getting an award. Neil was calm, at least on the outside, and he said something like, "I think that was a good question." I thought that it was a *great* question, and I may have said that out loud.

I knew it was a great question because I knew the answer. The judge had prepared the jury before they went into deliberations. I remember most everything she'd said. First, she had given them the usual instructions that apply to all trials, but the details pertaining to our trial are what I remember most. The jury was told they had three things to decide. She had already told them that under the law, she was able to find the doctor guilty of malpractice, so they did not have to decide that part.

Because of a legal course I was required to take when I went to school for health information management, I knew that when the evidence speaks for itself, a judge can take a decision away from a jury and make it herself. That is exactly what Judge Freedman did when she directed the jury's verdict in our case. According to an article that appeared in the February 2–8, 2001, issue of the *Pittsburgh Business Times*, which cited court documents from our trial, Judge Freedman denied the request for a new trial on December 19, 2000. In response to the claim from Health America and the doctor's attorneys that Judge Freedman erred when she directed the jury's verdict, she replied, "Simply put, there is no jury that could have found that Dr. Ganti acted responsibly in this case, and this court acted entirely correctly in directing a verdict against Dr. Ganti on the question of liability." According to this article, which continued to cite the same court documents, Judge Freedman also answered the defendants' claim that Mr. Renk could have known to ask for a colon screening because the guidelines for such preventive tests were discussed in newsletters that Health America had sent to its subscribers. To that argument, Judge Freedman wrote, "Frankly, it is ridiculous to suggest that Mr. Renk could be held to be guilty of contributory negligence for failing to read literature when that literature may have been discarded by his wife before it even reached him." These were the defense attorney's basic arguments for the appeal.

When the lawsuit was appealed and reviewed by the Pennsylvania Superior Court and the Pennsylvania Supreme Court Judge Freedman's decisions were upheld. It was a wise decision on the judge's part that she asked the jury to decide other matters in this case. Neil said the courts are less likely to overturn a verdict when the jury makes the decisions. The jurors were to decide if they believed that Bob had told the doctor he had blood in his stool. In the medical record, the doctor had stated that Bob had perirectal symptoms, but Bob said he specifically told the doctor he had blood coming from his rectum on a particular date in question. Next, they were to decide if Health America was guilty. And this is the part I remember: she said either way, Health America would be financially responsible. I think Health America was responsible because they were the employers of Penn Group, which was the group that employed Bob's primary care doctor. Either way, the reason under the law is not important for the purpose of my story. Lastly, they were to decide a dollar amount for the award. One amount was to be awarded to me, and one was for my husband. Each amount was broken down into different categories on the form, and the judge had provided a space for a dollar amount to be assigned next to the reason for that portion of the award.

As I said, I knew we were getting something. I remember when we were all walking back to the courthouse, Neil told Bob that they wanted to settle and make an offer. The defense had been getting nervous, which was when the phones began to ring. If I recall, people were having trouble with their cell phones dropping calls, too. Lots of phones were ringing, and the jury was on its way back to the courtroom. When Neil asked Bob if he wanted to settle, Bob did not hesitate for one second. His reply was, "No, the jurors have worked too hard and given too much of their time to this trial, and I don't want to take this away from them." That was my husband. He was such a sweetie, and I miss him.

The jury was an active participant in the process, which I believe is the intent of our jury system. That is why our system works: jurors take this responsibility seriously and get involved in the process. They bring their life experience but don't allow their biases to get in the way. We came to find out that our jury was perfect, because after the trial, many of the jurors wanted to speak to us. They wanted to ask some questions and have the connection with us that is forbidden during the trial. I know they came to care for Bob and me.

The very first question that a woman juror asked me after the case was, "Why were you late this morning? You are never late. Where were you?"

Think about this. I had to tell her I was at Magee-Women's Hospital, getting my results from my breast biopsy. She started to hug me when she found out everything was okay and then said, "I can't believe you went through all of this at the same time." That just goes to show the strength God gave me. I hope she is reading this now. That is what really gets me excited when I write. The thought that this story could come full circle and hopefully impact other people's lives is one of the things that keeps me typing away. I want all who touched my life to know that they had a positive impact on me. Well, really what I like to think is that God used them to bless me, and hopefully knowing that will have a positive impact on them.

The lawsuit brought power to my husband because truth is power. All the jurors believed Bob had told the doctor about the blood in his stool. Bob was freed of the thought that this was somehow his fault or that he had done something wrong. The medical record spoke for itself, and I believe God used this healing to extend Bob's life. It gave Bob confidence in himself, and I know the money took away some of Bob's worry. He wanted to be able to provide for me even after his death. That was who he was, and he took that seriously. He loved me and always wanted to take care of me and do things for me. He believed it was his most important job, and everything he did centered on that belief. He found his meaning in his relationship with me. So, you see, that is why this is such a great love story. By now you probably have been able to sense the love Bob and I had for each other.

The Money

At the beginning of the trial, of course, the subject of money came up. Not that we asked for a certain amount or anything, but Neil, Tony, Bob, and I discussed it. The trial hadn't started. I think it was when they were in the jury selection process. At the time, we had somewhat prepared our case, and I remember Neil saying something like, "Don't worry. The truth comes out in these trials. It's just a matter of whether the jury interprets the law in your favor. I've been to trials when the jury believed the person and felt she was deserving of an award but didn't think she was legally entitled to it. That is what this trial will decide." If I recall, that's how we got on the topic of the money.

Neil also said that jurors in Western Pennsylvania do not award amounts as large as they do in the Philadelphia area, for example. He said that in the Philadelphia area, there was a different mentality than there was in the western part of the state where our trial would take place. Around the time of our trial, our state's doctors, trial lawyers, and legislators were grappling with the issue of skyrocketing medical malpractice insurance premiums. Physicians and insurers claimed these high costs were because of exorbitant jury malpractice awards. However, trial lawyers claimed that insurers and physicians who refused to arbitrate and settle out of court were the problem. I can say in our case neither the doctor nor the insurer would arbitrate with our attorney to reach an out of court settlement and their refusal resulted in us being awarded much more money than what we would have settled for through arbitration.

We were all feeling pretty confident after preparing our case and someone said, "How much money do you think you'll be awarded?" Everyone stated a number, and I remember saying, "Oh, I think we will get much more. It's a young jury, and they watch *Who Wants to be a Millionaire?*" Love that humor of mine sometimes!

After the trial ended and before the jury returned, Neil and Tony apparently discussed the topic of the award amount again. They both wrote the amount they thought it would be on a paper, but I had no idea they were doing this at the time. They each wrote an amount of over one million dollars. They didn't show it to each other until right before the jury came in. Guess it's a lawyer thing. I saw them show it to each other, and that is when they showed it to me. Again, I motioned higher with my thumb.

The case was tied up in appeals. One year after our trial was over, Health America made the first offer of a settlement. By then, I knew I wasn't bitter anymore. In fact, I appreciated that we could possibly have the money while Bob was still alive. I just wanted to settle. I saw Health America as being caring when they offered this settlement, but when I thought Bob might die before he saw any of the money, I just remember getting angry and saying to Bob, "We better take the money now, because when you die, no amount of money will take away my pain." I tried to explain to Bob that I wanted to settle because I wanted him to be around when we received the money so that we could do things together. At first, Bob didn't want to settle with Health America because he believed I could get all the money once all the appeals were over. When Bob saw how emotional I was getting at the thought of it taking years and that he might be dead before I received any money, he started to rethink things. He could see how upset I was getting just thinking about getting that money after he was dead. That is when I think he finally understood that without him, the money didn't mean much to me. I said, "Even if I get every penny once you aren't here with me, I won't enjoy that money." I remember having such mixed emotions, and I was crying off and on because I was thinking of a future without him. As long as he was with me, the thought of doing things or buying a house in Pennsylvania held an appeal for me. Even though I wasn't blaming Health American anymore, I was angry at the thought of losing Bob. "I don't know what I'll be like when you die," I added.

Neil convinced us to allow him to negotiate for more money even though I just wanted to accept Health America's first offer. Neil said, "We have nothing to lose, and we can always agree to their lower offer." Bob and I agreed that that made sense, especially because we were just beginning the negotiation process. When Health America raised its offer, Bob agreed to take the settlement. He didn't want to take the chance of putting me through all of those emotions from the unfinished business. He understood it wasn't about the money, but he wanted to take care of me in the only way he knew was humanly possible. Neil and Bob both understood that the money wouldn't replace the loss of Bob's love, and Bob understood the depth of my love for him, even when I yelled at him at times or bickered with him over stupid insignificant things. But I don't think about this anymore, because all I can think about is how merciful my Father was for each day he gave me with Bob. He rewarded me by adding to Bob's life.

Health America was held responsible for paying the award, penalties, and interest over the amount the doctor and Penn Group were liable for because in Pennsylvania, the law does not require doctors to be insured over a certain amount. There is a ceiling to the award amount doctors are required to pay, but this is not true for HMO's, hospitals, medical labs, and other such businesses. Health America benefited financially by settling with us in exchange for a quick settlement. We weren't worried about the case being overturned when it was under appeal, and Neil wasn't, either. Then again, you never know. It was a remote possibility. We eventually received the maximum amount from the doctor and Penn Group that they were required to pay under Pennsylvania law. As I said, I just wanted my husband to enjoy some of the money he had a legal and moral right to be given. Although Bob didn't agree to a settlement at first, when he saw it from my point of view, he thought it was the best decision, too.

The trial's outcome was in the *Pittsburgh Post Gazette* because of the amount of the award, I'm sure. So, if you want to know, the information is out there. The amount we finally agreed to settle on with Health America is an amount I am legally bound not to disclose, but I can tell you this: we got a nice fat check.

I certainly wouldn't wish for my husband to get sick and die for any amount of money. Winning that lawsuit wasn't a dream come true. Bob was my life, and the only dreams I had were about spending more time with him, a lifetime. Who would ever wish to have a terminal illness in order to win a lawsuit and get money? It wasn't my husband's dream, either. No one would wish for this. Just today I saw an older couple helping each other at the grocery store, and I felt jealous—or maybe the word is envious. My dream was that Bob and I would grow very old together, but things changed, and we had to adjust. During the trial, it was our dream that Bob would live long enough to see the money, enjoy the money, and beat the cancer. Bob didn't make it to eighty, but he did live eight more years after the trial, so that is saying something. He wasn't expected at that time to live more than a year because he had had that reoccurrence, if you recall.

The award money we received was such a blessing. When Bob had to go on a very expensive blood thinner that cost over $18,000 a year, we were able to afford it and not worry about the cost. So, the award money helped make life easier. I think that helped Bob live longer, too, because all of his worries about money were alleviated. When you have cancer, that is enough of a worry, so anything that helps lessen the stress is most beneficial.

To this day, I look on all of this as a gift from God. Now I use some of my blessings to give back to God what he has given me. Only then am I truly happy with this money. It can never mean anything more than that to me.

For Bob, it was never about the money. Although he was appreciative of the money, no amount of money would ever be worth all the pain and suffering he endured or the emotional toll it took on his life and our family. Still, Bob was never bitter about his situation.

That's my Bob. I keep telling you he was special. He was a great guy. God broke the mold when he made him.

Furthermore, the case confirmed that Bob was an ideal patient and a doctor's dream. Bob continued to be exactly that, because he still believed in doctors. So do I. They give us good medicine, and the very best doctors give us a good dose of hope, too. I dedicate these chapters, "The Trial" and "The Money," to both the doctors and the lawyers. In their own ways, they can both be healers.

I know I have alluded to the fact that when Bob learned of his cancer and prognosis, he worried about not being around to take care of me financially when he died. I believe that the award money was an answer to Bob's prayer that God would take care of me. Bob never told me this, but I think it was just another one of those answered prayers that I now have the privilege to see. It is amazing to me how the same thing can look so different when our eyes are opened to all the possibilities of God. I know my husband was in constant prayer with God. We were awestruck about our settlement, and we did thank God. I just never fully made the connection until now.

A Dream Come True

When I named this chapter "A Dream Come True," I was really thinking about my entire life. I thought meeting Bob was the beginning of my dream come true. I always had that dream of being happily married. My life changed dramatically after I had my mental breakdown and again after I was divorced. I think accepting Christ and turning my life over to him piece by piece was what has brought me to where I am now. At times, I still try to control certain situations and areas of my life, but fortunately I am learning to recognize when I do this. I pray that God will help me learn to let go and trust him with everything. It is still not always easy for me, because I think I am a problem solver by nature. I did become free from all of the guilt and burdens attached to the sins and mistakes I had made up to that point, and that helped me to heal. Part of my breakdown had to do with the insanity that was my life, and I am certain some had to do with the choices I made and the guilt I carried. I want you to see how wonderful my life turned out to be in spite of my past and Bob's cancer. I also want to clarify that even before winning this lawsuit and being so financially blessed, my life was everything I hoped it would be because I had Bob and Jesus. What more could I really want? I had a wonderful marriage in every sense of the word and a loving God who was always with me.

I do not buy into the idea that accepting Christ will bring us financial rewards here on earth, but I also don't deny that God blesses us, we are to bless others, and sometimes those blessings are financial. It's up to God to give us whatever gifts and blessings he wants us to have. I've given a great deal of thought to why we would be so financially blessed. Part of me likes to think that God is using these blessings to get your attention and maybe mine. I just believe all good things come from him, and I thank him for what I consider to be a gift from him. I can say that I never asked God for all that money we were awarded during our trial. I am not going to say that the money is not a good thing, but it also carries with it huge responsibilities of being a good steward. I take those responsibilities seriously. Sometimes it's hard to accept that God really was the one who orchestrated this blessing, but I think there are reasons that he did. I don't think for God it had any relationship to the cancer. This reminds me of Ecclesiastes 3:1, which says, "There is a time for everything, and a season for every activity under heaven." We are not immune to life's troubles, but I believe that having trust and hope that God will bring us through is not wrong, either. God keeps his promises in his own timing, not ours. There are times in my life when I feel like I am in the wilderness, but those are the times I know I need to wait and depend on him even more. I hope you will keep all of this in perspective, but I will not hold back on telling you about the wonderful blessings Bob and I experienced any more than I did on telling you about our struggles. I want to say one last thing about having money, however. If you love money, you will never have enough, and money does not protect you from the problems in life. It can make certain situations easier, but it is not the end all to life's problems. I still would be much happier to have less and struggle with money the way Bob and I did when we were young than to have money in the bank and be alone without my husband's love and companionship. So with this in mind, I want to tell you about what happened after the trial.

Bob and I went back to Florida around the beginning of June 2000, but not before we went to visit my mother who was then in a nursing home because of her dementia. She knew us, and that was a blessing. I told my mother about the trial and she smiled, but I don't know if she truly understood. I remember telling my mother to rely on Jesus. I wanted to have that conversation one more time before I went back to Florida. I didn't know if she would understand anything the next time I saw her. I brought a picture of Jesus and put it on her dresser for her to look at when she felt the need.

When my mom had dementia, all I really could see was her heart. She was finally able to accept the fact that her memory and mind were not the same as they once were, and she allowed others to help her. At first she tried to hide it from us, and then she went through a time when she was very easily agitated and frustrated, which was unlike her. Then later, I remember her telling me that she just couldn't think right and I said, "I know." I said that I was sad about that, and she said that she was, too, but then she seemed to accept it somehow. When people treated her like she still had no memory loss, I could see the frustration in her eyes. She knew and understood that there was something wrong. We were being honest and real with each other. I don't know if this is true with other people with this disease, but I know it was with my mom.

The last time we visited my mom, my Aunt Peggie and Uncle Anthony were visiting, too, along with my sister Norma and her husband Jim. We had such a nice visit. My aunt was trying to have a conversation with my mom, and she said, "Kay, have you been playing any bridge lately?" This was something my mom and aunt used to do together over all the years.

My mom replied, "I can't even play bingo because I can't remember my numbers, so I wouldn't be able to play bridge." By the frustrated and maybe even the angry look in her eyes, I knew pretending her mind was still the same was not the right way to handle this memory loss and confusion.

That day, I told my mom that there were people at the care center to help her with the things she could no longer do and that I didn't want her to worry. I just wanted her to relax and have fun doing what she was still able to do. I knew she had already made friends at the care center, because one time when I was in Florida, I called her on the phone and she said she wanted to hang up because her friends were down the hall and she wanted to go be with them. When I got off the phone, I cried because I knew that those days of our long phone conversations we'd had over the years were over. I felt such a loss, but I was also so happy that my mom wanted to be with her friends. When I visited her in her room that day, I pointed out to her how wonderful it was that she still knew and recognized all of her family and friends. I said that we should be thankful that she had the most important part of her mind still working. She smiled and said, "Yes, that's good." We were truly blessed. I know she understood because when her mom had dementia, little by little she started not to know some of us. My mom told me she felt sad that Nana couldn't remember my mom's younger brother Anthony, and she thought it upset him. I think seeing her brother that day helped my mom realize how blessed she was to still remember us. At the end of her life, Nana only remembered my mother. I don't think we will ever understand why, but I know it is hard to accept what this disease can do. Nancy Reagan captured it when she titled her book, *The Long Goodbye*. It truly can be.

When we returned to Florida, I told Bob, "Let's go on a trip." There I was, making plans to go away again. I started planning a second trip to California. In case you haven't realized it yet, I was the travel agent in our marriage, and Bob was the willing traveling companion. The first time we had gone to California had been for only a few days when we went to San Diego and put our toes in the Pacific Ocean. I wanted to drive the coast from San Francisco to San Diego for our second trip, so Bob and I flew out to San Francisco and rented a car. We stayed in San Francisco over the Fourth of July holiday. We rode the cable car, went to China Town and Pier 66, and walked up and down Lombard Street, which is famous for its tight hairpin turns. We took the San Francisco Municipal Railway and connected to the BART, Bay Area Railway Transportation, so we could visit my cousin, Anna, whose friend was the person who indirectly brought me to PWP, where I had first met Bob. Another day we drove over the Golden Gate Bridge, saw the California Redwoods, and went to a winery in the area. After we left the San Francisco area, Bob and I made stops in San Jose, Santa Cruz, Monterey, and Carmel, drove along the Big Sur, and stopped at Hearst Castle for a day. We went to Pismo Beach, Solvang with its picturesque windmills, and then onto Santa Barbara, Ventura, and Malibu.

When we arrived in the Los Angeles area, we decided to visit my other cousin, Linda, who was Anna's sister, instead of spending time in the city. Linda lived outside of Los Angeles. We grew up together and were the same age. I hadn't seen her for over twenty years. She had MS, multiple sclerosis, and was in a wheelchair by the time I saw her. She still drove, however. When we went out to lunch, she insisted on driving us in her car and almost wrecked. Bob said, "Hey, Linda, I haven't survived this cancer for you to kill me. I'm driving home." And then he said to her with his great sense of humor, "Did you see the guy's face you almost wrecked into?"

"Yes."

"He went straight home," Bob said.

"How did you know that?" Linda asked.

"He had to go and change his underwear."

Linda laughed so hard, but I know she got the message because she told that story to her sister when she decided to stop driving. I know she didn't want to give that up, as it was one more piece of her independence. She eventually moved to Sun City and drove around in a golf cart. A few years after moving there, she died of what the coroner ruled a heart attack. It was good to have spent that time with her, and I know she and Bob had a lot in common. Neither one knew what was ahead of them.

Really, we all have that in common, but when all is going great, we forget that this life on earth is not eternal. We delude ourselves into thinking this is all there is. I like to live for today, look to eternity, and skip worrying about tomorrow. I am learning only to look back to reflect on where I've been, to see that God was there with me, and to ask for forgiveness if my sins are brought to mind. I can honestly say I don't do this every moment, but I am getting much better with God helping me learn to live this way. It is hard sometimes, especially when I need to make plans for my tomorrows. I know I need to do that to accomplish the plans God has set before me, and I ask God to show me his ways and reveal his plan for my life. That searching and praying keeps me pretty busy. I look with great anticipation to the work God has for me to do, and I find it exciting. I don't think of it as boring or burdensome, but I do see it as a challenge—mostly with regard to discovering his will for me. I think writing this story has been part of that plan, but it is just the beginning. I am learning to trust that God will come through for me and that if it is his will to work through me, it will go well. I have the best mentor and teacher in him. For someone who is a perfectionist at times, it is a relief that God's work is not my responsibility alone. I call on God to do his part, and then I know it will turn out just right.

Now, let me continue to tell you about our trip to California and the happiness we were feeling at the time. After we stayed the day with Linda, we continued our drive south to San Diego. The trial was behind us, and we were anticipating getting the money. We both knew that Bob might not live to see any of that money, which was one of the reasons we took the trip. Another was that we had been talking about this trip since we were first married. When Bob worked at U. S. Steel in Pittsburgh, he was once offered either extra pay or six weeks extra vacation. He took the vacation, and we worked on refinishing our kitchen cabinets. We didn't have much money at the time, but we decided we could justify taking the time instead of the extra pay if we did something worthwhile with our time besides just having fun. We just wanted to spend the time together. You know, getting to go back to bed after the kids went off to school, having uninterrupted conversations, being able to just be the two of us and work without the demands of parenthood for a few hours while the kids were in school. Plus, we were newly married and wanted the time alone that you don't get when you're remarried with an instant family. We had also talked about taking that time off and going on a trip with the kids across the country, with California as our final destination. We just didn't feel like we could spend the money, which is why this second California trip meant so much to us. It was another one of those dreams come true.

My mom had put the initial desire in our hearts to take that trip to California. She talked so much about the things she saw that we wanted to go and see them, too. She always returned from her two-week vacations out there looking so happy and refreshed, and I guess going there was a dream come true for Bob and I, too. My mom always had a dream of going with my dad, but I think he really had a fear of flying or maybe was afraid because he was sick and didn't want to go that far from home. So, my mom started to go to California after my dad died, and she would visit her sister and brother and their families. In later years, she visited her sister-in-law and her daughter, who happened to be the very same cousins of mine whom I visited out there, too. Our trip was wonderful. I had so much fun planning it and making the hotel reservations and daydreaming about what it would be like when we got to each city I had plotted along the map.

Ironically, while we were there—in fact, the day before we were to return home—we received a call from my sister that my mom had died. It was July 15, 2000. Even though my mom was eighty-two years old, I wasn't expecting that she would die so soon. My mom died of cancer and not from advanced Alzheimer's, and I think God showed great mercy. Her death was not long and difficult, which was a blessing to me.

I didn't realize her cancer was even close to that point. I was okay about not being there, because even though I yelled at my mom when I was younger, she and I always got along and were very close my entire life. Over the years, my mom and I had spent so much time together that I couldn't ask for more. I was just happy I had talked to my mom about Jesus the last time I saw her. I told her to focus on him and not to worry so much about other things. I told her she could relax because my sister and Jim were there to see that she would be okay, and she understood that and agreed with me. At the time I had no idea they would be the ones to be by her side those final days. I knew my mom's heart and that she loved Bob and me, too. She knew my first place was with my husband, and she didn't want to cause any tension or stress for me. When my mom was living in Florida with Bob and me, she had told one of my aunts that she did not want to be a problem for us. She knew Bob had cancer and wanted us to have time together. She knew she might have to go to a personal care home one day, and we made that decision because she needed more care and I had to set my limits. I wasn't able to care for her and Bob at the same time. I was not torn about it, either, because I knew it was time for her to be taken care of by someone else. I knew I didn't have to prove anything to anyone, and I was free to make whatever choice was best for Bob and me. So I was really okay being with Bob in California when my mom died. We spent that last day at the San Diego zoo and changed our flight to Pittsburgh instead of Sarasota, Florida, so we could attend my mom's funeral. It all worked out for the best.

As I said before, having a breakdown and accepting Jesus put an end to my being motivated to do things out of guilt. It is so wonderful to be free in Christ. I was thankful that my aunt told me about the conversation she and my mom had, because I knew my mom would be okay about my decision, too. She easily adjusted to going to the personal care home that my sister and Jim wisely chose for her. They visited her often when they were in Pennsylvania, and many friends would come to see her, too. She had the best of both worlds. She was able to spend several years living with Bob and me in paradise in Florida, and then she was able to go back home to be with her old friends and make some new ones, too.

It was really fitting that I was in California when my mom died because Bob was having a great time, and I know my mom wouldn't have wanted it any other way. I also did not want Bob to go through seeing my mom die of cancer knowing that that could be his fate at any time, too. I am sure my mom would agree, and in a way, it was like returning a favor. You see, when I had my breakdown and was in the hospital, my mom had her California trip planned. Even though my children really needed someone to watch them, I gave her my blessing to go on her vacation and not spend her two weeks off from work taking care of my children. I know she was torn about it, and we talked it over. Everything worked the way it was meant to then, too.

It was all in his perfect timing and in his wisdom. My dad died of heart disease when I was almost eighteen, but when I learned to forgive him and myself for all of the fighting we had done over the years, I was able to look back with an honest perspective. I know he didn't die of a broken heart. He shared with me that he knew Jesus, and writing this has revealed the rest of the puzzle pieces to me. We were raised Roman Catholic, and we were not taught to say the sinners prayer or to confess we were saved. My dad spoke of going to be with Jesus and said not to worry about him. Only God truly knows what is in our hearts, but I believed my dad when he spoke those words to me. I just hope that I've lived long enough that my claim that I found Jesus matches the way I live so that my children will never have a doubt about my salvation, either.

In May of 2001, when we learned that Health America was willing to settle their part of the lawsuit, Bob and I returned to Pittsburgh, anticipating receiving the check. We began house hunting for our summer home in Cranberry, Pennsylvania. It was so exciting to go house hunting for that second home. We were going to have the best of both worlds. We would spend six months in Pennsylvania and six months in Florida. Now that was what I called paradise. I had my time with my children in the summer, and I still had my two dogs with me all year. So, you see, life couldn't get any better for me. I remember how blessed we were to find this beautiful home, and I cried when we went to look at it. The woman who was living there cried, too, because we bought it the first day it was listed. She and her husband and children were moving to Texas, and he had to start his new job soon. We later came to find out from our realtor that she had been praying about selling the house, just as we had be praying about buying one. At the time I had been thinking about how God works for good for those who love him. I thought it was neat that he matched us together. I hadn't thought about it since, but now I am thinking it was really something special. This is a common thread throughout my book. I think God puts people in our lives to accomplish answered prayers.

This house would have a special meaning to us because it would eventually be the home where Bob and I would spend a lot of time with our first granddaughter, Megan. When Megan was born, we decorated our nursery, too. My daughter-in-law, Colleen, generously let Megan spend days at a time with us. Bob and I just loved that time together. It was so much fun for Bob and I to see each other as grandparents. We could dream about what it would have been like to have a baby together, which made it extra special. That home was just so beautiful to us, and we would enjoy so many special visits with our children, our extended family, and our friends. Those few years we lived there were great.

While we lived in Cranberry, we found an awesome church to join called Northway Christian Community Church, which was where I first felt the calling to claim my Bible verse, Jeremiah 29:11: "'For I know the plans I have for you,' declares the Lord, 'plans to prosper you and not to harm you, plans to give you hope and a future.'" I knew God had certainly prospered us with earthly blessings, and I knew he was not the one who caused Bob's cancer. I understood he had plans to give me hope, and I already was receiving so much hope since Bob was still alive. But I struggled with the plans for a future. I knew I had my future in heaven, but I felt God had a specific plan for my life. I remember thinking that he wasn't going to waste all the trials he helped me through. That is when I began my quest for what would be my ministry. I felt he had a calling on my life, but I wasn't sure what exactly it was. I wanted to know what his plans were. I think this is when I developed my strong belief that God had a specific plan in mind for Bob, and I wanted to fulfill the purpose he had in mind for me.

If we weren't already blessed enough to have a second home outside of Pittsburgh, we were even more blessed because we bought a brand new home in Osprey, Florida. This house was our dream home and the first and only brand new home we ever owned. We had looked at a similar model several years before, but it had been out of our price range, and it had been too uncomfortable for us to even think about building a home. We originally were going to build an addition onto the house we owned in Punta Gorda after winning the lawsuit, but when we decided to remodel, things started to feel unsettling. We took a drive back to a housing plan we had seen when it was first under development. We had actually seen this model home before, and now there was a stripped down, less expensive one for sale in the inventory. We both loved that model more than any house we had ever seen, and I had saved only that picture and floor plan out of over more than fifty model homes we had looked at over the years. When we decided to remodel, I threw out all the real estate magazines along with all the brochures from the model homes we visited over the years. It was the only one I had kept, because for some reason, I couldn't part with it. As I said, it was our favorite model.

It was a hobby of ours to look at model homes, and when our friends or children came to visit us in Florida, we would drag them with us to look at the latest models. We thought they would enjoy it as much as we did. I came to find out that some did, and some hated the experience. By now this housing plan was more developed than when we had first seen it, and we really liked it. Naturally, the model house we liked had been sold, but they had built a similar house with fewer upgrades on a small lot, and the original buyers had opted out of the sale. Once again, the price was reduced, and the upgrades were exactly the ones we would have chosen. It was very affordable compared to the model. Also, it was move-in ready, which was one reason we never considered building a house. We didn't want the headaches and stress, plus a one-year wait was not welcome in our lifestyle. It was so uncomfortable for us to plan that far ahead. We made an offer and ended up purchasing that home. We were now only a few miles from the beach and that, I think, was our biggest incentive to move from Punta Gorda to Osprey. It was only a few miles south of Sarasota, and it would be less than a half an hour from our favorite beach, Siesta Key. The house was only ten minutes from our closest beach, which, as the crow flies, was less than two miles. And, as life would go for us, we had no trouble selling our other house in Punta Gorda. We held out for a good price, which we were able to get.

Again, we were living in paradise. That's a saying all the snowbirds use to describe Florida. But to us, it really was a paradise, and Bob was living on all this blessed time that God had graciously given to us.

This was also when Bob and I visited the Brooklyn Tabernacle church in New York City. I read the books that Pastor Cymbala wrote, and they had a profound influence on me. In fact, one testimony stuck out so much that when that person came to visit at our church in Cranberry, I immediately recognized him from reading about him in one of the books. It was so awesome to have that happen, and I saw God working in me and thought this was no coincidence. Looking back, I see how one thing just led to the next, but God would have been able to do that no matter where we have moved. It was just neat to know his eye was upon me in each place I lived, and he was working out his plan for my life. It is truly magnificent when I think back on it. So much good came to us from Bob having cancer—so much that no one would have ever believed it could be possible.

The following years went by pretty fast, and we spent several of them making only routine visits to Moffitt for evaluation, which included blood work, PET scans, CAT scans, and MRIs. Our oncologist, Dr. Garrett, knew Bob didn't want chemotherapy if at all possible, so the plan was that he would not have chemotherapy unless we could see a measurable increase in his cancer or if he started to have symptoms. Bob went about six years without any treatment. The cancer finally started showing up on the MRIs, and it appeared to be in his peritoneal cavity, which is the space where various organs, such as the colon, liver, stomach, and lungs, are located. The cancer was growing so slowly that it could hardly be measured on the CAT scans, but the CEA level continued to rise. At one point, I think the CEA was around nine hundred, which is pretty high.

However, Bob and I had learned long ago to ignore the CEA level. We weren't putting much stock in it as a predictor of Bob's life expectancy anymore because even though his CEA level fluctuated, it didn't coincide with how Bob was feeling or explain how he was able to live so long with those elevated CEA levels. There was actually a time when the CEA level had dropped considerably, and Dr. Garrett asked Bob if he was taking any herbal treatments. Bob said he wasn't, but that he had been on the South Beach Diet. The doctor said, "Whatever you are doing, just keep on doing it."

Later, one of the oncologists at Duke told me that cancer feeds on sugar—something I admit I have not heard since from any other doctor—so maybe that is why Bob did so well on that diet. The only problems were that Bob could not maintain a healthy weight on that diet because he got so thin on it, and besides, he loved to eat forbidden sweet things like chocolate cake. So, eventually the South Beach Diet went the way of all such restrictive diets: out the window. Whether or not it's true that cancer feeds on sugar, sugar is not good for us, which is a good reason to encourage each other to stay away from it. Maybe the effects of sugar on CEA levels or cancer would make for a good clinical study.

Aside from the South Beach Diet, Bob took a multivitamin, garlic, vitamins C, D, and B, calcium, and maybe a few other supplements. I recently heard that doctors believe vitamin D may help to prevent cancer, so maybe that will be proven. Then again, it may go by the wayside like vitamin E, for all of you who remember the theory of vitamin E.

When Bob's cancer was first discovered, I read about all the vitamins that were thought to prevent cancer and had Bob take them. There was and still is no proof that these actually worked, but they could be labeled the "hope" vitamins. We hoped they worked, and Bob believed it was possible. It was good for him to have all of the positive reinforcement he could find to help him believe he might just beat his cancer.

I am by no means promoting either the South Beach Diet or the use of any vitamins for cancer treatment; I am merely telling you what happened. You can decide for yourself if you want to take vitamin D, stop eating sugar, or try the South Beach Diet. Check with your doctor. Unless your doctor says otherwise, none of these should be harmful to you if you don't have any health issues that would be contraindications, and I personally believe we all could do without refined sugar, white flour, and processed food. I don't always do it, but lately I am trying to be more aware of what I eat. I am trying to eat more like my grandmother, who lived to be ninety-eight years old. She rarely ate processed food. We were a meat, vegetable, and potato family, and we also ate pasta and olive oil. I know my grandmother ate an apple every day. What's that old saying? An apple a day keeps the doctor away? She was in excellent health until her late eighties, when she ended up with dementia. She also ate cheese, drank red wine, ate a lot of lentils, ate northern beans, ate tomato sauce, cooked with olive oil, and ate Italian bread fresh from the bakery without all the preservatives. We had chicken, fish, pork, and beef, but we always had variety. My rule still is nothing in excess.

In the spring of 2004, Bob and I flew up to Canton, Ohio, to visit our son Rob and his family. We had a great time with Megan.

She was getting older, and it was so much fun to be with her. When we were staying at Rob's house, he suggested we go look at some new condos being built a mile or so from him. We went to see them, but I told Rob I would never consider them because they had a large pond steps from the deck, which wasn't a place for a grandma to live. I would worry about Megan falling into the water. It was too close for comfort, even though there was a railing around the deck. However, we met a realtor, and she showed us several other condos in the area. Now, if you recall, Bob and I loved to look at real estate just for fun, and this was what were doing—or so we thought. When we returned to Florida, I couldn't stop thinking about one of the condos we saw and how nice it would be to live so close to Megan. Tracy and her husband David had already moved to North Carolina and my mom had died, so if we decided to move our summer home from Cranberry, Pennsylvania, to Canton, Ohio, it might work out. After constantly looking at the condo on the website, Bob and I seriously considered making an offer. Because we only saw the condo once, I actually made arrangements with the realtor to have Rob do a walk through and describe it to me over the phone. After hearing more details, Bob and I mailed back our first offer. We had to do some more negotiations because our realtor called and explained that another offered had come in. Both Bob and I and the other couple had one chance to give a final offer. To our delight, our offer was the one that was accepted. We closed on that property on May 31, 2004. It only took three weeks to close at that time.

We put our Cranberry home on the market in the middle of May, and we had it under contract before we even returned to Pennsylvania. It sold quickly, and by the time we returned in June for the summer, we were able to get into our condo in Ohio and start moving some of the smaller things. It was a fairly easy move that way, and we had such a good time buying a few more pictures and some living room furniture. My daughter Tracy laughed because she said, "I thought you were downsizing." I guess that wasn't the right word I used to describe the difference between our condo and our Cranberry home. We were going from a two-story to a one-story. The condo had a finished walkout, though, so it was still quite large.

I liked living in Canton, and having Rob and his family so close was really a blessing. We were able to go out to dinner with them and even play cards some nights. We had Megan sleep over often because we were only four miles away. We were still only a little over two hours from our friends and family in Pittsburgh. It turned out to be a good decision, and this is where I currently live during the warmer half of the year.

Duke or Death

In the winter, we continued to live in Florida, but Bob was starting to experience some back pain, and our oncologists in Canton, Ohio, and Tampa, Florida, agreed Bob should resume chemotherapy to help slow the cancer and control the pain. I must admit, I was getting a little worried, and the prospect of being by myself in Florida if Bob should die started to concern me. We also had a new grandbaby in North Carolina, and Bob and I wanted to get to spend time with her as we did with our granddaughter Megan in Canton. So, we talked about moving to North Carolina. I told Bob that he had had his time in Florida. It had been nine years, and it was my turn. North Carolina was the state I loved.

It was September 2005, and Bob and I agreed to look for a house around Pinehurst, North Carolina. If we found a good deal, we would consider moving there. Naturally, when you really aren't ready, a good deal comes along. We found a great home whose owner was building a new house, so she jumped at the chance to sell us her current house and then rent it from us from September to April while her new house was being built. That would give Bob one more winter in his beloved Florida, so that is what we did.

We put the Florida house on the market in January 2006. This was the end of the housing boom, so our house took almost a year to sell. We still were ahead of the terrible market that eventually would cause prices to drop and make it nearly impossible to sell a house in Florida. I consider it a blessing because the timing was perfect for us. I think Bob and I were under more stress than we realized the year we had three houses. In the end it did work out, but I often falsely wondered if that stress added to Bob's pain. Worry can have such negative influences on us, but looking back, I know I was wrong. We continued to pray about the house selling, and for the most part, we were able to turn it over to God. However, being human, I do remember worrying more about selling the house than I cared to admit.

We came to North Carolina in April 2006, painted the house, had carpet installed, and cleaned and cleaned to get the house the way we liked it. We had our granddaughter Sarah with us for a week while her parents went away, and I taught her to crawl. She was having a hard time because she couldn't get her arms going; she would just move her legs and then topple over. I got on the floor, lifted my arms up, moved them forward in an extreme motion, and then slammed my hand to the floor, so Sarah could watch me. And watch me she did. She imitated me and crawled exactly the same way. We laughed so much, but my daughter didn't find it so funny when Sarah had this unique way of crawling. She had to explain to everyone that I had taught Sarah to crawl. Sarah also was singing the chorus to "Old MacDonald." She would sing E-I-E-I, but no O. One day Bob sang the O in a loud low note, and Sarah mimicked the exact deep note that he had just sung. We laughed so hard we had tears in our eyes, and we knew we had made the right choice to move to North Carolina and spend time with Sarah. Bob loved to watch her play, read to her, and sing with her. We had fun preparing the house, too, and we had some new furniture delivered so we could sleep on the pullout sofa in the living room and eat at our new dining room table.

At the end of April, we took a week off to go to Aruba with my son and his wife. Colleen was expecting our newest grandchild, and it was going to be a boy. The four of us spent hours floating around in the lazy river at the resort, thinking of baby names and just getting really silly. We returned to Pinehurst, finished putting the house in order, and then drove to Florida to pack up the Osprey house. By the end of May, we were ready for the movers to pick up our belongings in Florida, and we cleaned our Florida home one last time.

We drove back to North Carolina, and a few days later, the movers arrived with our things. I stayed up late and had the entire house unpacked in a few days. I was motivated and organized. We now were ready to go north for the summer. We had moved from our Cranberry home in Pennsylvania to the Canton area in Ohio because our son had moved farther west and was no longer an hour's drive away. I used to joke and tell Bob, "We don't stay in one place long enough for the cancer to find us!" We were constantly on the move.

The previous September, in 2005, we had taken a Mediterranean cruise. Who would have ever thought Bob would be alive, let alone travel out of the country? Bob had promised me a trip to Italy for our twenty-fifth anniversary, but then he got cancer and we thought our trip was only a pipe dream. I was so excited at the thought of going to Italy, because it was the country where all four of my grandparents were born. It was a few years late in coming, but we did get to take that trip. It was so awesome. We went in between his chemotherapy treatments. Our oncologist, Dr. Schmotzer, said, "Just go and have a good time. The extra few weeks off would be good for Bob, because his blood work was borderline at best." He actually postponed Bob's treatments one week so that he would be in good condition for the cruise. We went on the cruise with some friends from church. We later found out that they had been worried about Bob getting sick on the trip, but we didn't know it. They told us that Bob put them to shame, as we were dancing and they were just sitting and watching us. They commented among themselves that Bob had just finished up several rounds of chemotherapy and was wearing his colostomy bag, but he was dancing and having fun. They said we were such an inspiration to them.

A year later, in September of 2006, Bob was still here among the living. Not only had we taken that wonderful Mediterranean cruise the previous September but we had also taken an earlier trip to Athens, Greece, and the Greek Isles in April of 2005. I loved everything about that trip. Bob was in between his chemotherapy treatments, and being able to do so much traveling was truly a dream come true. For many reasons, the trip to Greece was my all time favorite. Maybe it was because we followed in the footsteps of the apostle Paul to places like Corinth and also because we saw the cave on the island of Patmos where John may have written the book of Revelation. The trip was so wonderful, and I thank God for blessing me with the memories of these two experiences. I wrote a poem about my Greece trip, which was when I realized God was gifting me with the ability to write poetry. I had always written a few lighthearted poems or love poems to Bob, but this poem surprised me. I will include it for you at the end of the book, along with a few other poems I have been blessed to write.

Bob had been okay on these trips and was able to enjoy them and keep up the hectic pace of being a tourist, but both times when we returned home, he had terrible back pain from the long flights home. Over the previous year, he had received several different courses of chemotherapy. The chemo was being given to slow the progression of the cancer that was now in his sacrum, or what we know as the tailbone. The chemo was not given for curative reasons but rather for palliative treatment, which means to help treat symptoms rather than cure the disease. I knew this, but I never discussed it with Bob. I am sure he was aware of it, too. In conversations with doctors, they causally mentioned it a few times. Still, when you are getting chemo, you're hoping to be cured. So that was what we focused on. We told each other that maybe the chemo would work and really kill the cancer cells, and we continued to have hope, or should I say faith, that God would continue to keep Bob alive and well.

In our case, I think we had an almost perfect balance because Bob had chosen not to have treatment for six years. When he resumed chemo from April through September of 2005, his pain and the cancer remained under control. Once the pain settled down after the long flight home from the Mediterranean cruise, the chemo and pain medication seemed to help again for a while. However, the summer of 2006, Bob seemed to be having more and more pain.

By September of 2006, his pain had become so intense that he had to go to the emergency room and was admitted to the hospital to treat his pain with IV pain medication. A few doctors were called in to consult, and the pain management doctor agreed to inject an epidural into his spinal column. He thought maybe the pain was coming from a ruptured disc. Though that was not really the case, the epidural did help to bring Bob some temporary relief. For a few weeks, his pain was controlled because of that epidural and a change in pain medications. Dr. Schmotzer, our oncologist, decided to take a break from the chemo at that time because the chemo was no longer giving Bob any pain control and the doctor wanted to manage Bob's pain with just pain medication for a while.

I remember when Bob came home from the hospital, we made plans to take a trip back to North Carolina for a few weeks. We wanted to spend some time there with our daughter, Tracy, and with Sarah, our granddaughter, and we really hadn't had a chance to enjoy the house we had moved into in May. I drove, and Bob tolerated the drive just fine, but when we arrived, Bob's leg began to swell. The next day, I was out doing some yard work with Bob, who insisted on helping me, and I noticed he was having trouble moving. His leg was noticeably swollen by then, and he was feeling very uncomfortable because of it. At the time, I didn't know that Bob's leg had swollen just a few weeks ago when he had been in the hospital in Ohio. I later found out from my son Rob that when he was visiting Bob in the hospital, the doctor was discussing Bob's swollen leg, which was when the doctor ordered the compression stockings for Bob to wear. It is not unusual to wear stockings when you are in bed to prevent a blood clot. Rob only remembered it after I told him of Bob's swelling in North Carolina. That was one of the reasons I was always afraid to leave the hospital: something might happen that I would not know about, and I would not trust anyone entirely to oversee Bob's care. Now his leg was getting worse, so I made him an appointment to see our primary care doctor in Pinehurst.

When Dr. Antil saw Bob, he ordered Bob to go to the hospital for a test to determine if he had a blood clot. The results were negative, so Dr. Antil made an appointment for the wound care nurse to see Bob and wrap his leg. A few days later, we went to that wound care nurse, and she put a wrap on Bob's leg. Bob's leg was getting much worse, as was the pain in his back, so I became frustrated and started calling around to some of the doctors up at Duke University Hospital in Durham, North Carolina. Rob was also encouraging me to go to Duke because of its fine reputation. In 2006, it was among the top ten hospitals in the country, and we all agreed it would be the best place for Bob to be seen. So, one call led to another, and eventually I spoke to someone at one of the clinics there. I do not remember which doctor's office or which clinic I reached, but the woman who answered the phone gave me this advice. She said that if we wanted to be seen quickly, we should come on up and go to the emergency room. That would be the fastest way to be seen by a doctor. She said that if we tried to make an appointment, it could take weeks.

Well, I've come to learn it's all about perspective. Yes, compared to waiting weeks, it was most certainly the fastest way to be seen by the doctors, but let me tell you, we were in the emergency room for over twenty-four hours. I still can't believe that we were there so long. We were finally taken back to the treatment area after eight hours, and an intern saw us. Yeah! Or, so I thought. The intern asked for Bob's medical history. Fortunately, I knew it by heart, but even though the intern took all that information down, the doctors still wanted written reports. I remember being on the phone and calling Dr. Garrett at Moffitt Hospital in Tampa, Florida. He had most of Bob's records because Bob had been a patient at Moffitt from September of 1997 until April of 2006, and the records also included Bob's medical history from 1995 to 1997. I spoke to Dr. Garrett personally and explained the situation. He transferred me immediately to his nurse, and she faxed the records over.

Something good comes from being the star patient, or at least I like to think so. Dr. Garrett is such a great guy. When we were living in Florida and Bob was under his care, he even called Bob at home one Sunday to discuss Bob's test results from the PET scan, if I recall. I don't remember the details; I only remember how impressed Bob and I where that he personally called us at home on a Sunday. What a great doctor! There's another cute story that comes to my mind about Dr. Garrett. Bob and I were in New York City at Times Square, and Bob ran into Dr. Garrett while walking down the street. Bob was so excited to see him. The two of them spoke for a while, and Dr. Garrett mentioned he was there for a medical conference, if I recall. Bob couldn't get over seeing Dr. Garrett among the thousands or hundreds of thousands of people who passed by us those few days we were in New York City. I like to think it also did Dr. Garrett's heart good to see Bob out there enjoying life. It is ironic that under Dr. Garrett's care, Bob never had any treatment. Dr. Garrett recommended a course of chemotherapy treatment, but a local oncologist in Sarasota is who gave it to Bob. Dr. Garrett actually recommended that Bob have this treatment in Sarasota because it was so much closer to home and more convenient for Bob. One thing Bob always got from Dr. Garrett was a huge dose of hope. He always gave Bob personal attention and made him feel cared for, which is very important when trying to heal someone. We would go to Moffitt every three to six months for testing, and on our visits with him he would go over the results of Bob's scans and blood work. Then we would talk about our families and travel plans. How appropriate was it that they should meet in Times Square?

Now, even though we had all the records faxed from Moffitt Hospital, the doctors at Duke wanted Bob's records from his original surgery in 1995. When I made the phone call and tried to retrieve those records, I learned that those records were so old that Jefferson Hospital had purged them from their system. Imagine that. He wasn't even supposed to live a year, and after eleven years, the records were no longer available. The doctors at Duke also wanted the records from Bob's original radiation treatments. I called Dr. Katz, who worked out of Jefferson Radiation Oncology Center in Pleasant Hills, Pennsylvania, a suburb of Pittsburgh. Fortunately, those records were still available.

While I was making these calls, Bob was in pain, having trouble with his leg, and hadn't even eaten. We were able to stay in a treatment room with a bed, and thankfully, Bob was able to sleep some of the time. I finally insisted that they feed him, too. You normally don't get fed in the emergency room, but Bob finally did get a few meals. We had many doctors come in to consult. I think Bob was there almost twenty-four hours before he was admitted to the oncology floor. There are good and not so good things about a university hospital, but that is true of any hospital, really. There were extremely long waits at Duke, and it did not help that we came in through the back door, so to speak.

Admission Number One

The good thing about Bob being admitted to Duke Hospital was that he was seen by a multitude of experts in their fields, and Bob would have access to the latest treatments. While Bob was in the hospital, doctors from different specialties saw him and made their recommendations for the course of treatment they thought would be most beneficial. If you were to try to follow these recommendations and did not understand the system, you could go insane. Those of you who have experienced this, whether because you or a loved one had a very serious condition, especially if it was unique or rare, can relate. One time you think the doctor is going to do this, and the next minute another doctor is going to do that. I remember when Bob had a strange reaction to his medicine on one of the admissions I told the doctors that our experience was like the TV show *House* from the 2006 era. The interns got my meaning and smiled.

So, as I was saying, if you don't understand a university hospital, it is a think tank. The doctors will eventually come to a decision and make their recommendations, and you more or less give them your blessings. The idea of more radiation was being tossed around, as was the idea of more chemotherapy. I told some of the doctors that Bob was on a break from the chemo because his blood counts weren't very good and it was no longer helping his pain. At the time, I was also concerned about his leg being swollen, which I expressed. During this visit, doctors determined that Bob had a clot in a vein in his groin. I think when the doctors had checked Bob for a clot in his vein when we were in Pinehurst, it either did not show up yet or maybe they did not go up that far to look at the vein in the groin area. Bob was started on Lovenox injections twice daily in the abdomen area, which I think was because of the clot. The doctors hoped that using this course of treatment to thin the blood would prevent more blood clots from forming and help this one to resolve on its own without any other intervention. I remember when we left the hospital, we had a hard time getting the prescription filled, but we eventually did find a pharmacy that had some and could order in the rest. When Bob returned home, his leg worsened, began to swell even more, and started to weep slightly. He then started to show a lot of bruising on his stomach at the injection sites.

We were to return for our first appointments with the oncologist and the doctor who was planning on administering radiation treatments. We were given appointments upon discharge with the radiologist and with Dr. Nameless, whom we chose to be our oncologist because he was the attending oncologist during that first hospital stay at Duke. I recall that every two weeks a different attending oncologist was in charge of the interns. I think that the over the course of the six times Bob was admitted to the oncology floor, we ended up seeing four different attending oncologists. You will later understand why I have chosen to call this oncologist Dr. Nameless. He was the doctor who would take over being in charge of Bob's case on an outpatient basis, and we would see him at the oncology clinic at Duke.

So, the doctors determined that Bob would resume radiation treatments to see if they could slow down the cancer and alleviate some of his pain. The doctors all agreed that they did not think Bob's pain had anything to do with a ruptured or bulging disc, so no one wanted to administer more epidurals. Because there are limits to how much radiation a person can tolerate, there was some question about resuming radiation treatment, too. However, Dr. Christopher Willet was confident that Bob would be helped and could tolerate a little more radiation. I think there was a debate about this among some of the doctors, but they finally decided that it would be okay for Bob to have twelve more treatments. Too much radiation can damage the body's tissues.

I know Bob was concerned about the radiation, but we believed it would help with his pain, slow the cancer growth, and buy him more time. We had confidence in Dr. Willet. Bob lived two more years, so I believe it worked. It also helped with Bob's pain for a while. I had also been thinking that Bob had had enough chemo and that it was time to do something else. I knew Dr. Schmotzer was concerned about Bob's blood levels and that the chemo was no longer controlling Bob's pain.

Bob's leg started swelling even more, and he eventually would be readmitted to the Duke Hospital. Because we hadn't officially had our first appointment with the Dr. Nameless, the oncologist, at Duke, we were told that Bob wasn't officially his patient yet. I remember arguing with the woman who took the call and then I told Bob to "get in the car." When I spoke like that, Bob listened, and there was no arguing with me. Now, on the way there, we did argue about my driving abilities, but that's a story I'm not willing to put in print. Let's just say that mechanical things like cars and computers aren't my forte. We made the two-hour drive up to Duke and again had a long wait in the emergency room, but our wait to get to the oncology floor was fairly short. I joked that we seemed to be getting some clout there, too. Bob said, "I don't know if that's a good thing or not," and we laughed. We had developed a sick sense of humor by then, but laughter is good for the soul. Isn't that what they say? And we needed to treat our entire selves, not just Bob's physical body.

Admission Number Two

Once my husband was again admitted to the oncology floor upstairs, the doctors resumed his Lovenox treatment. That time, we had our first attending oncologist who was a woman, Dr. Jennifer Garst, and she believed Bob's swelling issues were because the cancer was affecting his lymphatic system. She told me in private that his legs might never get better. She gave me a hug that last day we were there and wished me her best.

I remember going home with the plan that we were to see the previous attending oncologist and the radiation doctor that next week. Bob would be going to be getting the radiation treatment, and the oncologist would be following up on his Lovenox treatment and talking to us about other possible chemotherapy treatments.

We went for our first appointment with Dr. Nameless, the oncologist. He saw Bob's leg, which was now even more swollen. I pointed out all of the bruises on Bob's stomach from the injections of the Lovenox and asked him if that was normal. He didn't answer. I told him how I was frustrated with the system because I wasn't able to talk to him prior to this visit and that we ended up going to the emergency room. I said Bob had been readmitted, which was the only way we could be seen. He assured me that I could call his nurse the next time and gave me her card. Then he told me Bob could continue with the Lovenox injections. I said I was having trouble finding a place to give the injections and asked how long Bob would be on this medication. He replied, "indefinitely," and said patients were on it for years. I told him that I would not be able to find any places on his stomach that were not bruised and that I did not think I would be able to give him those twice daily injections much longer. He made a phone call to another doctor and said he would get back to us about scheduling an appointment at the cardiovascular thrombosis clinic. He said he wanted to make a few more phone calls and would get back to us. I think that at this visit, he sent us over to the other clinic to see his nurse, and she said to use an ice cube on Bob's stomach before giving him the injections in order to prevent this purple bruising. So, I did that prior to each injection, but it didn't help at all.

We stayed over night in Durham because Bob had an appointment on Wednesday to see the radiologist, Dr. Willet. By then, Bob's stomach looked like an eggplant with round sores that looked like the skim that forms on cooked chocolate pudding. Bob also had little black marks on his legs and on his fingers and hands. I hadn't heard back from Dr. Nameless, so on Tuesday afternoon, I called his nurse to find out what our next step was. He eventually returned my call after seeing his patients and told us to go to the cardiovascular thrombosis center on Friday. He said someone would get in touch with us.

The next day was Wednesday, and we went for our appointment at the radiologist. Dr. Willet was going to be getting Bob ready for the twelve radiation treatments by making a cast and pinpointing where exactly he would receive the radiation. Sometimes they will actually give you tiny tattoos to mark the spots were they will direct the radiation. Bob had those tattoo markings from his first radiation treatments in 1996, so I was somewhat familiar with what they were planning to do. As I said, we were feeling confident that Dr. Willet was going to be able to give Bob a little more radiation and that this might help to slow the cancer and help with his pain. The doctor had spoken about the fact that radiation treatments in 2006 were more specific than what Bob had been given in 1996. Plus, Dr. Willet was very thorough in his dosage calculations, which was why he believed Bob could endure twelve treatments at that time. Since Bob already had what was thought at one time to be the limit, it was crucial to get it right.

When we went to see Dr. Willet, he began to examine Bob and saw Bob's swollen legs and all of the sores on his legs and hands. Then we showed him Bob's stomach, and he said that he could not possibly give Bob the radiation with him in that condition. Then he asked if Dr. Nameless has seen us. We said that we had seen him on Monday. The radiologist wanted to know if Bob's legs looked like that at that visit, and we told him that they did. His reply was, "Well, what does he plan to do about this?" We said that Dr. Nameless told us to go to the cardiovascular thrombosis center some time on Friday. Dr. Willet's reply was that this couldn't wait until Friday and that Bob needed to be admitted to the hospital right away. He continued to tell us that he did not have privileges to admit because he just performed outpatient radiation at the clinic. He said, "Let me call Dr. Nameless and ask him to admit you."

Admission Number Three

Bob was then admitted, and I was glad we didn't have to go to the emergency room first that time. We had never before and were never since seen by so many doctors. We had oncologists, dermatologists, wound care specialists, hematologists, urologists, and also some specialists in infectious disease. When I included all of the attendings, interns, and residents who came to see Bob, it was mind-boggling. I honestly cannot tell you the names of all of the doctors who came in and out of the room. I did have to eat and do my maintenance for daily living, so there were times I wasn't in the room. Bob would later tell me that doctor so and so was there. Bob would always know their names. I would say, "Well, what kind of doctor was he?" Sometimes Bob would know the specialty, and sometimes he would just shake his head. Then, in his own words, Bob would try to relay what the doctor said. Poor Bob, I think I frustrated him because I would say, "Pay attention!" What was I thinking? He was living this nightmare, and it was his body, so I am sure he was paying attention. I was there scolding him because of my frustration. Bob understood and just would smile, give me a kiss, and tell me to try not to worry. We had come a long way from the first hospital stay when he learned of his cancer. Now we were a team and, I'd like to think, an unbeatable one. He was such a nice guy that all of the doctors went the extra mile for him. I was the pushy wife who kept them on their toes.

The dermatologist ordered a biopsy of the little black marks on each of his thighs. The result turned out to be negative for cancer, and there was no indication as to what might have caused these markings. When the injection site bruised even after the nurses were giving the injections, I think the doctors concluded that the bruising was not because of the way I was injecting Bob. They were also able to see a pattern in how these sores at the injection sites were developing. Bob also had numerous blood tests, but nothing could explain why Bob was having those issues. At this point, they decided to discontinue the Lovenox and switch Bob over to an oral medication called Coumadin.

Bob remained in the hospital until the Coumadin was at the proper level, and only then was he discharged. His legs were still swollen, and I think this was when they began to excessively weep from all of the swelling. After he was released, we needed to go back to the cardiovascular thrombosis center every few days to have the Coumadin levels monitored to try to determine its proper dosage. We continued to stay at a hotel in Durham because Bob was also going back to the radiologist to prepare for those radiation treatments.

Before Bob was discharged, one of the doctors had taken pictures of his legs, hands, and stomach for publication in a medical journal. The picture would not show his identity. I knew from all of my schooling that Bob's identity would be kept confidential. I also knew that unusual cases are published in journals in order to be made available to doctors throughout our health care system. I know Bob's reaction to his medication was rare, but the information would then be available in case other patients exhibited similar reactions. I don't know for a fact whether Bob's case was ever published, but one of the kind doctors did give us a copy of the picture of Bob's legs with all of the sores on it. It was given as a sort of souvenir or, as I like to think, a medal of honor. I can remember how pleased Bob was by the kind gesture. He would proudly show that picture to our friends and family. What a remarkable guy, that husband of mine. Now you may begin to understand the Bob I love.

Bob was finally ready to get started with his radiation treatments. According to the schedule, we were planning on being done just before Thanksgiving. Bob wanted to be home for Thanksgiving because our children were going to come to our North Carolina home that year to celebrate that holiday with us. We planned to stay overnight in Durham Monday through Thursday and return to our home in the Pinehurst area for the weekend, and then we would do the same thing the following week. Bob eventually tolerated the radiation, but only after surviving a panic attack right before his first treatment. I wasn't in the room at the time, but I know they had to postpone the treatment. They came to get me and explained that because of Bob's panic attack, he could not stay still and they were not able to give him his first radiation treatment. Bob wanted to get that first treatment under his belt, so to speak, so Dr. Willet said he would try again later that day. They put Bob in one of the treatment rooms and called me in to stay with him. Bob was determined to do it that day, and he told me that he wanted to get started and conquer his fear. Bob then explained that the doctor had prescribed some Ativan for his anxiety.

It was getting closer to closing time and Bob was still very restless, so the nurse came in and gave him a second Atavin to help him relax. He finally managed to get his panic attack under control and was able to remain calm enough to get the treatment.

I think that all Bob had been going through was getting to be too much for him. I couldn't believe he was able to endure all that he had up to that point in his battle with cancer. And I know he was truly scared, because he and I talked about his fears. All of our discussions about the extra radiation and the possibility that he could lose his bladder control were weighing on his mind. However, prior to all this, his bladder had been showing evidence of some retention, and I mentioned that to him. His legs were also still swelling because of the clot, so there were many problems going on all at once. You see, his legs ended up getting so swollen and weepy that I was placing disposable diapers on them to absorb the fluid and then wrapping them with ace bandages. Bob normally wore a size ten shoe, but his feet were so swollen that he could only wear open-backed size thirteen slippers.

We managed to finally get through the radiation treatment, which actually took all of five minutes, but between going to the lab for blood work because of the blood thinner he was on and the anxiety attack, we were the last ones to leave the clinic. If I recall, his blood level was also off that day, and we had to go back to the cardiovascular thrombosis clinic after Bob's radiation treatment so Bob could be given vitamin K. It was well past five o'clock when we were leaving, and it was pouring down rain. This was also the day the parking attendants misplaced our car in the parking garage. It just seemed everything was going wrong. I think what happened was that my ticket got wet, and the number that corresponded to my car wasn't right. I just remember waiting for them to find the car while Bob returned to the clinic to get the vitamin K shot. I was starting to worry that maybe the car was stolen. It took more than a half an hour for them to find it. Though it eventually worked out okay, it was just one more stress to what would become known to me as the day from you know where. As you read about the rest of my day, you may agree with my assessment.

Then we ended up in heavy traffic just outside of Durham. I was driving, and I didn't know the area. Bob was my copilot. I have already told you about my driving, haven't I? We decided to stop for something to eat and found this pretty cool hamburger joint. It was decorated in the art deco style, with a lot of chrome, and there was music from a jukebox playing. It looked like a fun place to eat. We sat down at a high top table, ordered our food, and were talking when Bob said he had to go to the bathroom. He wasn't looking too good and was slurring his words a little. He went over to the entrance and just stood there, and then I realized he was really out of it. I was afraid he was going to pull his zipper down and pee right in the restaurant. I hurried over to him and brought him back to the table. Now his burger came and he picked it up and he started chewing. Only thing the burger was still on the plate. I called over the waitress and told her to please pack up our food and bring me the bill. I looked over at Bob and he was still chewing the burger that he never picked up—the invisible one he was holding in his hand. Those anxiety pills had kicked in. I had told the radiologist not to give him two, because he had a low tolerance to that medication. He had been given it along with the IV pain medication when he was in Canton and had had a similar reaction. I knew he couldn't tolerate Atavin that well.

I managed to get Bob in the car, and we drove to the hotel across the street. I went to the lobby and checked in, hoping and praying that Bob didn't get out of the car. Thankfully, he didn't. I drove around the hotel to get as close as possible to the entrance where our room was located. I was parked alongside the hotel and not in a parking space. I managed to get out of the car in the pouring rain and somehow get this smiling guy who was slurring his words out of the car. Anyone who saw him would have thought for sure he was drunk. Wearing his furry size thirteen slippers that could hardly stay on his feet, he stepped in a huge puddle of water that was running along the curb. I then escorted him into the room with the help of God; Bob was six feet tall and could barely walk, and I am only five foot one. I made numerous trips back to the car to unpack it. I finally got him undressed and into bed. Every minute or two he would pop up and would start to talk. I just had to laugh; what else could I do? I was in a hotel room with Bob, with his swollen, soggy, wrapped leg and his matching soggy slippers, and I was just thankful he was smiling and had made it through the first treatment without having a stroke. I eventually got him washed up and rewrapped his leg, but I had to stay awake most of the night because every so often he would wake up and try to get out of bed. He couldn't even stand, and I didn't want to add a broken bone to the list. It is amazing the things we can get through.

To this day I am not sure how I got through that day, but I know God had to have been with me. My strength was superhuman; it was beyond what I could normally achieve physically, mentally, and emotionally.

We drove back home to Southern Pines the next day and spent the weekend at home, trying to recover from all that had happened. Then we returned on Monday to continue with Bob's treatments as we had planned. Bob managed to get a few more treatments in that week before he was readmitted to the hospital on Friday because of all of the problems he was exhibiting.

Admission Number Four

We stayed at a nearby hotel during the week so that Bob could continue his radiation treatments at Duke. I remember it was Friday, and Bob had received a total of six treatments by then. We finally were able to get an outpatient appointment to see the wound care physician's assistant. He wrapped Bob's leg at last and said that it would help with the swelling. We all hoped that because of the blood thinner, the clot would eventually resolve and that the compression wrap would help improve the venous circulation and eventually reduce the swelling and fluid that had accumulated in Bob's leg. I think it had something to do with the lymphatic system, too, but I am not certain. The physician's assistant said how amazing it was that Bob had survived those eleven years and that he could not have possibly done it without me. He emphasized this and said he was being very serious. He was commending me for all I had been doing to see that Bob was taken care of through his battle with cancer. Of course, Bob told him he knew that, and he told the doctor about how I had saved his life when he had the nicked bile duct. Bob truly believed that I had saved his life because I kept after the doctors to do something. Bob said he knew that he wouldn't still be alive without me, and it was so good to hear both of them say that. Their words were a Godsend to me because I was so weary from those past three hospital stays at Duke and the one in Ohio right before we took the trip to our North Carolina home. As I write about this and know what was ahead of me, I am totally sincere when I say there is no way I could have endured all of this on my own strength.

I am writing about all of the problems we had at Duke not to bash that hospital or any of the doctors, but to help you see how God was there for me through all of this. The doctors at Duke never gave up on Bob, and they finally did get all Bob's complications resolved. I also believe God was able to use all of this for good, and as you learn of the final outcome, you may agree with me.

Now, the irony is that all the praise I had just been given would change in an instant. I went from feeling like I was such an important part of Bob's healing by being his personal nurse and advocate to feeling like I was the blame for all his trouble with his blood sugar and sore legs. You see, we had an appointment at the cardiovascular thrombosis center to draw Bob's blood and check on his Coumadin levels. If any of you are familiar with this drug, you will know it is important to have the blood levels monitored to make sure that the blood is neither too thick nor too thin. As I said before, Bob's blood was so off the week before that he had to be given the vitamin K to get it back into a healthy range. The doctors were having such a hard time trying to find the appropriate dosage, and it seemed that his blood levels just would not adjust properly. At this time, Bob was also taking Prednisone to help counteract the effects of the Lovenox. The steroid was playing havoc with Bob's blood sugar, too. He was also on medicine for his diabetes, and I had to constantly adjust his insulin. I was doing this on my own with very little direction from the doctors. I was using the sliding scale that I had been given when Bob was hospitalized in Ohio. Bob's blood sugar was out of control, so it was good that we had an appointment to get his blood levels checked. We saw Dr. Becker for the monitoring of Bob's Coumadin, and he noted how swollen Bob's legs still were. I think that is when Dr. Becker said he would like Dr. Nameless to come see us. Dr. Nameless worked at both the oncology clinic and the cardiovascular thrombosis center, where Dr. Becker was the director. So, Bob and I impatiently waited in the treatment room for Dr. Nameless.

By then, Bob and I were very tired, and it had been an extremely long week. We were looking forward to going back home to Southern Pines for the weekend before returning for more radiation on Monday. Dr. Nameless eventually came in, and we started to talk. He asked about Bob's leg, and I mentioned I was concerned about Bob's blood sugar readings. I remembered telling him how I could not get Bob's blood sugar under control and that Bob's readings were so high that I was very worried. I told him I was using the sliding scale that I had been given at the hospital in Ohio to try and determine Bob's insulin amounts, but that it didn't seem to be lowering his blood sugar levels. I mentioned that I had gone to nursing school and was comfortable fixing and giving his injections, but I just wasn't able to get the levels under control. I explained that Bob was having some blood sugar readings that were almost five hundred.

As we were talking, Dr. Nameless started to unwrap Bob's leg. At that point, I just remember feeling that I was ready for a straightjacket, because I was about to lose it. We had literally waited weeks to get Bob seen by wound care. I told Dr. Nameless we had just come from wound care and that Bob had just had that wrap put on his leg. He said he needed to see it. I agreed, but I was very upset and told him that he should have been coordinating all of these appointments so that this would not be happening. I said Bob was to keep his leg wrapped and that we were to return to outpatient wound care in one week to have it check and rewrapped. I also said that the last time Bob was an inpatient, wound care never even came to see Bob for some reason, even though the attending oncologist had requested a consult from them. I continued to tell him that the nurses had no orders, so I had wrapped his leg myself while the nurse just got me the supplies I needed. I explained that I was worried that if I did not keep Bob's leg wrapped, he would slip and fall because his leg and foot were so wet that he literally would have a small puddle if he had his foot on the floor for even a few minutes.

Dr. Nameless then said, "I heard your were upset with me, too." He wanted to know why and what he could do differently. I said that I had already told him the last time I saw him why I was upset about the Lovenox and I continued to explain that I thought he was our main doctor at Duke, so I expected him to help us navigate the system, get us in for appointments, and oversee Bob's care in general. I told him I wanted him to be the captain of the ship. I think he understood that term because he nodded his head. I then said that I had to go to wound care on my own and that Dr. Willet from radiology was the one to help get us that appointment. Then I brought up Bob's allergy to the Lovenox. He replied in the language of what I like to call "atoms and neurons." He said Bob was not really allergic to the Lovenox. That was when I lost it completely. I didn't say another word to him, but inside I felt I was going to explode any minute.

I remember having to take care of the paperwork for Bob to be admitted to the hospital again. I kept thinking, *Why did Dr. Nameless decide to finally admit Bob now that he had his leg wrapped and we were to go home for the weekend?* If I had been thinking clearly, I would have realized that Bob's blood sugar readings were reason enough to admit him. Now, maybe Dr. Nameless had that planned all along, but he and I did not communicate well together, so I had no clue of his thought process.

As soon as Bob was wheeled away to go from the clinic to the hospital side of Duke, I ran down in tears to see Dr. Willet. First I saw his nurse, who went and talked to Dr. Willet. He then came out, saw me crying, and said he just couldn't talk to me right then about all of it. He said he would have one of his assistants talk to me. I know he really cared for Bob and me and that he was getting personally involved, too. That is when he sent one of the other doctors we knew to talk to me. This doctor compared Dr. Nameless and me to being like oil and water: we just don't mix. He then said, "You two are just having a personality clash." After I explained that Dr. Nameless didn't think Bob was allergic to the Lovenox while every other doctor said he was and that I was going crazy because the doctors were not agreeing, he just listened and did not say another word. Then Dr. Willet came back in to see me after we both calmed down and said, "Please go to a hotel and get some sleep and then go back home to Southern Pines for a while. You are exhausted." I know he could tell I was about to have a breakdown, but there was no way I was leaving Bob alone in Durham. However, I did check into a hotel that night. You see, I usually stayed at my husband's side and slept in the reclining chair whenever he was admitted to the hospital, but I was so exhausted. I promised Dr. Willet that I would at least go get a good night's sleep, and I didn't put up a fight.

Now you would think that with all that Bob and I had been through, it would be smooth sailing from then on. No way! First, I found out that Bob was retaining urine and that they inserted a catheter, which was, I am sure, a good thing. It probably was another reason Bob's blood sugar had been elevated, and I am sure Bob was producing a great deal of urine with those high readings, too. Besides, I think having all of that urine retention could have led to kidney problems on top of everything else. I think Bob had retention of twelve hundred cubic centimeters of urine, which is a pretty large amount. I had so many questions for the doctor. I was worried about Bob's blood sugar and the fact that he was taking Prednisone, which I knew raised the blood sugar, too. I was also worried about Bob having an infection, because I think he was running a fever. There was no way I was leaving him there alone.

However, I did end up leaving the hospital. I checked into the hotel that was right up the street from Duke. Despite my questions for the doctors, I was so exhausted that I slept in and missed the morning rounds.

When I arrived back at the hospital, I asked our nurse which doctor was the attending physician that morning and then went to seek that oncologist out to talk to her about all of the problems Bob was having. One of the nurses pointed the female oncologist out to me, but she was on the phone. I patiently waited quite a while for her to get off the phone. We were both at the nurses' station, and I know she saw me standing there, leaning against the wall. After she finished her phone call, she walked right past me. I said, "Excuse me, can I speak with you?" I introduced myself by telling her I was Robert Renk's wife and her reply was, "I know who you are." By her tone, I concluded that my reputation had preceded me. I told her I had a few concerns. I asked if they had tested Bob for a staph infection, and she reassured me that of course they had. I could sense she resented my question. Next, I mentioned that I was also worried about other blood infections. I told her Bob still had some sores on his hand and said, "You know, he has that colostomy and I was worried he could get an E coli infection. Could you please mention to Bob that he needs to wear gloves when he takes care of his colostomy."

She said, "You know, the skin is a natural barrier," and she went on about it.

I replied, "Yes," as I thought to myself, *I learned that in Nursing- 101.* I was in agreement with her statement, but I was also sort of puzzled because I knew Bob had open sores. I was not really processing very quickly. I merely continued with my original idea about the gloves. At that point I think she instructed me about hand washing. I was arguing with her in my mind because he had open sores and it was hard to wash his hands. I just reiterated that with all of the sores on Bob's hand, I just thought the gloves might be a good idea. I mentioned that if she talked to Bob about it and went over the importance of hand washing, he would listen to her because Bob always follows a doctor's orders. I don't know if I said that part out loud or just thought it, but I just didn't want Bob to see me as his pushy wife. Looking back, maybe that was exactly what she thought of me. I was the pushy wife who was getting into all of the doctors' business.

Now, the next morning when I went into Bob's room, he told me about the gloves he was to wear when he used the bathroom. I was so happy and thought *all is well.* Not long after, the female oncologist came into Bob's room with several interns. She was standing next to me and talking. Something she said brought a question to mind, so I began to ask it. I sensed that she was annoyed, so I apologized for interrupting her and told her how tired I was and that all of this has been too much. I then told her if I didn't ask the question during the natural flow of the conversation, I might forget with all that was on my mind. She then said that I was interrupting her and she had a lot on her mind, too. She walked around to the other side of the bed. She started talking directly to Bob. There was a very distinct chill in the air, and it wasn't the air conditioning. Even Bob noticed it because after the all doctors left Bob said, "Boy, she was rude to you."

"You noticed?" I asked. Coming from Bob, that was quite some statement. He never had an unkind word to say, and he usually didn't notice these things, so it must have been really obvious.

Now, I am not a genius. I think I've said that before, but for a nonprofessional, I am a quick study when I need to be. I needed to be involved in my husband's treatment; I was his advocate. Just the previous day, Dr. Nameless had been talking very technically—way over my head—in our Lovenox discussion. Dr. Nameless may, in fact, be the genius, but I did actually understand his point. My question to him had been, "Now that you know what you know, would you do anything different if you saw Bob with these sores on his stomach?" Dr. Nameless defended his decision to ignore the purple stomach, swollen legs, black bruises, and every other symptom my husband had. But what he needed to realize was that we didn't expect him to have those answers the first time we walked into his office. He was only to ask the question, "Why?" I don't care if he is an attending doctor or not. Ask the question, and in God's infinite wisdom, and with a team of doctors working together, we will find the answer.

So there I was in the hospital room with Bob after having that icy conversation with the female oncologist, and I was about at my wit's end. I went out into the hall and sought one of my favorite nurses. I told her what had happened, and she listened and suggested that I call the complaint line. I called without giving any details, and they said someone would get back to me.

Later that day, a man came in the room and said he was from administration. He said, "I understand you are having some problems." Where to begin? He sat and listened to me complain about the hospital. I told him about our trouble getting wound care to see Bob and a few other complaints about the room and so on. I didn't dare tell him about the female oncologist because she was taking care of Bob and I was already on her wrong side. And I didn't want to bring up Dr. Nameless, either. But this man sat there and said he could wait until I felt comfortable to talk, because he wanted to know everything. So we made some small talk and then he just kept sitting there. I had the distinct feeling he wasn't leaving until I opened up to him about what was really bugging me. So, eventually I told him about how confused I was and that all I wanted to know was if Bob was really allergic to Lovenox or not. He wise reply was, "If it walks like a duck, talks like a duck, looks like a duck, and acts like a duck, wouldn't you say it is a duck?"

I said yes. Now who's the real genius? In my mind, the genius was the man who handed me his card and said, "If you need anything, don't hesitate to call me." After he left, I read his card and saw that he was the director of pharmacology at Duke University. And, I might add, he was one of the most patient and wisest men I've ever met. He brought healing to my mind, peace to my spirit, and a sense of calm in the middle of a war. I thought he was there in response to my call to the complaint line, but after looking at the card he handed me, I wondered if he might have been there not because of my phone call, but maybe because someone who cared about Bob and me sent him. I believe that many professionals knew of my dilemma and my need for clarity. I will never know. I believe in angels, and some of them are doctors, too.

By that hospital stay, Bob had been off the Lovenox. Bob's stomach wasn't nearly as purple, and those little areas that looked like the skim that forms on the top of cooked chocolate pudding were all gone. He was now just taking the Coumadin for his blood thinner. All of the black little spots on his hands and legs weren't nearly as bad, but he still did have some open sores that were slowly healing.

Because the female attending doctor only wanted to speak to Bob, I communicated with her by way of the blackboard in the room. It was a teaching hospital! This board was actually white, and I used the blue markers to write down my questions. Every day as a question would come to my mind, I would ask the nurse. If she could not answer me, then I would write the question down so that when the doctors came around in the morning to do rounds, I did not have to be there. That was good for me, too, because I could sleep in a little. I think God used this for my good, because he knew I needed the rest. So, once again, something good came out of something bad. It was Bob's job to see that the answers were written back to me. And, if I might add, I asked some very good questions. I am going to brag, because the day Bob was discharged from the hospital, one of the interns was going over all of the prescriptions Bob would be discharged on, and one was for Prednisone. I questioned him and said that I thought the nurse had mentioned Bob was now off of it. He said, "No, he is still on the Prednisone."

"Okay," I replied. "Maybe I misunderstood the nurse."

Bob and I went down to the cardiovascular thrombosis center that day, and while we were waiting to see Dr. Becker, the receptionist said there was a phone call for me. It was the intern. He said, "Mrs. Renk, are you going to be there for a while? I need to see you."

"Yes, we haven't been seen yet," I replied.

"Please wait for me," he said. I did, and when he showed up, he asked for the script back for the Prednisone and said, "You were right. Your husband was off the Prednisone."

Now, I'm not sure if an intern is able to decide the prescriptions on his own or if the attending doctor is the one who determines what medicines the patient should take when discharged, but I know one thing for sure. This intern respected me enough to go and recheck the medical record. He smiled, thanked me, and once again said, "You do know what's going on."

That was the best ending to that stay, and once again I was given kudos by a caring, soon to be great doctor. He learned something important on that rotation, or maybe he already knew it. Either way, he listened and researched and made an informed decision. He also learned that sometimes a family member might have something helpful to say regarding a loved one's condition. I do not think I am the only person who has something important to say. I also know that not all family members are as blessed as I was to have had a recent medical background that would prepare me for all of this. I like to think that while I was at Duke, a few people learned something from me. And I mean no disrespect when I say this, and it is with all sincerity. You see, I believe God put us here to learn from one another. I know I learned more than I ever cared to learn from this experience about medicine and people in general. And doctors, after all, are only people, too.

We all agreed that Bob's body had a strange reaction to the Lovenox and that he should never use it again. In fact, the doctors did not even want Bob to use Heparin because it is so similar to Lovenox. All I wanted from Dr. Nameless was for him to be perfectly clear about what we learned from the experience. I would imagine talking to Dr. Nameless, asking, *Don't you know who you are talking to here? I am not your peer. I am the wife of a very sick man. I have a lot on my mind. My husband might be dying, and you want to talk about atoms and neurons. I'm not really that smart.* I guess I should have been flattered that he thought I was that smart and would understand him. As I said before, we weren't even on the same page.

But I do believe that even though we had our differences, God would use this for good, too. It got us noticed at Duke, a large hospital, and Dr. Becker took us under his wing and went that extra mile for my husband. It was my hope that in time Dr. Nameless would realize that when I asked him if he would have done anything different once he knew what he knew, it wasn't a trick question. I just wanted him to realize he learned something new, too. Sometimes we all can learn something new. He wasn't expected to know what was happening with Bob; it was such a freaky development. Hopefully, if Dr. Nameless saw another patient with these symptoms he would say, "Oh yes, I've seen this before and I know what to do." More than that, I hope he learns to question everything unknown and realizes that he doesn't know everything. Only God knows all. I hope in time and with distance he has come to that conclusion on his own. If not, I hope he is reading this and gets it now. I learned a great deal in the thirteen years that my husband battled his cancer, and it was more than I ever really wanted to learn. It cost me a great deal to learn all of it, but I am glad to share what I learned from my experiences with anyone who wants to learn, too.

I want you to know that I call this doctor Dr. Nameless to protect his identity. I really mean him no harm. I just want to tell my story and show how in the end, God ruled, as God is the Great Physician. I also want you to have some idea of just what I went through so that you can understand the magnitude of what God is capable of and how he will work all things for good. I hope this is a huge dose of hope for you.

Bob lived in a positive world, and I think that was what made him shine and made so many doctors want to go that extra mile for him. Bob was also so accepting of everyone and had the greatest respect for doctors. They really liked and respected my husband, too, and they understood the battle he was fighting. He had volumes of medical records to prove it.

Bob would often go home only to have so much trouble with the swelling in both his legs that he could hardly walk. Dr. Becker, the director of Duke's cardiovascular thrombosis clinic, had seen

Bob at the clinic many times. On numerous occasions he had teased me about seeing Dr. Nameless. We really never said much, but Dr. Becker would smile and ask if I'd like to see Dr. Nameless. I would say, "No thanks." Sometimes I would say, "We have an oncologist in Pinehurst." He always would put his arm around me and say he would take care of us. He gave me his card to call if I had any problems. Well, the day after Thanksgiving, Bob was getting much worse. His testicles were swollen, too, and Bob was in so much pain. I called the number on the card that Dr. Becker had given me. A man answered. I said with surprise in my voice, "Is this Dr. Becker?"

"Yes, this is my number you called." I told him who I was and that I was surprised he answered the phone himself. He said he happened to stop in the office. I told him what was going on with Bob and that Bob had had his last radiation treatment on Wednesday. Dr. Becker said, "I think we really need to put a stent in the vein where his clot is located. I don't think Bob is getting much venous flow, which is why he is has the swelling, leakage, and so on with his leg. We have waited long enough, and I don't think this is going to resolve itself."

Admission Number Five

So, Bob went back to Duke and was admitted for the fifth time. I think it was the Sunday or Monday after Thanksgiving. We did get to have our family Thanksgiving dinner, and all three of the children were with us to celebrate. Sadly, Big Rob came alone and told us he thought he and Laura would be getting a divorce. He wanted to talk to us about it. Life goes on, even when a family member has cancer. We were sad to hear the news, but Bob and I had both been there. In our minds, we didn't think the reason was good enough, because Bob and I had been through so much more. It really wasn't our place to judge. Maybe they ended things at just the right time.

Laura is still in my life, and now we have being single in common. We have our girl talks. So, that is a blessing. Bob enjoyed Thanksgiving, which ranked high among his favorite holidays because Bob loved to eat. He also loved helping me cook, doing the dishes, and being a part of all of that kitchen-focused activity. I used to get a lot of extra attention when I was at the stove because, you see, food is a way to a man's heart. But this Thanksgiving was different. He was able to eat, but that and enjoying the family were about the only things that were the same. I was so worried about him, but somehow I was able to pull it all together and make dinner. Because Bob didn't clean up, my son-in-law David and our two sons did the dishes.

So, as I was saying, Bob was finally admitted to Duke so that doctors could insert a stent to help resolve his problem with the blood clot. It just was not clearing up. I think it became a matter of whether to take the risk or watch Bob die. He was getting worse as each day passed. He was in the hospital for a few days before the procedure because he had to go off the Coumadin, get his blood levels to reach normal levels, and have some testing to locate the clot. I know you cannot have your blood too thin before a surgery, as you could bleed to death. This was the hospital stay when the lymphedema nurse came in to talk to us. Bob also saw someone from the wound care department this time. I know that the procedure to place the stent in his vein was successful and that there were no complications. After the surgery, the biggest issue was trying to readjust the Coumadin to a therapeutic level, and that took a while to regulate. He was actually doing pretty well once the stent was in place and the venous blood flow was working properly.

At one point I started to stay at a hotel again. I think Bob was doing so much better that I didn't feel like I had to sleep in the chair in his room. Once Bob was out of pain or could manage by himself and wasn't really sick, I would consider leaving. Everything seemed pretty good, so I checked into the hotel that was right up the street from the hospital. I would walk home and Bob would look out the window and accompany me home with his gaze. We would talk on the phone as I walked. It was usually around midnight when I would head back to the hotel. I used to stay with him and we would watch TV, play cards, or play games. I remember one of the women who cleaned Bob's room during this hospital stay told me that she thought Bob and I were so sweet together and that it was nice to see us enjoying each other's company even in the hospital. I thought to myself that we were still sweet as I walked back to my hotel from the hospital that night. Before I entered the hotel, I would wave goodbye to Bob as he looked out his window. Then I would get in the elevator, where the call would drop, and I would always call Bob back once I was in my room and had the door locked. I felt safe then, and Bob would stop worrying about me then, too. I had a room that faced his room. We would both wave, but we really couldn't see each other. It was just a game we would play. I'd say, "Can you see me waving?" Then he'd do the same thing back to me. Writing this makes me realize just how inseparable we were.

That hotel was so convenient. I could just leave my car parked there and not worry about finding a parking space at the hospital or having to wait for parking attendants. Besides, if I didn't leave the hospital by a certain time I would have to call to get someone to bring the car around, which was a pain after a long day.

There were even times when I would go out for a few hours because Bob was doing so much better. I remember that Tracy drove up one day and took me out to the mall so I could get a break from the hospital routine. At times like these, Bob was pretty self-reliant, which meant things were good. It was those stays when he was in pain or had many unresolved problems that I dreaded. It's funny how I even ranked the hospital stays. It all centered around how well Bob was feeling. If he was good, then in the end, it was all good. So with that in mind, I will add that his very last hospital stay was the best. You'll understand this better as you read further.

Bob was finally discharged, and it was amazing to see how well his legs were doing after his swelling had started to go away. It is remarkable how fast our bodies can heal. It is also so spectacular to see how advanced medicine is today. We are truly blessed to live in a country with such great health care available to us and to see the advancements firsthand. When I talked to some of the staff and some of the other patients' families, I learned about some amazing things that were being done at Duke University Hospital. When I was waiting for the parking attendant to bring my car one day, I had an opportunity to talk to one of the nurses at Duke about some of the remarkable things that they were doing at the university, too. I think she was talking about some treatment that the doctors had administered to a patient right in the middle of a surgery. It was very wild. She was impressed that they stopped and performed that advanced treatment while the patient's body was still opened up. I am not sure if it was radiation or some nuclear treatment, but it was impressive nonetheless.

Admission Number Six

Unfortunately, about a month later Bob had the same problem and Dr. Becker made arrangements to have the procedure done again. Big Rob flew in to be with Bob and me during part of this hospital stay, and he was there for the day of the actual procedure. I was glad I was not alone, because I was worried that Bob might not make it through that surgery. The doctor had gone over the risks, and all of the possibilities for what could go wrong started to weigh on my mind. I was beginning to have trouble sleeping. Now, I normally did not think this way, and I know that all that had happened prior to this procedure was catching up to me. I also think that when other people were around, I didn't need to be as strong. I relied on them to give me a break. Unfortunately, when I didn't have to take on all of the responsibility, I would actually feel worse. I was so glad to have Big Rob's company, and Bob was always happy to see Big Rob, even if it was for a lousy reason like surgery.

As a side note, this was the one time we chose not to go back to the oncology floor. After five previous admissions, I requested a different floor.

Now, for the past month, Bob's legs had been doing well and the swelling had gone down. All of a sudden, however, his legs began to swell again. Also, we had been having a hard time getting Bob's Coumadin levels to stay in the proper range. During this admission, the doctor switched Bob over to a once-a-day injection of Arixtra. Bob would end up staying on this medication for the rest of his life.

I think this hospital stay ended up being a long one, too, because of the transition time from one medication to the other.

When Bob went home, I gave him Arixtra injections in his stomach once a day and he tolerated them well. He would only occasionally have a little bruise if I hit one of the tiny veins in his stomach. I just remember that we had to stay away from his colostomy area and his hernias and his scars so it was a good thing he only needed one shot a day because it was hard to find enough sites for the injections. He was now on insulin all of the time too. I hated giving him the shots, especially the Arixtra, because I was always afraid that I would hurt him. Bob would say, "Just do it. It hurts when the nurse does it, too." Eventually he would learn to give himself the shots because he hated seeing the look of pain on my face when I had to do it.

Bob was starting to have some problems with his bladder retention, but all of the sores he had on his legs and hands were gone. Between the steroid treatment and the fact that he was no longer taking the Lovenox, those sores finally healed. By then Bob had to use the catheter occasionally to make sure his bladder was completely empty.

At the hospital, Dr. Michael Miller was the doctor who put the stent in the vein in Bob's groin area. He wanted to talk to me afterward, and he told me that that was absolutely the last time he would do that. He said that he could do more harm than good by going in there again. That had been in the beginning of January. Bob's back pain was pretty good and his leg had actually healed from all of the sores, so we were thinking he was out of the woods. Bob was doing well except for his few bladder problems. We visited the urologist that Bob had in the hospital, and she had the nurse teach Bob how to self-catheterize. We were able to do this with little trouble.

Toward the end of January, Bob's best friend Al and his wife Nancy were going to the Florida Keys and invited us to come down for a week or two. We talked it over and decided to go for about a week or so around the end of February to the beginning of March.

We purchased our tickets and were all packed and ready to go a day or two before we were scheduled to leave, when Bob's legs started to swell again. His legs were getting swollen fairly quickly. I again called Dr. Becker, and he made arrangement for Bob to have the test done to look at this vein again. We did this test the day before we were to fly to the Keys. It worked out because Duke and the Raleigh Airport are not that far apart, so after the test we went to the hotel near the airport and flew out the next day. But looking back, who would go to the Florida Keys under those conditions? Maybe we were foolish to go on that trip, but it all worked out okay. We had just learned to trust God and not to be fearful of taking advantage of opportunities to enjoy life.

Dr. Becker said he would have the best radiologist at Duke read the films and see if there was any cancer growing and causing the stent to clog. There had been cancer cells present when they analyzed the cells that had been clogging the stent the first time it was replaced. My theory was that since Bob had cancer in his system, maybe those cells were just the ones circulating in his blood and helping to form the clot but not necessarily growing into the vein. I discussed this with Dr. Becker. I always got the impression that Dr. Becker enjoyed talking to me and listening to my theories or questions. He would always smile, and sometimes when one of his associates would come in, he would encourage me to tell his associate what I had just talked with him about or he would have me ask his associate the questions that were on my mind. He was always respectful to Bob and me, and I truly appreciate him. After all, he was one of the doctors who helped give me more time with the man I loved. That was a priceless gift. Anyway, I like to think he was impressed with my knowledge for just being the wife of a patient, or maybe he found my theories or questions either amusing or amazing. I'm not sure. So, as I said, the debate was whether the cancer was pushing on the vein and causing it to clot or whether the cancer had indeed penetrated the vein. Dr. Becker said he would see what the radiologist thought after looking at Bob's test results. He said, "You may be right, and that is what I hope to find out." He made arrangements for the assistant doctor to call us with the results.

When we were in the Florida Keys, Dr. Becker's assistant called us and said that he had good news. He said that the radiologist who read the film said there was no cancer growing into the vein or, he thought, even around the area at all. So we were going to have the chance to have the stent replaced. The doctor told us to come to Duke after our plane landed on our return trip from the Keys.

Admission Number Seven

As soon as our plane landed at the Raleigh Durham Airport, we drove directly to Duke Hospital in Durham. Dr. Becker had made all the arrangements for Bob to be admitted, and the plan was that Bob was scheduled to have his third stent put in. Everything went well with the procedure. Dr. Miller removed the old stent that had clogged and inserted another one. When he talked to me after the surgery, he told me he put a longer stent in that he hoped would work. However, he said that this would absolutely be the last time he would do that surgery on Bob and that he had told Dr. Becker the same thing. He then said, "I did not want to even do it this time, as you already know from the last time we talked, but I did it as a personal favor to Dr. Becker."

I must tell you the best part of the story. When Bob was admitted to the hospital after that third stent was put in, Dr. Becker came to visit Bob in his room. The nurse who had been Bob's nurse on and off for six out of the seven hospital stays called me out of the room. She said to me, "Bobbie, who was that doctor that came in to see you and Bob? I didn't recognize him."

"Oh, that was Dr. Becker."

"Who is he? I don't know that name," she said. I explained that he was the director of the cardiovascular thrombosis center.

"You must really be special," she said. "The directors never come on the floor to see the patients."

Now, she was confused. You see, we weren't special. It was Dr. Becker who was special. He saved my husband's life. As I said, Bob was able to live almost two years after that, and he would get to spend time with our grandchildren. That was wonderful, because those grandchildren remember Bob, and we keep talking about him together, looking at his pictures, and keeping his memory alive. Not only that, but I think God used Dr. Becker to make something good come out of something bad once again. The way I see it, we stood out at Duke because of something bad that happened to Bob. Out of all of the patients who were there, we had so many problems, but those problems made us get noticed. So many doctors went the extra mile to give Bob the very best care they possibly could, and these doctors took risks to save Bob's life. I like to think one reason they did it was because they saw the love that Bob and I had for each other. Really, they were just seeing Jesus, because without him we would have never shined so brightly, especially through all of this.

I was shocked in a way, but in another way I wasn't at all. When we saw Dr. Miller for the follow-up, he told Bob the same thing about it being the absolutely last time he would operate, and when he finished, this is what I said to him: "I believe that doctors do the possible, and when you can't do anything anymore, it's up to God to do the impossible." I thanked him and said, "The rest is up to God, and I think he will do a pretty good job, too." Now I want you to know that that had to be the Holy Spirit speaking through me, because I said it with such confidence. I also want you to know Bob lived almost another two years, and never had any more problems with his legs. When Bob had all of the problems with his legs, I know I was getting scared. I thought, *I don't want my husband to die this way. What an awful way to die.* Some ways, I guess, are better than others.

When Dr. Miller saw us for the last time, Bob's legs had cleared up again, and the swelling had gone away. Dr. Miller suggested that Bob should wear a stocking on his leg to help return the venial blood flow back up Bob's leg. I don't know if he really needed to wear the stocking all the time, but Bob did because he always followed the doctor's advice, of course.

When Bob died, he had two truly perfect legs. One time, we read an article about what constituted a perfect leg. Bob and our friend Nancy passed the perfect leg test, but Al and I did not. We used to laugh about it over the years. Bob died with those perfect legs, thanks to Dr. Becker and Dr. Miller. Over the next years, Bob's leg was to receive hundred's of kisses from our grandson. Every time Ryan, who was around two years old at the time, saw Bob, he would kiss his leg over and over. He did it when he came into our house, sometimes in the middle of the visit, and then again when he would leave. Bob wore that stocking, and Ryan knew Poppy had a booboo. So, of course, that's what you do. You kiss the booboo. We loved to see Ryan doing that, and Bob got so much joy out of this ritual, too. And believe me, with Ryan it was a ritual.

The Final Battle

It was the summer of 2008, and we were back in Canton, Ohio. Bob had been doing fairly well, although he was having increased pain and was taking more pain medication than ever before. It seemed like he was getting so many bladder infections, and he had been self-catheterizing to release his bladder for some time. I know he had been on the chemo, which had given him painful, tiny cuts on his hand. We would try all types of lotions to help prevent or heal the cuts, but nothing seemed to work. This chemo didn't have too many other side effects, but these tiny cuts really bothered Bob because he found it hard even to wash dishes or do any detailed work with his hands. Bob loved to work because he loved to help me, so this added to his frustration. Although this part of his treatment was the most recent, it is all a fog to me. I vaguely remember him getting sick and vomiting, which was so unlike him. We weren't sure if it was from the antibiotics for the chronic bladder infections, the oral pain medication, or the patch he was wearing for pain management. Whatever the reason, he never had that reaction to any of his other treatments before, so it was rather shocking to me. It seemed his cast-iron stomach, which is what I always called it, was getting weak.

The pain medication did not seem to be working again. We didn't wait this time for the pain to get out of control, as we had learned our lesson. We spoke to Dr. Schmotzer about referring us to the pain clinic again. When we went to the pain clinic, we discussed the possibility of getting a pain pump for Bob with one of the pain management doctors. A pain pump is an internal device placed in the abdomen that has tiny tubing that leads directly into the spinal column to disperse pain medication. Since Bob's pain was mostly lower back pain, the doctor felt this would work well.

So, Bob was admitted to the hospital in Canton, Ohio, to have his pain pump inserted, which would be such a wonderful remedy for Bob's pain management. However, Bob did have a rough time of it in the hospital prior to the surgery. He was in a lot of pain and was on an IV pain pump, but the doctor had to constantly increase his dosage because it was not giving him any relief. They were trying to convert his oral pain medication over to the IV morphine dosage. He was on a large dose of morphine and was really out of it, but he was still in tremendous pain. I think the combination of trying to find the right dosage of a different medication and the fact that he was sleeping on those uncomfortable hospital beds or sitting on the hard chairs in his hospital room seemed to exacerbate his pain. Bob often had such trouble with what seemed to be routine medical treatments, and things often did not seem to go easily for him. Bob lived so long with this cancer that I guess for all of the treatments and hospital stays, there were bound to be obstacles along the way. This was to be another one of those times. I don't want to dwell on all of the details, especially the negative ones, so we will fast-forward to the end and say the pain pump that the doctor finally inserted was such a wonderful relief for Bob. In a few days, the doctors found the proper dosage of the medication, and Bob did terrific with that pump. Our entire family concurred that we just wished Bob had done it so much sooner.

It was toward the end of July then, and we were going to be taking our annual Myrtle Beach vacation with Tracy and Rob and their families. Bob and I drove to our home in North Carolina to stay for a week before heading to the beach. Bob did all of the driving and all seemed to be normal. The only thing I noticed when we arrived at our home was that Bob seemed to be doing some strange things when he was helping me. For example, he cleaned the toilet and then carried the toilet bowl brush through the house, and it was dripping all over the floor. This was not at all like Bob, because he was always so careful when he worked. I just remember getting so frustrated and asking him what was he thinking. I thought to myself, *We have brushes that stay in each bathroom, and couldn't he see he was dripping water all through the house?* Then he hosed off the pollen that was all over everything outside, and the water started coming in under the door. He even hosed down my artificial plants that were under the porch, and the containers became full of water. He didn't seem to realize that was a problem, either. I just attributed it to him being on so much pain medicine that maybe his thinking was a little off. I was so busy doing odd jobs in the house and getting ready to repack to leave for the beach that I did not think anymore about it.

On Saturday, Bob, my daughter Tracy, my granddaughter Sarah, and I headed to Myrtle Beach. Bob drove, and everything seemed to go fine until we were only a few blocks from our time-share. The traffic was very heavy, so we were not moving too quickly. It was start-and-stop traffic. We were approaching what was to be our last turn before we would be on Kings Highway, and suddenly Bob had no idea where he was going. My daughter picked up on this immediately. I have trouble with directions, so I was a little slow to see the significance of it all. I didn't realize how close we were to the time-share until we made the turn. Tracy told her dad he needed to turn right, and then she just looked at me with a fear in her eyes. Now I started to realize how confused Bob was. Bob continued to drive those last few miles, but Tracy had to give him specific directions the entire rest of the drive. We were thankful that we arrived safely.

To make a long story short, Bob ended up getting more and more confused by the minute, which was when I thought he probably had another bladder infection. Only the previous month, he had had such complications from a bladder infection that I had to call the paramedics because I thought he was having a stroke. At that time, he wasn't even able to talk or stand up, and they took him to the hospital by ambulance. That was the worst time because Bob wasn't even coherent enough to talk to me, and I was in a panic. I had to call my neighbors because I was falling apart. I could not function without him. The other times Bob had been to the emergency room those past six months were because he had bowel blockages. I had to drive and rush him to the hospital on three other occasions, but it had not been that unnerving to me, because Bob had had his senses about him those times. Even though he was in pain and vomiting because of the blockage, he was still mentally with it. At those times, he gave me courage and strength, and together we had one good mind. He would keep me calm and comfort me, and I would see to it that all his medical needs were attended to, so all was well.

But at the time, Bob wasn't thinking very clearly, so I took him to a local walk-in medical clinic close to our timeshare in Myrtle Beach. After a long wait, the doctor confirmed that Bob did indeed have a bladder infection. I was feeling somewhat relieved, because I had been thinking it was just the bladder infection that was making him so confused. I know that can happen, especially in the elderly, and even though Bob wasn't what I considered elderly, all of those health issues were really starting to take their toll on him. My relief would be short-lived, unfortunately, because his confusion never did totally resolve. He was not even able to fix himself a bowl of cereal. He had become almost totally helpless. He was still able to walk and talk, but he could not do any routine task. He could not brush his teeth or figure out how to dress himself, so he became totally dependent on me.

So, in a few days, when the confusion did not go away, we ended up returning to the clinic. The doctor said Bob still had the infection, so I did not panic. I also had my children with me, so that helped, too. At least I didn't feel alone. Well, toward the end of the week, Bob seemed not to be getting better, so I decided to take him to the hospital emergency room. We saw the doctor, and after she performed a urine culture, she said that his infection was cleared up. She stated that maybe he was getting too much pain medication from the pain pump.

We managed to get through the rest of the week, and Bob seemed to be doing a little better. I was also getting more used to his new state. We were able to go to the movies, and Bob enjoyed *Mamma Mia!*—the last movie we would ever go to together. We even went to the beach and went out to eat. Bob also was able to float around the lazy river at the time-share, but he kept sinking, and I was afraid he would drown. He didn't seem to be able to stay in his inner tube properly. Somehow, amazingly, I was able to enjoy some of the vacation and sleep at night, but I knew something was wrong. I just kept telling myself to be patient and that we would get to the bottom of it when we arrived back in Canton. You see, I was planning on going to the pain clinic and asking the doctor to lower the dosage of Bob's medicine. I agreed with the emergency care doctor who thought maybe Bob was just getting too much medicine. He had not had this pain pump very long, and the doctors were trying to regulate the dosage.

So, on Friday night, I drove Bob, Tracy, and Sarah back to our home in North Carolina. The day Bob drove to Myrtle Beach would be the last day he would ever drive. The plan was that our son Rob would meet up with us on Saturday in Pinehurst, and I would follow him on the drive home to Ohio.

Since Bob wasn't able to do much on his own, I had to go into the bathroom with him to empty his colostomy bag and to catheterize him. I tried going into the men's room and having Rob stand guard, but we were in there too long and I was very uncomfortable having the men wait outside. In fact, one time, one man wouldn't wait. I walked out of the stall with Bob to find a man at the urinal. So, from that moment on, Bob came into the ladies room with me, and we would use the handicapped stall.

We managed to drive home in one day, and I was okay doing this because Rob was right in front of me. We stopped at the Dairy Queen on the way home and got some fancy ice cream parfaits. Bob enjoyed his and was able to feed himself, although he had chocolate all over his face. Rob just laughed, because there was Bob enjoying his chocolate. At one time, I asked Bob how he thought I was doing with my driving and he said, "You're doing great, but what do I know? I'm confused." We all just started to laugh, which is how we always ending up dealing with these problems. We had each other, and no matter what happened, that's what counted.

At the same time that Bob was having all of his confusion in Myrtle Beach, my daughter-in-law Colleen's father was admitted to the hospital. He lives in Myrtle Beach and ended up going to intensive care at a hospital in Georgetown, which is about twenty miles south of where we were vacationing. He was very ill, and he was not expected to live. So Colleen's sister drove down from Chicago, and the two of them, along with my two grandchildren, stayed behind to be with Colleen's dad. Sometimes when it rains, it pours. So that is why Rob was driving home in the car by himself, and Colleen and the children would later drive home with her sister. Colleen's dad ended up recovering, and he is doing much better now. So, you see, you never know.

We managed to get home safely, and I got Bob into the pain clinic first thing Monday morning. While we were in the treatment room with the doctor, he mentioned that I might want to call the oncologist and ask for a brain scan. He did lower Bob's dosage, but he thought the cancer might have gone to Bob's brain. I left and was very angry that he would say that, especially in front of Bob. That was the first time it had crossed my mind that that could be what was happening.

I called my oncologist, explained the situation, and asked if he thought Bob could be getting dementia or Alzheimer's. Here we go again. The power of denial is strong. The oncologist said he did not think so, and he had his nurse make an appointment for us to see him later in the week. Well, by Monday night, Bob was not even able to walk straight. He was literally walking into the walls. I was exhausted and made the decision that we were going to go to bed and deal with it in the morning. I just knew I needed to sleep before I could deal with it. I had never done anything like this before and haven't since, but I just did not think it was an emergency. I did not think he was going to die that night—and he didn't. I just did not have the energy to drive to the emergency room and spend all night there. I really believe that God helped with that decision because it was so unlike me.

Bob and I got up in the morning, took showers, I got us dressed, we ate breakfast, and I gave Bob all his medications. I did everything I needed to do, because I was preparing for another long hospital stay. I called Dr. Schmotzer, Bob's oncologist, and explained that Bob had lost his sense of balance, and the doctor told me to take Bob to the emergency room for a brain scan. I gathered the things I would need for the trip and then packed the suitcase for Bob. I packed Bob's catheters, Depends, pajamas, slippers, socks, ostomy supplies, and toiletries. Off we went to the emergency room.

Our oncologist called ahead and ordered the brain scan for Bob, so when we arrived at the emergency room, the personnel were expecting us. We did not have to wait a long time to get into the treatment area, and the emergency room doctor immediately made the arrangements for Bob to get the brain scan. It wasn't that long of a wait until the doctor came back with the results, either. The cancer had definitely gone to Bob's brain. He said that Bob's brain was very swollen, and the doctor did not think Bob would live more than a week or two without some life-extending intervention by Dr. Schmotzer. It didn't seem that much of a shock to me. I think God had prepared me for that when the pain management doctor told me he thought the cancer was in Bob's brain. In an instant, I believe God transformed me to be able to hear and accept that news. I cannot offer any other explanation for how I would go from fighting for Bob in every instance for thirteen years to then knowing that that would be Bob's final battle. I just remember praying to God that Bob's death would be the easiest God could make it. I wasn't afraid. I trusted God. Where else could I go? I knew he had been there through every complication, every treatment, and every surgery, and I just knew that I needed him then all the more.

Bob was admitted to the oncology floor once again. Dr. Schmotzer came to see Bob and explained that he could help Bob with some radiation and oral steroid treatments. He said the steroids would help reduce the swelling of the brain and give Bob some relief. I remember Bob was just ready to end all of this treatment and really did not want to do anymore. The doctor said, "You have fought too long and too hard, and I do not want to throw in the towel." He thought he could help Bob think better and still have some quality time with us. He said that if the radiation became too hard for Bob, it could be stopped at any time. The doctor really urged Bob to consider that.

Now, when I spoke to Bob, he said he did not want to do that anymore. He did not seem depressed, but he seemed to accept that it was his time to die. However, I agreed with the doctor that Bob had come too far to just give up. I told Bob, "I know this is not going to cure you, but it will give me a little more time with you, so as a last gift to me, will you just try this?"

I promised him that if he wanted to stop, I would not object. By the next day, the steroids had started to work. Bob was starting to think a little clearer, and he agreed to continue the steroid treatment and try the radiation to the brain. I know he did this because he loved me and he knew I needed to have that extra time with him. I told him it would be his last gift to me, and he just smiled and kissed me. The doctor said that the Prednisone would help and that Bob would start to be able to think clearly again and have some of his brain functions return. The doctor was right. It was only a few more days before Bob seemed to be doing much better. He was back to joking around, and he gladly went to the radiation doctor to get ready for his treatments. A blessing was that the pain pump controlled Bob's pain, so he was actually feeling pretty good.

Bob was finally discharged, and he would receive twenty radiation treatments in the coming weeks. We were told that he might be able to live up to a year if this worked, but I knew he would not live that long. It wasn't that I lost hope, but the Holy Spirit revealed that Bob would soon be with the Lord. I just remember feeling thankful and, in a way, fearless.

The doctor who had operated on Bob and inserted his pain pump had come to see Bob as a courtesy when he heard Bob was in the hospital that last time. He asked me to come out into the hall, and he spoke this truth to me. He said, "The cancer is peppered all through Bob's brain on both sides and in both lobes. It is totally inoperable, and don't let any doctor suggests an operation." Then he pulled me close to him and hugged me while I cried. At that moment, he was an angel to me. He would later send me a letter of sympathy. He represented so many wonderful doctors who took care of my husband those thirteen years.

The day we received the news about Bob's cancer was August 5, which was Ryan's second birthday. So even though it was a day that I will remember as the start of Bob's final fight, it is also a day of such blessing for our family. It represents life to me. Life comes with the ups and downs, but in the end God makes it all good. Bob did well with his radiation, and the steroids gave Bob an even bigger appetite. It was good to see Bob able to eat and eat with such gusto, as my mom used to say.

During this time, Bob's brother Rich died, and Bob was able to go to the funeral to see his brother one last time. Bob had not seen him for over a year because Rich had had too many contagious infections. Bob had been receiving the chemo, and we could not risk any more problems. It was a blessing that Bob was able to go to the funeral, and all of our family and many of our friends from Pittsburgh were there and able to see Bob, too. Everyone said how good Bob looked, and he jokingly made the comment to our niece that he was so sick of hearing how good he looked. She said, "Okay, Uncle Bob, you look like crap." The two of them laughed so hard that everyone wanted to know what was so funny, and the joke was passed around the room at the funeral home. I must say Bob did look good for someone who had so many things wrong with him. He had lost all of his hair, but he looked cute bald, and I jokingly say it left me with an attraction to bald men.

That was around the August 25 when we made what would be our last trip together to Pittsburgh for Rich's funeral. Ryan was at the funeral home, and when he saw Bob, of course, he kissed his booboo. I could see the tears in some of our loved ones eyes as they witnessed this tender act of love, and I am sure they were thinking about how Bob would not be around to see Ryan grow up.

Death is not easy, but it is these moments that make us want to fight to live. I know Bob wanted to hang on because he loved us all so much, and he wanted to stay and just have fun with all of us. That is the kind of guy he was. He loved life, and he loved people. His favorite song was "What a Wonderful World," by Louie Armstrong. When I first met Bob, he told me that he just loved that song, and long before his cancer, that song would bring tears to his eyes. They were always tears of joy.

Another good thing that came out of having this extra time was that I was able to go to the attorney and make sure our legal affairs were up to date. My sons and I went to the funeral home and made the arrangements for the upcoming funeral.

A few weeks earlier, I had been having trouble finding some important papers, and I had been getting so upset. I said to Bob, "I can't believe I can't find those papers. I hope I didn't lose them when we were traveling back here from NC."

Bob said, "Don't worry, Bobbie. They show up."

Then I said to him, "I hope I won't lose your ashes when I am traveling back and forth from Ohio to NC, either."

Bob just started to laugh and said, "Bobbie, that is one of the things I love about you. You are so funny, and you always make me laugh."

When we went to the doctor's for our last appointment, Bob told that story to Dr. Schmotzer, and all three of us had a good laugh. Sometimes it is better than crying.

Dr. Schmotzer told us that the radiation really did not work the way he had hoped and that there was nothing else he could do. We knew that, too, because Bob was starting to have trouble doing things again, and at times he would have trouble walking. Then he would seem to be okay again. I think it probably depended on the swelling in his brain. The doctor had been trying to lower the dosage of the steroids during his radiation treatment, but now that the treatments were over and the steroids were lowered to the maintenance dosage, the signs had started to return. Even though the doctor increased the steroids to the maximum dosage again, Bob did not improve.

That day we returned to Dr. Schmotzer's office for what would be our final appointment. We were seen right away. Usually when we went for our appointments, we could wait there for one to possibly three hours, but that day we were seen immediately. The doctor said that it was time for hospice, though he would not see us anymore, he would still be in charge of Bob's treatment. He said to Bob, "I will see you in heaven." That pretty much said it all.

It had been almost thirteen years to the day since Bob had first had his colon surgery when we were told there were no further treatments possible. It was September 27, 2008. Dr. Schmotzer told us to take all of the time we needed and to let the nurse know when we were leaving. We were in that room for what seemed like an eternity, and we just cried and held each other. It was hard to let go of the fight, but sometimes there is nothing left to do or say. After we left the office, Bob said, "Let's go out to lunch." He wanted to enjoy our favorite pizza again. In case you haven't realized it, Bob liked Italian food and, of course, chocolate cake and apple pie.

After lunch we went to our son's house to tell him and his family the news. Megan was there, and she ran to see Poppy. She hugged him and said that she was so happy he was not going to die. You see, she knew he had come close to dying during his last hospital stay. It was ironic that she would say that at exactly that moment in time. It was hard to keep it together, but for her sake, we all did. Why ruin a happy moment for a five-year-old? There would be time for her mom and dad to prepare her again for Bob's death. Bob and I went out to the Olive Garden for dinner. He ate four helpings of the all you can eat spaghetti, five bread sticks, and the salad. For a moment, I thought about how high his blood sugar was probably going to be, but then I told myself to just let go of the worry. We reminisced about all the times our family had gone to different Olive Gardens over the years we were married. I guess you could say this would be our last date. We were still in love, and Bob was happy. We were so blessed to enjoy this time together.

We were able to spend more time together before Bob died on October 11. We would talk about heaven and how we believed we would both be there for eternity. Sometimes we would just stay in bed together, but it seemed as though there just wasn't enough time to even do that as much as we would have liked. You see, in those last days, Bob talked on the phone to people. He had many friends come to see him and, of course, many of the family members came to visit, too. If you could have a perfect dying experience, his was it. He ate up until the day before he died, and he got to see the Steelers play Monday night football and win. He even commented on what a great game Ben played, and he knew Ben's stats for the night. On Tuesday, the dogs went to the groomer's, and Bob noticed they were not at home and wondered where they were. I said that the dogs had gone to the groomer, and when the dogs came home, Bob noticed their haircuts and said that they looked so cute. I want to remember all of the good things that happened that week, and one of them was that I was able to take care of Bob with so much patience. Prior to that, when Bob first had become very confused, I had been so nervous that I yelled at Bob for some of the things he was doing. I had become anxious trying to give him his medicines and take care of him and the house and cook his meals, and it just seemed like too much for me. Then I would cry and say I was so sorry. He would hug me, and he understood. But I was not yelling anymore. I was smiling and just taking care of him. The children were around to help, so I was able to hold it together. One day when I was taking care of Bob, he reached over and touched my face with that look of love in his eyes that he had that first time he made the comment about love at second sight. He never could hide his feelings for me. They showed on his face. I really miss him. He was the love of my life; what else can I say?

Death or Birthing a Baby

I have reached the point in my story where I am going to write about the last days of my husband's life. I would like to take you through what our family experienced during those final days. But before I do, I want you to know that I believe it was a privilege to be a helpmate to my husband at this special time in his life.

When my children were grown, I went back to school. I wanted to work, and I thought then would be a great time in my life to help Bob with the financial aspect of our life together. We had a dream that Bob could retire early if I went back to school and landed a good paying job. That never happened because right when I graduated and was planning on getting that job, Bob learned of his cancer. Everything changed. Thanks, in a strange way, to the cancer, Bob was able to retire. That was the way we viewed it. I decided not to work because I wanted to spend all of my time with Bob, and then we made that decision to move to Florida. When we first learned of Bob's cancer, we never dreamt that he would live another thirteen years. I thought, *I have my education, and when Bob dies, I will go to work.*

I wasn't going to worry about money at that time. I just wanted to be with Bob, and we were financially able to do that. I knew the money we had probably wasn't enough to last my lifetime, but

I really didn't focus on that because I was just enjoying the extra time with Bob that God had given us. I got to use my education in the health field to help Bob, but instead of it helping financially, it helped with all of the things centered around the medical aspect of his cancer.

Finally I was going to have the opportunity to help Bob in a way I never dreamed I would be brave enough to do. I was going to help him through the dying process. I got to serve as Bob's helpmate in a very special way that people whose mates die suddenly don't get to experience. In a strange way, it makes me sad for them. I found it to be a wonderful blessing that I could share this experience with Bob.

I know we all should live like we are dying. I think someone even wrote a lyric to a song about that, but more importantly, Bob and I lived like we would never die. That may seem like a strange statement. Some live that way because they are in denial about the existence of death. I want to be very clear here: I know we are all going to die someday, but I'm not talking about the physical death of the body. Bob and I lived like we would never die because we lived in the hope and promise of eternal life. What a wonderful way to live. That is what gave Bob the belief that all things are possible when we have faith. Without that, I don't know if he could have survived having cancer for all those years. I used to say that some people die from cancer right away because they are scared to death. Now, I don't mean that in the literal sense; it is more a metaphor. I believe that God had revealed a promise to us. He said, "You are going to live forever with me in a place called heaven." He told us the name of his hometown. When death appeared to be near to Bob those thirteen years ago, we both focused on the eternal life that brought us peace. It was in that peaceful state that I think Bob lived and also healed.

It was also in that peaceful state that we accepted his eminent death. We were able to go through the dying process without fear and trembling, and I never thought that would be possible. When Bob first learned of his cancer, I think I was more afraid of his dying then he was. I remember feeling that I could not survive without him. Not only was I afraid of living without him, I was also afraid of facing the death process. I didn't think I could watch Bob die. At some point I, too, surrendered all and asked God to be with me as I helped usher my husband on toward his eternal life.

So, when Bob's final days on this earth arrived, I was somewhat prepared for it. I didn't know the day and hour of his death—only God knew that—but we all knew it was soon. The hospice nurse told us Bob was well into the process of dying and that he needed quiet time. They can tell when the time is getting closer by changes in vital signs and other bodily changes that they see. She explained that Bob had work to do. She told us some of the ideas about the dying process and gave us literature to read that went into more detail about the dying process. According to the literature, the dying go through a time of inward reflection. We don't know all that goes on in the mind and heart of a dying person, but there is a drawing into the self that can be sensed. There were times early on when Bob would transition in and out of this deep sleep. Sometimes he would just wake up. We had someone always quietly sitting by so that if Bob woke up, he wouldn't be alone and feel scared. Sometimes he would talk a little and then go back into this deep sleep. We kept the room quiet and had no TV or radio on because those things might have held Bob to this life longer. No one knows for sure. It was a time to separate, not hold on, and I trusted God about that. It was hard, however, to express that to others. When I think back on it, my daughter was the one the nurse talked to about this. I would stand and listen, but looking back the nurse could sense I wasn't quite ready to let go. I knew it was the end, but my heart just wasn't ready to let go of Bob. I was emotionally trying to distance myself from him so that I wouldn't hold him on this earth any longer than he needed to be here, so I had to physically stay away from him more.

We accepted the fact that he was going to die soon and that the roles we had previously played in doing everything to keep him alive had changed. We had to accept our new roles, which involved keeping him in as little pain as possible and taking care of his daily needs. At first, I needed help attending to some of Bob's daily care, and my children encouraged me to accept that help. The hospice aids would come and help Bob with his shower, which was a tremendous help. Bob was still able to get into the shower with help, and it saved my physical strength to do other things that needed my attention. When Bob no longer had the strength to enter the shower with help and needed the nurse to bathe him, I noticed the frustration in Bob's eyes. I knew it was time for me to bathe Bob myself, and I wanted to do it because those were to be the last loving acts I would be able to do for my husband's physical body. I see that God was there, coaching me, because I had never been with anyone through the dying process, and I wasn't quite sure what to do. I can look back and see myself tenderly taking care of my husband, and it gives me great comfort when I think about those final days. When all my children were gathered around helping Bob, I could only see their love for him. It gave me such comfort, even though I was going through such an emotional time. I know Bob felt it, and it is my hope that if they haven't already accepted that as one of the greatest acts of love that they could ever show their dad, I hope their eyes and hearts will be opened and that they will clearly see it the way I remember it. It will forever be the time I was the proudest of my children. We were such a team, and we all worked in sync. Our goal wasn't to save Bob's life; it was to give him our love and to make him comfortable, and we did exactly that. Even though Bob was dying, my heart was full of joy when we were all there taking care of him. Oh, to see ourselves through God's eyes and hear him say, "Well done." I sensed that this was how God saw us.

Now I don't want you to think I was looking at Bob's death through rose-colored glasses. We had our moments. There was tension and stress as each one of us went through the process of losing this man. Also, two of my children were staying with me while Bob's was dying. We had many visitors, as well, and the hospice nurse was coming in and out during those final days so that she could support us and help us help Bob through his dying. The kids were busy grocery shopping, running for takeout food, washing dishes, and doing laundry, and they had to juggle all of that because they had their own families, too. Even a death doesn't stop the hands of time, and life still goes on. In between all of these tasks and comings and goings, we were making our final plans for the funeral and going through all of the family photos in order to make a DVD to share with our friends and family. That was a very intimate time for our family, and maybe some of it wasn't to be shared with others. I had mixed emotions about that, because I wanted to be generous and give others the time with Bob, but I wanted to have time alone with him, too. So I hope you will see my struggle and understand my resentments. I wanted the visitors even though Bob was ready to be alone, and at one point, he even said that to me. I was trying to take care of everyone, and in the process, I forgot to take care of myself. My children were trying to take care of me, and I know our roles became intertwined, because I was trying to take care of them, too.

I used to look at those final days negatively and think about how I could have done them differently, but now that I look at them clearly, I wouldn't change a thing. I just needed to accept that I did the very best I could, with God's help. I believe that things happen for a reason, and I know as I sort through all of this, God will use this story and its realizations to help others the same way he used them to help me. That's my hearts desire.

I can say one thing for certain: when you go to visit a dying person, put on that special pair of glasses you own, because you'll need them when you look death right in the eye. If you're confused about which of your glasses you should be putting on, it's the pair called love. Now, I probably didn't need to tell you that, because if you're like my friends and family, you already knew that. Otherwise you wouldn't have come to visit someone dying.

I know as you read this you will be able to see just what a blessing my children were to me when my husband was close to death. Writing this opened my eyes, and I was able to see the beautiful present they gave me. I know that without them, I never could have taken care of Bob at home by myself. My kids know me, and they knew my heart's desire was to take care of Bob. It was in that giving of themselves that I was able to see the great love my children have for me. You see, I was blind. I thought they were doing it just for Bob, but now I see it was their gift to me, too. Even though I felt at times that it was such an intimate time for Bob and I, I knew I had to share him with everyone else who loved him too. I don't know if there is ever a right way to do it. Maybe I would have changed some things, and maybe not, but I know if I am ever to find true peace, I cannot hold any resentment for sharing Bob with the ones who loved him. I just need to look at my sharing him as a giving back to everyone who loved Bob. When I see it that way, I know that everything was exactly as it should be.

There is no perfect way to let go. I know my children and I did the best we could, and, in fact, I can honestly say we did a great job. I also see that some things were meant to be for our eyes only. I don't think anyone should be concerned about keeping up appearances, and sometimes it was just hard to cope. I also know that when you look at the family dealing with death, it is no time for judging. It is a time to show grace. It is also a time for the immediate family to make their wishes known and not feel guilty for any decisions that they make for themselves. That is why you need to know when to speak up and not be afraid to say no to visitors or to set limits on the amount of time for a visit. That may have been the one thing I wished I had done, because it was exhausting for us and especially for Bob. The hospice nurse kept saying to make the visits short, but I really didn't understand her reasons at that time. It may also be a time to ask for help without embarrassment if help is needed. I think friends and extended family members often look for cues from the family for what is expected of them, because they may not know what to do, either. I suggest being as honest as possible, and keep the lines of communication open.

The day before Bob went to be with the Lord, he ended up in the hospital again, which was a struggle for me. Bob experienced some seizures. We used all the medicine we had to control the seizures, and there was none available at any nearby pharmacies. So, the hospice nurse suggested taking Bob to the Palliative Care Unit at Aultman Hospital. She said he might not make it to the hospital and could possibly die in the ambulance. For some reason, that made me very upset. I had promised Bob that I would take care of him at home. At the time, I did not know that Bob wanted to be home and have me take care of him, but that he did not want to actually die at home. He told our daughter-in-law Colleen he didn't want me to remember our home as the place where he died. I did not know any of this at the time, but later Colleen would tell me all of this information because she and Bob had talked about it. When we were riding in the ambulance, the paramedic told me that Bob's vital signs were not good, and he didn't know if Bob would make it to the hospital. Once we left our street and were going down the main road, the paramedic took his vitals again. He said to me, "I don't believe this. He is rallying, and I don't think he is going to die on the way." I felt as if Bob knew the ambulance was the last place I wanted him to die. We made it to the hospital, and the kids were all there. This was late Friday night. My daughter and I stayed the night and slept in the large room they gave him.

Though I didn't want Bob to die at the hospital, I now see why it was important. It was not only Bob's wish, but also it would free us to take care of the most important task of all. At the hospital, the nurses could step in to take care of Bob's physical body. We had other work to do. We were at the hospital because we were birthing a baby. I hear you say *what?* Yes, that is how Colleen described it, and she was right on target. You see, dying can be painful, and not all deaths are the same. Some are quick, and some take days. You've all heard the cases of the long labor. Well, Bob had work to do, and there was still some unfinished business. On the advice of the nurse, we called those loved ones that either hadn't had a chance to say their final goodbyes or maybe were holding on to Bob. The nurse said that he was waiting for something. I made the calls and put the phone to Bob's ear so that the people God brought to our minds and hearts could talk to Bob. Bob's sister, Patty, and his sister-in-law, Judy, were able to speak to Bob, too, along with a pretty lengthy list of our family members. I don't recall everyone who talked to Bob, but that isn't important now. You will remember Bob's brother Rich had died only six weeks before Bob. It was during this time that Patty told Bob not to go and die on her, too. I know Patty was going through such a tough time, and Bob was worried about how his death would affect her. Bob and I talked about what she had said to him. So, when the nurse asked if someone might be holding onto Bob during this birthing process, naturally Patty came to my mind. I know some of you are wondering, *What in the world is she talking about?* We were ushering Bob or coaching him to take that first step into his eternal life. I stand corrected; it was his second step. He took the first step when he accepted Jesus Christ as his Savior. Colleen had tried to comfort me because she saw all the pain I was in while watching Bob suffer, which is why she compared Bob's death to giving birth. She said that dying is hard work, but in the end it will be great. I know she really had no idea how profound and wise and true her statement was, because she does not even remember saying it to me. It makes me wonder if once again the Holy Spirit was using her to deliver this message. We were birthing a baby boy named Robert Renk, who was going to his new home to be with his heavenly Father and with all of his earthly family members who were waiting there for him. When I told Bob he needed to go, I had those people in mind. Then I know I also said, "Go and be with Jesus." Our children were there for the birth, and they were coaching him to go to heaven, too. You see, this was a journey Bob need to take alone. All I said to him was that he needed to go but that I was there with him just like I promised I would be. I said, "Bob, you are not going to recover this time, and it is your time to leave us. I will be with you until you take your final breath, and in a blink of an eye, you'll be with Jesus."

A few minutes later, I went to the foot of Bob's bed, turned my back on Bob, and out loud asked God to "take Bob right *now*." I was being very demanding. Now I see that God was being so kind to me, too, by waiting for me to let go. So, when the nurse asked if someone might be holding onto Bob, I now see it was I. You see, even though I had told Bob to go be with Jesus, there was one person I had forgotten to talk to about this, and it was God himself. He was waiting for me to ask him. In all the thirteen years of Bob's illness, I never had asked that before. So I went and sat next to Bob toward the head of the bed, whispered to him, and then I just waited in silence. And praise God that he gave me my heart's desire. All of our immediate family was there. Now I know for sure Bob is with his heavenly family and with all the saints and angels, and they are singing and praising God. As Jesus said, "Today you will be with me in paradise." Now you see why I said that the last hospital stay was the greatest. It had the best outcome of all. It was a total healing. Amen.

When Two Become One Again

In November 2008, I saw my life change right before my eyes. I knew when Bob died my life would never be the same, but I had no idea how my life was going to look. I kept making myself do things like write the bills, clean house, call people and make plans to go out with friends, but it didn't feel natural. The awkwardness I felt wasn't just about missing Bob; it was also about being myself. I thought I had forgotten who I was because Bob and I were one. I started to think maybe I had never really found myself, but I see that this was not true. I know who I am. I am a child of God. Then I came to the conclusion that my real struggle was what was I going to do with my life.

I struggled each day without Bob and wondered, *What I am going to do today?* When Bob was alive, I knew exactly what I was to do. I was to be there with him and take care of him and pray for him, and I willingly and joyfully did that without question. I had a sense that Bob, God, and I were working together in the battle against cancer, and I had so much hope. When Bob died, I didn't feel that we lost the battle; I just believed God had called Bob home and that he was healed and happy in heaven. I rejoiced in that, and I still do. But I have struggled with what I am to do now and what the purpose was of Bob living so many years with cancer and what that had to do with my life now. I thought God had kept Bob alive for me, and that made me feel special, but it didn't make sense. Why Bob? And what glory did that give to God? I knew God had answered our prayers, but why us? I knew that if I did not continue to share this story and my walk with Jesus, then I would be turning my back on what I believed God had put on my heart to do. I wasn't sure what all this meant or how I would even share this story. When Bob was living, we shared our story with the doctors and all the medical personnel we happened to see when Bob was being treated, but that would no longer be the case. I actually wrote a letter and intended on sending it to the doctors to let them know Bob had died. In that letter, I implied that God had used them to do his will by keeping Bob alive and giving us hope, but I never sent the letter. It didn't seem like the right thing to do. Now, after writing this book, I understand it was not meant to be. I do not think that it would have led me to know that I was to write this book.

All I can say is that the first few months after Bob died, I was lost. I just went through the motions of life and kept busy doing everything that I needed to take care of, from giving his clothes away to the needy to moving my things around in my now very spacious closet. I hated to see the empty space, so I was glad I had extra clothes in a closet in the other room that I could add to my bedroom closet to make it look full again. It brought back memories of the times Bob would tease me about all the clothes I owned and that I was stealing his side of the closet because I was running out of room on my side. It made me sad to see only my clothes hanging there, however, and sometimes just going into the closet would bring tears to my eyes.

There were times I would be driving in my car when a song would come on the radio and I would have to pull off the road because I was crying so hard I could hardly see the road ahead of me. That is why I started to only listen to my Christian CDs at that time. It helped keep my focus on Jesus and my eternal life, and it made it easier to be without Bob.

Experiencing the death of my husband has not been what I expected. In some ways it is easier than I thought it would be and far less scary than I imagined, but in other ways it has been a very lonely journey. I chose to travel it with God alone and not to share my innermost thoughts and feelings with others until now. God created us to be in relationship with others. I am realizing that by choosing to travel this path alone, I may be robbing someone else of having the benefit of my experience, so I have decided to write a little about what is was like for me to grieve the loss of my husband.

A woman I know, who lost her husband only days before Bob died, took her own life just recently, and that is truly when God put it on my heart to share. The knowledge that there are other hurting people that I might reach helped me share with you that I have had times of despair and such sadness and loneliness that I wished God would call me home. I have wanted to be with God and Bob, but I also know that it is God's decision to make. When I had those moments, I called out to God, and in his mercy, he brought me comfort and the moments passed. I have had a lifetime of those moments, because I have had many hardships. I have also been blessed to be in the presence of God enough to know he is real and that I only need to wait, to hold on, and he will answer my prayer as I call out to him to take away my emotional pain. The thought that others might not know or believe this makes me want to share this and give hope to those who are suffering. I believe as I write this that God will find a way to reach them with these words.

It has long been known that artists, poets, and writers use their gifts to share their emotions and connect with others. I don't think my experience is that different from other people's experiences, but maybe I will reach an audience that would not otherwise hear. Mourning the loss of a mate, whether it is through death or divorce, is so traumatic. If you believe married couples are one as the Bible says, then when this loss takes place, your entire identity changes. It is totally appropriate to feel sad or lonely or even lost. That gives me comfort when I feel as if I will literally lose my mind. Even though I have accepted Bob's death, what I have trouble accepting is my life as a single person. It is not the life I wanted or chose. Does that mean I want to marry again? I don't think that is the question. It is not that simple. I honestly do not know what I want, and therein lies the problem. I do not know what to ask God for when I pray, because I do not know what it is I want or need. I think what I really want is to know my purpose now more than ever. I think that is the real question and desire. I want to live a life that is pleasing to God, but it is more than that, too. I want to connect with people, but I don't know how to begin to do that, either. I was so connected to my husband that I didn't even realize it. We were one. We shared everything and bared our souls to each other at times. We were just there for each other. Now I have to learn to live with a part of me missing: the part that reflected God's love for me, took pleasure in taking care of me and doing things for me, and enjoyed my company. Now I have to do all that for myself.

I jokingly said after Bob died that I didn't know how much work I was until I had to learn to take care of myself and do all the things Bob did for me. Bob was such a terrific husband. He not only wrote all the bills, but he also kept the files for our important papers, helped in the kitchen, did laundry, and sometimes even ironed my clothes. He walked and fed the dogs right on time, and the dogs appreciated it. He even did most of the grocery shopping. But what he did that I miss the most was he made me laugh and listened to me talk. Those are things I know God is doing for me now.

So, I am kept pretty busy now, and I am learning I need to love to take care of myself. I do love myself. That is not the problem. However, I have to enjoy doing things for me in the same way I did when I did things for Bob. I think in our society we get confused because we are taught that we are selfish if we take care of our own needs. That is what is expected of us when we are single. As hard as it is to make that transition when we marry and have to include or put our mate first, we have to learn the opposite when we become divorced or widowed.

Even though I joked about it being hard work taking care of myself, it really was so difficult to make my decisions—particularly my financial decisions—alone. Bob and I used to discuss everything, especially when it came to making financial decisions. Bob died the year the financial market was beginning to tumble. I had to make so many decisions and tried to learn to budget the money I was earning with my investments. I also struggled with getting a new financial advisor. I knew I could not relate to the one we had, and for reasons other than financial, I wanted someone else who I could feel had my best interest in mind. I prayed so much about this and had to forgive the manager I had before for not looking out for me when Bob was dying. I had some resentment to work through because of his management style or, shall I say, lack of it. At one point, because of all the mistakes that manager was making while handling Bob's affairs, I actually felt God was saying, "Stop trying to stay in this relationship." It was almost funny because I went overboard trying not to be unfair, and God showed me I needed to trust myself and know when it was time to make a change. At the same time that I was struggling about changing managers, I also had to learn to rely on God more because I was mistakenly finding my security in my money or, shall I say, my *insecurity* in watching my money shrink with the declining market. It was a hard time for me because I felt so scared. I remember confessing to God that I was sorry for not trusting in him. I also felt that I was not capable of managing the money or making good decisions about it. I finally came to terms with it when I realized my trust was in God, not my bottom line on my financial statements.

I believe God helped me choose wisely when I moved my money to a different manager. I found someone who had and still has my best interests in mind. He looks out for me, pays close attention, and helps to educate me, and we make the decisions together. He even calls me every month to tell me how much he deposited in my account. Every time he calls, it reminds me that God has found someone to help me with some of the things Bob used to do. I made a decision to live on my interest income only instead of depositing a set amount of money that my portfolio might not be able to support. It might be harder for the manager, but that is the way Bob and I had been doing it. We also gifted a lot of money when we first won our lawsuit, and I do not regret that decision for a moment. However, I do also now understand that I cannot give away the store. God has taught me to be a good steward of the money I have received.

Like others, I went through a crisis when the market went down. I figured out my expenses, made some major changes, and to my amazement, in 2009 I was able to live just fine without touching my principal. Most amazingly, I was able to give a double portion to God. I discovered that fact when I did my preparation for my income tax and compared my income and my giving. I am happy with the changes, and I like that I have input. I don't handpick each investment, as that's my financial manager's job, but I do understand and agree with the goals and tools we use to meet them. I realize that I know more than I thought about how to manage my money, and together my financial advisor and I have done things that have felt comfortable for me. It has been good to be involved and learn in the process and also to have some control over the decision making. I like to live in a trust relationship with God, and I believe he helped me pick someone who was trustworthy, hard working, and wanting to involve me in each decision.

I know God has blessed me beyond all I could possibly have imagined, and I just want to continue to bless others. That is a joy for me. Bob and I did not always tithe, but over the years we started to proportionately give. We continued to increase our gift until one day we were at the point where we were truly tithing. When we won our lawsuit, one of the first things we did was to buy a well in Africa, and that was something I was so excited to do. I want to continue to be a joyful giver. That is the most important thing to me. It is not really about how much I give. I don't really plan on an amount above my tithe, but it is just a heartfelt feeling. I trust God to put where and what I should give on my heart. Now that I am alone, I know God will continue to lead me all the more with my financial decisions, and I am feeling so much more secure this year. I am glad I have come back to that place. Becoming a widow was a scary time because everything changed and I had to learn to be on my own. No matter what, my bottom line is that I must trust this promise: "'Bring the whole tithe into the storehouse, that there may be food in my house. Test me in this,' says the Lord Almighty, 'and see if I will not throw open the floodgates of heaven and pour out so much blessing that you will not have room enough for it'" (Malachi 3:10).

The practical things in my life started to come together. I was able to take care of my finances and the legal matters I still needed to attend to that first year after Bob died. God has shown me that he is there for me, but sometimes it is a balancing act. I have heard myself say negative things, such as "I hate this" or "I am so depressed," but then I become filled with guilt. I went from mourning to self-pity, and I do not like either of those places. I am thankful that I have had the self-awareness to notice, and I ask God to change that negativity in me. Just as God has been there for me before, I have assurance that he is walking with me as I go on through this season in my life. I don't want to take forty years to wander through the wilderness because I am foolish and blind to God. I have faith that God has good things for me to do for the rest of the life he has given me, and I need to have great hope and expectations that once again he will give me so much more than I ask for or deserve because he is a loving Father. I just need to put my trust in him and listen to that still small voice that guides me and gives me strength, comfort, and all that I need. Maybe this is my season to wait upon the Lord, but I know the harvest is coming and that there is work to do. Somehow I don't think sitting around filled with self-pity and doubt is anywhere on God's list of things he has in store for me. He allows me to go through the refining fire because he is there for me, and he has confidence that I will become all he intended because I am his child.

It has also been a great year of healing for me because God has helped me to look back, which has helped me to confess some sins I had been holding onto without realizing it. I also realized I had some resentments and that I needed to forgive others, too. It was through this process of writing that I gained such revelations. I felt conflicted about writing about some of things I had forgiven, because I believed that when we forgive others, we forget. I think that was a false belief. I now think it is okay to remember, especially if it reveals how God helped me to forgive and helps others to believe that, in time, they will be able to forgive, too, with God's help, if they are willing to take that first step. I don't want to hold onto bitterness about those old hurts and injuries, and I pray that if there are more ahead, God will gently remind me of the past so that I can confess, forgive, and move on. I just need to pray and ask God to help me let go. Forgiveness is a process, and I believe God works with us to help us achieve it. What I know for sure is that God knows my heart, and with his help, I am willing and capable of forgiveness. That is my heart's desire. Beyond that I rely on him.

Most of all, I rely on God's promises. He knows the number of hairs on my head, and when one falls out, it reminds me that he is with me. Look how he cares for the sparrows and the lilies of the field. How much more will my father care for me? Jesus said, "Which of you, if his son asks for bread, will give him a stone? Or if he asks for a fish, will give him a snake? If you, then, though you are evil, know how to give good gifts to your children, how much more will your Father in heaven give good gifts to those who ask him!" (Matthew 7:9–11).

I know he hears me and answers my prayers. I just keep the conversation between us going. I turn my life over to him, sometimes minute by minute, and he works all things out for good. Since I have no husband, I find myself talking to God so much more than ever before. That is another good thing that has come from all of this. I learned to rely on God when Bob was battling his cancer, and I saw God answer my prayers. It was such a blessing to me, and it helped prepare me for my life as it is now.

I learned lessons along the way that prepared me for my next drama, crisis, or trial. I did this little by little as I looked back at each circumstance in my life and saw that God was there. I might not have seen him at first, or maybe I only saw a glimpse of him, but I thought there was at least a possibility that God helped me get through whatever the circumstance was. And when I started to believe it was true and looked back again, I saw him more clearly and felt a little more prepared for the next battle. I started to face life a little braver because I trusted God a little more. I would think, *Yeah, maybe he did show up last time. I just couldn't see him in the midst of it.* Then I learned to see him in the midst of my problems, which is when I really live and shine. Right there in the midst of it, I see him and trust him because I've been down that road before and know that it gets a little easier. And then when I face the next battle, it is almost exciting—like the drama in the trial. It may be emotional and painful, but it is not that scary because I know the outcome. Whatever comes my way is not going to rob me of God's promises. I will be prepared, and God will be with me.

Now, that does not mean I won't suffer. I know there is still suffering ahead in this life. I know I will have more sorrow, and I will either die soon or grow old and die. Please don't think I am being morbid here. It is reality. I know there is going to be more joy in my life, but the most important thing is that I know I've won. I've conquered. I am an overcomer. Now I can live life with excitement and hope, and I can look to the future without fear. I can almost see that reward, the one I know I don't deserve. I hear off in the distance a tiny little voice as I bend my ear toward it. Now that's my dream. I want to hear God say to me, "Well done, my faithful servant." I want to live in hope and inspire you to live there, too. Ask God for your purpose, and love God with all your heart and your neighbor as yourself. I think that whisper will become a little stronger, and the voice will start to get a little clearer. And for a moment, we both will have a little heaven right here on earth.

The Here and Now

As I wrote this sometimes it felt risky to put my thoughts out here for everyone to read, and I wondered what others might think about me. When I admitted that this is not all about me, but what I believe God has called me to do my fear left. I want this story to do something for you, too. I pray it opens your heart, give you hope, gives you encouragement, or whatever it is you need at this time in your life. I want my story to be healing to you, just as my life with Bob was healing for us. It was healing from the very beginning, when we first met and poured out our broken hearts to each other and helped create a beautiful love story. I believe God orchestrated this love story and that I am a big part of it. It gives me such joy to think I am able to give part of myself away to you so you can know me, know the pain I suffered, feel it, and believe it. Only then will you believe in the miracle behind my life, the miracle that God is real and personal and hears our prayers and meets our needs. Sometimes he doesn't meet our needs in the way we think he should, and it may take a lifetime to see that he knew best. I really hope you can believe it now, even if you haven't experienced it yet in your life. Then I will have given you my gift, hope. When I said, "hope," I don't mean the kind that hopes to become rich or have everything great in life. I mean hope that God hears us, answers prayers, has a plan for each of our lives, and that we have an eternal future with him.

As I reflect back over my life so far, what has given it the most meaning up to this point has been all the time I spent with my husband, encouraging him through his battle with cancer and sharing our faith and trust in God with others. Without the cancer, maybe we would have taken God for granted. In some ways, cancer was a special gift to us. Now, you may think that is such a strange thing to say, but God turned something so awful into so many good things that all I can say is what was meant for evil or harm, God used for good. I saw Bob's living thirteen years as a miracle, but it was no miracle for God. He can do all things. I see that in his creation. I like to call anything I can't do or that I think is humanly impossible a miracle, which is okay as long as I remember that the miracle giver is God. Our lives were dramatically changed over the years. We learned to put our trust in God for Bob's health. We also went from not having much money to becoming what I consider wealthy. I think God used that trial in some ways to get your attention and surely mine. It also was an answered prayer of my husband's. I know it is all a matter of perspective, but having cancer has changed our lives in ways we had not anticipated. I am so thankful that with God's help, I am able to view things this way and truly appreciate all his blessings. I am learning to look at difficult circumstances as opportunities for God to show up. I just need to patiently wait on him to answer my prayers. I need to not put him in a box and try to tell him what it is he needs to do for me, although I will admit that sometimes I do this. I just need to trust he has my best interests in mind because he loves me.

Bob loved life, and he lived it to the fullest. In some ways, cancer made us appreciate everything more. I am not going to lie to you. We did have our moments. We would cry and be down for a few hours, and I would say to Bob, "Okay, that's enough of that. Let's go out." He would agree that we weren't going to sit and cry too much, because that would be letting the cancer win. We didn't let ourselves dwell on what was ahead of us. We lived each day in the moment, which was such a special gift in itself. Without God's help, I don't think I would have been capable of doing it.

Once I started to actually write this story, I saw it as so many more things than just a love story or an inspiration for those with cancer. I saw my life unfold with each page I typed, and I saw God's hand in all of these writings, just as I saw him in all of my life. The fact that my husband lived a remarkably long time with a prognosis of only a few months is probably not unique. My feeling strongly that I need to share this with you may be the unique part. Sometimes I struggle, because I don't trust God enough to believe he has this purpose for me. That is really the bottom line. I easily become discouraged. When complete strangers who God has placed in my path encourage me, I doubt. He never gives up on me. I keep crying out to him for answers, and he makes his answers clear, but then I deny over and over again. I think of Peter and that even though Peter denied, Jesus said he would build his church on the rock that was Peter because the Holy Spirit had given Peter a revelation that Jesus was the Christ. It is very scary for me to believe and confess that God wants me to write this story and that I could possibly have something to say that he wants others to know. I am going to trust this to be a fact. I just want this story to give glory to God, and I am trying to be obedient to God by writing even when I feel discouraged that this is not really what God wants from me. When I truly believe he has called me to write this, I feel confident and excited. He helped me believe he wanted this written for his purpose by enabling me to write this story with such ease. Writing this book entirely by memory was another opportunity for me to experience God, because on my own accord, I would not have had the ability to accomplish such a task. As the words effortlessly appeared on the page, my belief that God is personally involved in my life increased, as did my belief that writing this was part of his purpose for me. I wonder if all writers are as excited and amazed when they write a story. I've heard some songwriters speak of this when talking about the song they just sat down and composed. I think when it's a gift from God, maybe the receiver of the gift is surprised, too. I also know that every gift doesn't reach its full potential until it is opened and used or maybe even given away for someone else to use. Maybe you are reading this story because someone gave it to you as a gift. I am planning on using 90 percent of the money from this book to grow God's kingdom by helping others. I joked with God and said, "I'll keep 10 percent." I know putting any royalties to work to bless others will be another way my husband's life will serve a greater purpose.

As I said before, when I first started to write this story, I was just doing it without really knowing why except that it made for an exciting love story and that it would be healing for me. I actually started to write it about eight months after Bob died, because I met someone and had the strangest experience. He had picked up a hair of mine that had fallen on my shoulder and held it up for both of us to see. As we looked at the hair, our eyes met, and it was as if I already knew him or that he would be in my future. It is hard to put this into words and make sense of it. I'll just say when I reflected back on that moment, it brought me out of the stupor I was in. I had been grieving for my husband, and it brought me back to life. I was feeling excited and hopeful about love and life. I was able to remember my life with Bob, and it wasn't painful to think about those memories because I believed it was possible to have a wonderful love like that again. I guess you could say that in an instant I had hope back in my life.

After I looked into this stranger's eyes and saw that certain look on his face and his smile, I started to remember the first feelings of love my husband and I shared. It had been too painful to remember this while grieving. Then a flood of memories of my life with my husband came back to me, and it was wonderful. Maybe some people never experience a love like the one Bob and I shared, but I started to believe I could have my memories and another love again, too. Once these memories resurfaced, I knew those feelings were stronger than any negative ones I was having over the loss of my husband. Maybe that is what is meant by the saying, "Love never dies." While I was grieving for my husband, the feelings of our love must not have been that deeply buried if a stranger could so easily bring them to the surface. I think once again God had intervened, because I believe with all my heart that God wanted me to write this story. I also believe he wants it to be a love story to each and every one of you who reads it. He wants all of us to know he is the initiator of love and that his love for us is far greater than any love we could have for each other, because his love is perfect. It is selfless and freely given, and I feel honored to be able to share the times I was aware of God's love for me.

Although that person was the catalyst to begin writing this book, he was more than that to me. He was the person I imagined was reading this book, and I shared that idea with him. He told me he was looking forward to reading it, which makes me feel happy. Besides being instrumental in my writing this book, the experience with him made me realize I am single. Even though that could be a sad realization, the fact that there was a mutual attraction gave me hope that maybe I could love someone else. This attraction was shocking and so unexpected. This person mistook me for almost ten years younger, which was his age, which was quite remarkable considering what I have been through these last thirteen years. I will admit that I spent a great deal of time daydreaming about him because I thought it might have been love at first sight. Now I have come to the conclusion that even though this was all a fantasy, similar to how I felt about the puppies I visited at the pet store, God used the experience to help me through this last year. I tried to lie to God and myself about my desires for wanting to know this person and possibly having him in my life. I also tried to pretend those feelings away. Now I keep praying that God would take these desires away because I honestly believe God is the one that put them in my heart. I see this man as an angel who God used to awaken me and bring me from a place of despair to a place of hope. For that reason, my angel will always hold a special place in my heart. I pray that God will watch over him and keep him from all harm.

Sunday, May 2, 2010, the day before I left North Carolina to come to Ohio, I heard myself say to one of my friends, "I believe God wants me to write this story, so I know he will find a way to get this published. I'm not going to worry. All I need to do is finish writing the story." I had it almost completed by then, but there were a few more things I wanted to add and rearrange. I had jokingly said to another friend that maybe I would speak at the Women of Faith Conference. I thought I might talk about some of the things I had written in the book. After I made that remark, I almost started to question my sanity. I was feeling very joyous, but to make that remark caught me off guard. My friend and I were laughing, and then she actually had tears in her eyes. Now, I said all of this even though I didn't know the first thing about writing a book, let alone publishing one or promoting one for that matter. At first, I thought self-publishing meant taking my book to a local office store or printer and having it printed up. I didn't realize that was self-printing, not self-publishing. I am almost embarrassed to admit this except to show just how far God has brought me.

After I arrived in Ohio, I was riding in the car one day and decided to reset the radio stations. As I continued to search for my favorites, a man's voice came over the radio and said, "If you feel God inspired you to write a book, go to [a certain website that publishes Christian books] and we will send you a booklet to help you get started."

I can't begin to tell you how strongly I felt God was directly answering my prayers. I had finished writing the book and was just at the stage where I was editing it myself to look for errors in grammar and spelling. I was in total shock; the timing was impeccable. I was also shocked because I had even given God a deadline of July 6, Bob's birthday, for when I wanted to send this book to the publisher. So, when I heard that advertisement on the radio, it certainly got my attention. It was as if God said, "I hear you, and I will find you a publisher."

Part of me was shocked, because when I talk to God and ask him for things, I do it in a joking way. When he answers me so boldly, I am in amazement. I don't doubt for an instant that the answer is from God, but before he answers I doubt myself, especially when a bold statement comes out in my conversation with him. Sometimes I feel such an intimate relationship with him that I joke with him. I feel he answers me back in a joking style sometimes, too, and it makes him all the more real to me. When I hear from him, I just start laughing sometimes. I don't laugh out of disrespect, but because I just feel so close to him and know I can be myself. We have a sense of humor together, but he knows I love him. We just relate this way. Sometimes I will even say, "You've got to be kidding me," because of the ways he finds to speak back to me. I am learning to recognize this is the Holy Spirit in me speaking out. I guess that is the most shocking part, but I am starting to see a pattern here. One common thread is the boldness on both my part and God's. Once again, God confirmed that he hears me and answers me. He did this so quickly that I didn't have a doubt that he wants this book finished and published. It motivated me to finish working on the book because I had some direction about how to get it published. I was honestly clueless up to that point. I knew I was willing to invest my money into this book, but I had no idea about where to go or how it would work.

I have become more confident about telling people I am writing a book, and I have even been sharing some of the things I've written. I've been going to the "Single Focus" small group at RiverTree Christian Church in Massillon, Ohio, and when I was sharing my beliefs about the Holy Spirit and about the way I like to praise and worship God, someone there suggested I might like the nearby Frontline Ministries International, so I have been going there, too. I met a woman at Frontline and told her about my book. She was going to get the name of a publisher from a friend of hers and e-mail it to me. I told her about setting the deadline to send my book in to a publisher.

I had been praying that God would confirm the publishing company I should use. At the time, I really only had that one in mind that I'd heard about on the radio. I was seeking confirmation because I wanted God to help me with my decision. I wanted to wait on the Lord and be confident that I was not doing this on my own.

About a week later, when I still hadn't received the e-mail, I decided to do a little research on the Internet. Right before I left North Carolina—in fact, the same day I proclaimed God would find me a publisher—I had looked through some of the books featured in our church's lobby. I had written down a name of a publishing house,

"Thomas Nelson: W Publishing Group" and noted their address. I left the computer, went to my purse, and took out the card I'd noted the information on, as I couldn't remember the name. At the time I had written this little note to myself, I remember thinking that I might mail my printed book, the one I mistakenly called the "self-published book," to Thomas Nelson, hoping someone would read it and decide to publish it. So, I went online to see if the publisher had a website, which is how I found WestBow, the self-publishing division of Thomas Nelson. Now, there is a bigger point to all of this. When I finally spoke to someone from WestBow, after talking about my story to him and learning from him about Thomas Nelson, he mentioned that his company was one of only two publishers that sell books at the Women of Faith conference. Then he said he thought my story would definitely appeal to women, and that this would be a good marketplace for my book. I said, "Bingo." I told him my story about jokingly saying I would be speaking at The Women of Faith conference and said, "I guess I will be speaking there through my book. This is the confirmation I'd been waiting for to make the final decision between these two companies that were put in my path."

I talked to God and said, since he is my co-author, "Which publisher do you want to use?" Now, I do this in a fun and playful way, but I also do take it seriously when I speak boldly and get an answer. When I talk to him like this it gets my attention and it helps build my faith that God hears me when I speak to him. So, I will leave it up to you to decide if you believe that you can sometimes ask boldly and expect God to answer those requests. Just remember, I do not believe in coincidences as random happenings. To me, they are God sightings.

I see how God is growing my faith as I go through this process. I am starting to believe he has a lot more in store for me to do. I am beginning to believe I will be doing some speaking engagements, but just as I've done before, I'll leave that up to him. One thing I am certain of now is if that is what he wants me to do, he will open the doors and provide opportunities for me to speak. He will find some fun way to communicate that to me, too. I told you before that we have a special relationship and that humor is how we relate to one another. I think he chooses this way because he wants me to have so much joy in my life that I will shine as I did when I knew Bob's medical history before our trial. This is how I see God working in me. Now, that may not be how you find him working, but that's okay. We are not all the same.

At that moment when I heard the radio commercial, I felt as if God had heard me asking him to help get my book published and as if he were answering me, "Yes, I will." So, just as he sent people to encourage me to continue writing, I believe he has been leading me literally every step of the way. From the moment I was inspired by the stranger to write this love story to the moment I chose the publisher, I believe God has been with me, encouraging me and inspiring me and leading me because we have work to do.

I don't know why I am always so surprised when I see God acting in my life, but it is a good surprise. It's like when my husband bought me flowers or brought me a card. One of my surprises to my hubby was when I wrote him a poem. Even though we were there for each other every day, it was the unusual things that surprised us. When it was time for the card, poem, or gift, we both realized it was the everyday kinds of things that really showed our love for each other. We would stop and realize how easy it was to take each other for granted. But maybe it was more than that. We just knew we could count on each other, and we expected to be surprised. That wasn't a bad thing; it was just love. I think it is the same with God. I take for granted all the things he does for me day by day. When he shows up with the flowers, so to speak, by preparing my way or answering a prayer, I am surprised, but then I see how he is there for me all the time. It is just love.

I am truly excited now, and I hope that my excitement is coming through to you and inspiring you to trust God no matter how bad or good a situation may be in your life right now. And please don't think that something like this could never happen to you. Remember, I had my share of problems like we all do, and I will just list the few I shared with you as a reminder. I was in an abusive marriage, I was a mental and emotional mess, I was divorced with no job and not much money to my name, I was a single mom, my second husband ended up with fourth stage cancer, and now I am a widow. In all of these circumstances, I just needed to be patient and recall God's promise in Jeremiah 29:11. "'For I know the plans I have for you,' declares the Lord, 'plans to prosper you and not to harm you, plans to give you hope and a future.'" He has fulfilled those plans.

When I was younger, I had glimpses here and there of the person I thought I was to become. Ever since I was a teenager, a part of me felt there was something I was supposed to do, but I didn't know what that something was. I think because my father was so sick and because he died two weeks before I turned eighteen, my world was rocked and maybe I lost sight of my intended journey. I've been thinking about my dad so much lately. I mourned him for years, which was a big part of my sadness when I was in my twenties. I remember the night before my father died and how separated I felt from God at the time. I had been living apart from God because of the wrong choices I was knowingly making. I clearly remember not being able to ask for healing for my father because I didn't think I deserved to even go before God to ask. I have always known that God forgives, but I also knew that I truly did not want to turn from my ways. I wanted to do what I wanted to do. I realize now how those bad choices were just one half of the equation. I did not believe God could forgive me because I could not forgive myself.

As I reflect back on my life, I see how much I have changed and how much God loves me. It was accepting his love that changed me. I accepted that love when I accepted that Jesus died for me and that I was and still am forgiven. No strings attached. It is because of that love and forgiveness that I willingly obey God's command to love others. So, if I am to love others, I naturally need to forgive them. That goes hand in hand. I saw that in both of my marriages. I learned it at the end of my first marriage, and fortunately, in my second marriage, I knew it at the beginning. I know I had to go to the pits of hell in my life before I could finally feel God's love for me. I just needed to learn some things the hard way.

Now I feel I am getting a "do over." I am writing more poetry, which was something I used to love to do. And a big change took place at the gym yesterday. I was riding my exercise bike and feeling frustrated because the music was hardly audible, and I was just not into that bike ride. Music is an important part of my self-expression, and I was upset that it was missing. As a rode, I watched a woman doing a boxing workout. The memories came flooding back of when my dad taught me to box. He taught me the jabs and a little of the footwork. My dad also had me trying softball and fishing. I was the son he didn't have, hence the name Roberta, daughter of Robert. Unfortunately, being athletic and coordinated are not in my DNA. Now, I am not saying I actually boxed. It was more like no-contact box dancing similar to what some gyms now offer at their workout classes. My dad and I also used to put on *West Side Story* and dance around the living room, and we had such fun. We'd make up steps, kick our legs up in the air, and pretend we were dancing as they did in the movie.

As I rode my bike and watched this woman hitting the punching bag, I so much wanted to do that pretend boxing that my dad and I used to do. My daughter was on the treadmill, and I took a walk over to her and told her what I was thinking. She said, "Mom, that's the class that's going on right now. Go back and watch them." So I did, and after a minute or so, I joined in. With my bad knee, I really wasn't able to do all the steps, but I was able to do some of them. It brought back some fond memories, and I got so into that class. When the instructor came over for my turn to punch her hand, I only needed to punch it a few times, and she said, "You got it." I had watched the other women having to be coaxed to give it their all.

The person I was created to be is alive and well and, in some ways, getting younger. I have dreams, and I am starting to live them. It feels natural now. I am dancing at home to my praise music, and I am enjoying dancing for God as a form of worship. I used to do that long ago when Bob and I first bought our second home in Cranberry after we received our settlement. Over the last years, I know Bob's health problems became the forefront in my life and that my time and energies were needed somewhere else. As I write this story, I am in awe of just how many health issues Bob experienced, especially toward the end. I guess what I am more in awe about is that they did not dominate our life. Still, I do also see that there wasn't time to do some of the things I am now getting a chance to enjoy. I am making the best out of the worst. I still miss Bob and would rather be with him than doing some of the things I am doing to fill my time. I think that is why I want to serve and do things that rate high up on my list, just as being with Bob used to do. I don't want to just keep busy. If I do things for God, then I know those will be the greatest things I can do, even if they are small. I just can't wait to see what's next for me. I think God will find me some interesting and joyful work.

I also think that I am receiving the gift of wisdom at this time in my life. It doesn't come from asking for it, though it starts there. I think it comes from looking at the past, seeing God was there in the middle of everything, and knowing that he can bring goodness out of the storm. I think it starts with faith and the belief that he will give me whatever I ask for if it is in his will. This has been the worst and the best year of my life. It has been very painful to go on without Bob and know that he will no longer be here for and with me. It has also been a great year knowing that God was here with me in the midst of my grieving. He is here to comfort me and give me hope in all things.

I am what some may call an optimist. I am forever waiting to see how God will make something good out of every situation I invite him into when I talk and pray to him about the details of my life. You see, he truly is my best friend, and he knows all about me. He is there for me, and I just need to be patient to see what he will do. I understand there is no magic wand, and sometimes he is working on someone else's heart to bring about a change.

So with that said, I want to tell you where I am now. I am somewhere that is maybe a crossroad. I know that this book will be the end of a chapter in my life with Bob, and that is a good thing. All is well, and I have been taken from grief to joy. At first, I thought maybe I would be speaking to others about Bob's battle with cancer and giving others encouraging words, but now I see clearly that this book will accomplish that job and that I am free to move forward. I am looking with joyful anticipation for where God will lead me next. As I said earlier, he and I have been joking around about whether he will bring another man into my life. My hair has turned very curly lately, and I have stopped using my flat iron for now. I jokingly tell people that I think God has some man for me who likes curly hair. Now, just today I thought I would wear it straight, and I honestly cannot find my flat iron. I thought I had packed it and brought it to Ohio from North Carolina. So, I said, "Okay, God, maybe there really is something about this joke I am making about the curly hair, because what did I do with that flat iron?" Now you may think I am a little crazy, but that is okay. It is conversation I have with God, and it makes me aware of him and, more importantly, brings me peace and joy. Sometimes I catch a glimpse of myself in the mirror and see a smile on my face. I like to think God is pleased that I am beyond my self-pity and that I trust him for good things.

I told God, "When you get sick of hearing me talk, maybe that is when you will find me a new earthly husband." The truth is he will never get sick of hearing from me. I know he loves me, and I am his favorite child. I hope after reading my story you will agree with me and say, "Yes, I am his favorite child, too."

The reality is that our God is so big that he has the capacity for each of us to be his "favorite child." Some of his children just haven't realized that yet. I pray all will.

As you might suspect, men are one of my favorite topics to discuss with God these days. I wonder if he really does have someone for me. I joke about the kind of man I want and that I'd like a perfect one. I hear God say that there is no such kind. So, maybe I won't be getting one after all, or I will have to lower my standards to accepting a human. I know at times I've made my husband into a saint. That's because he is, by which I mean he is someone who is in a right relationship with Jesus. This last week I met another man and I was talking to him about my book, a subject I find myself telling others about more and more. He asked if I had a title yet.

Surprisingly, I had just been struggling with the fact that I didn't have the title. He encouraged me by saying, "I think God will give you it tonight during your sleep. He'll wake you up with it in the middle of the night."

When I saw him the next day, I told him I had the title: *Love at Second Sight*. Because he had just heard about the first time I met Bob, he said, "That makes sense." Then this guy asked if I woke up in the middle of the night with the title. I said, "No, but it was late." We both laughed. Then I explained the other meaning about taking a second look at Jesus, and he said, "See? That's perfect." Later, this guy told me he wants to take me out for a filet mignon to celebrate my book being published.

I do not know where any of this will lead, but I know God is hearing me. For now, Jesus is my husband, so I do have the perfect one. In all seriousness, I want a man who knows and loves God. I know God already knows and loves him. I don't know if God has someone in mind for me. As I said after Bob died and someone asked me if I'd marry again, my answer remains the same: if God has someone for me, he will present him. I did join Match.com for a few months, but after a while, I really only logged on for the stories. I think that has served its purpose, too. I never went out or even personally met anyone through that website, though I was sent a few e-mails from some fellow Christians giving me encouragement. I did get quite a few winks, and many were from younger men, so that was fun. After talking to other singles and especially some widows, I know what I am going through is just all part of the process of becoming single again.

For now, I am just excited to see where God and I are going. I am thinking of going on a mission trip this winter, and I am also asking God where I can serve him best in his kingdom. I will be honest and tell you that my life is not all roses. There are times I really want to have someone in my life and times when I feel alone. But I know I've felt that way before, even when I was married. It was usually the time I needed to seek the presence of God. I have no desire to cook anymore, and I would love to have someone help me make the decision about what I should make for dinner or whether we should we go out and grab a bite to eat. I know that was always such a hard decision for Bob and I. He would say, "What do you want to do?" Then, I would say, "Well, what do you want to do?" Then he would say, "Well, what do you want to cook?" and I would say, "Well, honestly nothing." Then he would say, "Well let's go out to eat." I'd say, "Okay, where do you want to go?" He'd say, "I don't know; where do you want to go?" I'd say, "I don't know; what are you hungry for?" and then he'd smile at me and say, "Well." He'd explain that he had everything he wanted in me, and he really didn't care where or what he ate. He wasn't picky. I was the picky eater, and he knew if he said, "Let's go get a burger," I'd say, "I was really hungry for Chinese." This was just a ritual we would go through sometimes. And we would always emphasize the "well" when we asked each other these questions. Bob sometimes would get goofy when I'd say "well," and he'd say, "That's a deep subject." That is why we'd add the "well" to our silly conversation. We had that quirky sense of humor that two people can share only when they build a life together. We were a great team. I miss him. But now I think I'd like to go to a new restaurant and try something I've never tasted yet. Have any suggestions? I just bet that God and Bob are smiling now and saying, "That's our Bobbie."

Post Script

I just wanted to let you know a little about Bob's here and now. First of all, I think Jesus is a Pittsburgh Steelers fan, and he and Bob have been watching a few games. Now don't get mad at me, but I'll tell you how I know. Do you remember the miracles the Steelers pulled out the last few times they won the Super Bowl? What is really neat is that the Steelers won the season Bob went to be with Jesus. They weren't even expected to make the playoffs that year. And it was quite a miraculous finish, I might add. I believe they celebrated in heaven by eating some chocolate cake and apple pie. It is, I am sure, still full of calories and sugar, but not to worry: those will not harm us once we get to heaven. Remember, in heaven all things are as they were created to be, perfect. It is the new order, and there are streets of gold and many mansions. For sure, there is love. The Bible tells us, "And now these three remain: faith, hope and love. The greatest of these is love." (1 Corinthians13:13).

If you would like to send a comment or a prayer request to the author, please forward them to Roberta Renk at her e-mail address robertarenk@msn.com or contact her on facebook page at Roberta Renk.

Afterword: Love at Second Sight

Remember when Bob asked me if I believed in love at first sight, and I said no? Then he said what I always referred to as his famous line, "Well, this is the second time I've seen you." So, it is from this that I arrived at the title, *Love at Second Sight*. The reasons I have decided to go with this title are twofold. The obvious is as a dedication to Bob. However, the second reason is the most important and meaningful to me. It is my hope that because of this story, many people who don't really know Jesus will take a second look at him and fall in love with him. I pray that through this story, he has become real and personal to you, if he was not already. Bob believed, and I still do, too, that by his stripes we are healed. Because Jesus died for us, we will live for eternity with God. But just as importantly, we can have his power right here, right now, because the Holy Spirit is here with us. It is the deepest desire of my heart that you, too, will find not only healing from the sins and hurts in your life, but also eternal life because you have accepted Jesus Christ as your personal Savior. I also pray that you will know your purpose and will find joy in that purpose. Then I know God truly will have changed all the bad things that happened to Bob to good for all of you who have come to know a little about Bob and a lot about Jesus because of this story.

Some Bible Verses to Consider

When you pass through the waters, I will be with you; And when you pass through the rivers, they will not sweep over you. When you walk through the fire, you will not be burned; the flames will not set you ablaze. For I am the Lord, your God, the Holy One of Israel, your Savior. (Isaiah 43:2–3)

What does the Scripture say? "Abraham believed God, and it was credited to him as righteousness." (Romans 4:3)

But he was pierced for our transgressions, he was crushed for our iniquities; the punishment that brought us peace was upon him, and by his wounds we are healed. (Isaiah 53:5)

All the prophets testify about him that everyone who believes in him receives forgiveness of sins through his name. (Acts 10:43)

God our Savior … wants all men to be saved and to come to a knowledge of the truth. (1 Timothy 2:3–4)

God saved us, not because of righteous things we had done, but because of his mercy. He saved us through the washing of rebirth and renewal by the Holy Spirit. (Titus 3:5)

He lifted me out of the slimy pit, out of the mud and mire; he set my feet on a rock and gave me a firm place to stand. (Psalm 40:2)

God says, "In the time of my favor I heard you, and in the day of salvation I helped you." I tell you, now is the time of God's favor, now is the day of salvation. (2 Corinthians 6:2)

If you confess with your mouth, "Jesus is Lord," and believe in your heart that God raised him from the dead, you will be saved. (Romans 10:9)

And I am convinced that nothing can ever separate us from his love. Death can't, life can't. The angels can't, and the demons can't. Our fears for today, our worries about tomorrow, and even the powers of hell can't keep God's love away. Whether we are high above the sky or in the deepest ocean, nothing in all creation will ever be able to separate us from the love of God that is revealed in Christ Jesus our Lord (Romans 8:38–39 NLT).

I believe your reading this book was not by accident. If you already are a follower of Christ, God may have brought this book to your mind because you are to pass it onto someone else. However, if you are not in a personal relationship with Jesus, maybe God is using this book to soften your heart so you will understand the depth of his love for you. All you need to do is tell God that you want him to be in your life and that you accept his gift of the death of his son, who took your place on judgment day. Because God is a just God, a price had to be paid for your sin, but because God is also merciful, he has made a way for you to come to him. He sent his son to die as a substitute for you. Jesus is the sacrificial lamb who died once for all. This gift is unconditional. It is yours for the asking. No strings attached. It is the gift of eternal life. So, come before his throne. Just whisper the words. *I accept Jesus as my Savior. I want him to be the ruler over my life.* That's all there is to it.

If you confess with your mouth, "Jesus is Lord," and believe in your heart that God raised him from the dead, you will be saved. (Romans 10:9)

If you are not sure and still have questions about how to become a Christian, or if you want to know whether the Bible is true, this website may have some answers for you: http:www.allaboutgod.com/become-a-christian.htm

Appendix: Poems

Ever since I was in the sixth grade, I have written poetry. I actually won a ribbon for some of my poetry when I was in the seventh grade. I was on the junior high school newspaper staff, and part of my job was to write some timely articles or poetry for the paper. As I said earlier in my book, I came across some of these poems, as well as some of the poems I had written to Bob, when I was looking in my memorabilia bin. So, for nostalgia's sake, I will include one of my earliest poems. I find it so simplistic, but I have to remember I was twelve and this was 1960.

New Year's Day

On New Year's Day, we have a happy time.
New Year's Day is a favorite of mine.
Resolutions should be made,
You should have all debts paid.
New Year's is a time to cheer,
It is a beginning of a new year.
Now the year begins again.
This has been going on since I don't know when.
Vacation is over, and school will then resume.
This is quite a different tune.

It's funny, but I also used one of these lines in my "Memories Colored Blue" poem, which I wrote after my Greece trip. Now I can tell you that when I wrote the following poem, it just came out. That was when I thought maybe I had some undeveloped talent.

Memories Colored Blue

We met at the church with luggage in hand.
We were excited to fly to a distant land.
Some came from Ohio and New England, too,
But born in Florida only one person not two.
We boarded the bus and the chatter began.
Mysteries awaited; through the airport we ran.
The plane was on time; we flopped down in our seat.
Nine hours later, we were in Frankfurt with swollen feet.
Several hours after, to Athens we went.
We met our tour guide and a day was spent.
Our hotel in the city was crisp and clean,
Quite the contrary to the Athens' scene.
We drove to the Temple of Poseidon that beautiful night.
We were all amazed at the ancient sight.
Then off we drove to a restaurant by the sea.
Everyone was eager to eat, especially me.
We had smelts, calamari, fried zucchini, and such.
We found out this was only the beginning touch.
A full course of meat and potatoes next came.
After that meal, we were never the same.
With our tummies all full, and our heads spinning some,
We went home to our beds; by then we were numb.

Next morning we rose to more food again.
I had the feeling this would never end.
I'd been on enough cruises before
To know there's food each time you exit the door.
The sun was shinning so bright in the sky.
Off to ancient Piraeus our tour bus did fly.
The ride through the city was a sight to behold.

Ancient myth and folklore were then being told.
More buildings, and buildings, the port and Aegean Sea:
These sights were all so marvelous to me.
At the port, and the Aegean I cruise ship sat there.
We were all smiling and had not a care.
We went through customs, climbed the steps to the ship,
Some with creaking knees, others with a popping hip.
We surrendered our passports and entered our room.
Grabbed our orange life jackets to prepare for doom.
The crew was waiting to tie our jackets tight.
"If there's a wreck", they said, "This is your plight.
You must jump off the boat and peench your nose tight."
Then we bid you all a very good night.
It took me a day for my head to clear.
Then I realized the lifeboats were ever so near.
The story about "jump and peench your nose like these"
Was meant only to be told in jest.
Now we know the results of jet lag and sleep depravation,
So do nothing unless you have a prior reservation.

As we traveled the Aegean Sea,
We were kept as busy as a bee.
There were many things to keep you busy,
That is, as long as you weren't dizzy.
There were dance lessons, unpacking, and touring the ship,
Or sitting in the casino, watching cards flip.
We had lessons about blackjack, poker, and roulette,
Now we know what it means to "hold your bet."
Later that day, the whistle blew.
Off to beautiful Mykonos Island we flew.
Up the hill to the windmills we went.
Hey, how many euros have we spent?
We returned to the ship, and it was time to eat.
There were people from around the world to meet.
Each meal was an experience all of its own.
It's amazing we've gone days without a phone.

Each morning we awoke to new adventures, it's true.
There was so very much to see, to eat, to say, and to do.
We had waffles with ice cream, spinach pie, and pizza, too.
We saw kitties, stray puppies, changing guards, and a zoo.
We shared our stories, we laughed out loud.
We had fun together, we should be proud.

We saw ruins upon ruins, civilization so bright,
It made us stop to think and gave us a fright.
We learned that a very long time ago,
Ancient man was found to have an ego.
He had ideas and dreams,
And as strange as it seems,
We haven't changed so much.

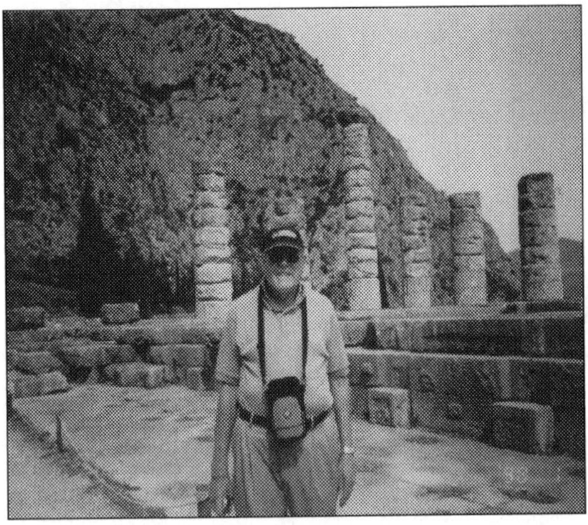

Some still have that special touch
To draw, to build, to write,
And to see the future bright.
As we looked upon the temples, the height at which they stood.
We were so amazed at all the things they could
Plan and make and dare to build,
And it seems they did not yield.
For we saw with our own eyes something that now can never be,

For the knowledge has been lost, maybe for eternity.
We saw Rhodes surrounded by walls of stone.
In some ways, it made me feel so alone.

To the top of Santorini, the cable car we did ride.
I conquered a fear, so I did it with pride.
We traveled to Corinth, Ephesus, Delphi, and Crete.
There was so much to see; the mountains were so neat.
There were statues, columns, amphitheaters, and caves.
Beautiful blue waters with small calming waves.
There were shopkeepers, tour guides, waiters, and maids.
It's sad to think as our memory fades
We might not remember their names or faces,
But hopefully we will remember the places,
And there will be warmth in our heart
Because each person played his part.
We were blessed to walk in the footsteps of the apostle Paul
And see some of the things that he saw.
We received the gift of the gospel because of this man,
And it's been my privilege to travel this land.
I came home and am learning to pray
That someone somewhere might say
That because of me, the good news they heard.
That is the heart of the living Word.

I had a silly thought the other day:
People from another world might be willing to pay
Many dollars, euros, cannoli, or such
To see how I lived and had so-o-o-o much.
This trip made me think about my life so far,
And as I gazed upon a star,
I know for certain that one thing is true:
What I value most about the trip is my time with you.
We have memories to cherish and a God we share, too.
I'm so glad for Jesus. Because of him, I met you.

Here are some of the poems I wrote to Bob. The last, of course, I read at his funeral. I wrote it in the middle of the night in about five minutes, two days before the funeral service. I felt it was God-inspired.

September 18, 1976

My Dearest Bob,

Once I was a restless child, my heart was on the roam,
But now I am a woman, and my heart has found a home.
For me, life has so much to offer; the years, a treasure awaits.
In the past I had no future, so I turned my life to fate.
Since I've come to know you, I have just begun to live.
I am so very happy because of all you give.
Each day I wake excited with all life has to bring.
I feel like a flower amid the breath of spring.
The world seems ever-changing; I see it as never before.
It's all because of you, the you whom I adore.

February 14, 1986

My Dearest Bob,

With pen in hand, I'll show you my heart.
You are the place where I shall start.
I love you dearly, I really do,
For all the things you say and do,
Because even when I don't agree,
I always know you'll still love me.
The days have come and the days have gone,
But the memories shall linger on.
There are so many so precious to me.
Come hold my hand, and you shall see
With words we can journey again
To happy times, remember when—
Mount Washington, our honeymoon, Boyce Park, a flower, a smile—
Does that take you back a while?
A ride to see the changing leaves,

The cemetery in the breeze,
Beaches and walks in the sand,
Especially when we went hand in hand,
The many times we together danced,
The many hours we romanced,
The lovely home together we made,
The special times we have prayed,
Rides we've taken in our cars,
The times we've gazed at the stars,
A lifetime of dreams still to come
With you, you are the one.
We have cherished memories to make come true,
And I want to make them all with you.

A Final Gift To My Love: My Gift From God

Oh Bob, where do I start?
It's hard to find words with this pain in my heart.
I know you hated to see me cry.
Just know, my love, that you'll never die.
You loved the poems I wrote to you,
But now they all seem way to few.
I wish I took the time to write you more,
But you know I spent so much time at the store!
I believe your spirit is here today,
And once again, we're together to pray.
God brought us together when we cried out for a mate.
We knew we loved each other on our second date.
Remember the first time we talked on the phone?
We knew from that moment we were never alone.
We hadn't even seen each other yet,
But I had this feeling you were a sure bet.
As we learned to live our life together,
We managed to find joy, no matter the weather.
We had times when I made life harder by making such a fuss.
We had sunshine with each grandchild given to us.
I learned so much from you with your quiet way.

I pray I'll remember you more with each passing day.
I'll see your face glowing and your beautiful smile.
I might just have to wait a little while.
Just know I'll always continue to pray,
And don't worry about me another day.
You were living proof, God answers our pleas,
And you know he will meet all of my needs.
Know in your heart, I am in peace today,
Because I'll be with you again someday.
As all gather to say our last goodbyes,
Do not be upset when you hear our cries.
It's just the Holy Spirit's way
Of helping us to pray today,
For sometimes there are no words to say
Until we see each other on the last day.
Know I love you with all my heart,
And yes, I think you were very smart.
I know you were such a humble man.
Now you will see that was part of God's plan.
That was the part of you I loved the most.
Now go be with Father, Son, and Holy Ghost.
Until then …

Following are two of many poems I have written since Bob died. Writing them seems to bring me closer to God.

The Desires of My Heart

God, you alone know the desires of my heart.
I come to you and do my part.
I question if you placed them there.
I bring my doubts and my care.

I try to hide just what I need.
I try to reason and to plead.
I try to hide my desires from your sight.
I try to mold them and make them right.

Then in this dance I hear you say,
Will you fear another day?
You cannot your desires hide, you see.
When will you learn to trust in me?

Do not fear to tell me all.
Do not question when I call.
Just learn to live with endless hope.
I'll make it strong; I'll make the yoke.

Patience and trust, I am teaching you.
When will my words finally get through?
I know you find me in the struggle,
But I don't want it to be this much trouble.

If only you could finally see.
You have everything you need in me.
I know your wants and your heart's desire.
I'm the one that set your heart on fire.

Just live your life with me each day,
And then you can truly say,
He knows my heart, my desires, my needs.
He knew them long before my pleas.

He knew them before he gave me life.
He knew my battles and my strife.
It is so hard to comprehend,
He has no beginning and no end.

It is even harder to know I'll fly,
And be with him when I'll die.
Then my heart will finally see
All he made me to be.

For then I will be truly one,

And to the banquet I will come.
I will understand his way.
I know he loves it when I pray.

So God, to you, I give my all.
You knew me even before the fall.
It is so strange to think,
You made me with only a wink.

It is so hard to grasp your love for me.
I whine and holler; how can that be?
To trust you knew me and still gave me life
And strengthened me to deal with strife.

Now as I look to see your plan,
I want my life to expand.
I want my destiny I have in you
To be what now will come true.

But even when I follow your call,
I still may wonder, *is this all?*
For that is how you made me to be,
Because in the struggle, I seek thee.

The Glory of God

The Glory of God I cannot see.
Can it be found when I behold a tree?
Maybe with the changing leaves in the fall
And the sun magnifies the beauty of it all.

In the tree's beauty is not where God's glory is found.
It is only when I look around
And think upon the creator himself and seek
That the awesomeness of him makes me weep.

The glory of God my mind cannot capture
But I may know of it in the rapture.
For God and his marvelous light
May I get a glimpse if I look just right.

I get a foretaste as I gaze at the galaxy so far away
And for a moment I stop to pray.
But God's glory is so much more
I get a glimpse when I see it pour.

But it is not in the rain itself that God's glory be;
It is so much more than that you see.
It is not in a song or a tune.
It is not even in the flowers in June.

I cannot understand it yet,
Though poets and artist have tried to capture it.
God's glory is such a wonder to me;
It is beyond all captivity.

My mind cannot even understand electricity,
But how much great can God's glory be?
He is magnificent all knowing and wise,
But that is only a speck of the prize.

There are no earthly ways to describe it to man.
I cannot even see it in the grains of sand.
There are no paintings to capture his face.
I cannot even understand outer space.

How to explain God's glory to you?
I cannot imagine it in a drop of dew.
My mind is so small there's no way to seize it all.
So how can I tell of God's glory in the fall?

When I think of every song that's been sung
Or a smile of a child when she is young.
That would not begin to touch God's glory.
There is so much more to the story.

But it is not really in a story;
That is not where I find God's glory.
In the Word I may find a clue,
But even the Good Book will not do.

Is God's glory found in his son?
No, not even there am I done.
God's glory cannot be seen in his love for me,
But I know it is in my destiny.

God's glory is so above us all.
Maybe Adam and Eve saw it before the fall.
But somehow I don't think that is true.
Can we find it in a rainbow or the color blue?

I feel in my heart that God's glory is near,
But then as a human I begin to fear.
To seek the glory of God, do I ask?
Or am I hiding behind a mask?

The only time I can capture a trace
Is when I look around this place.
I see the tangible, and I know I exist,
But beyond that I am amiss.

There are words like "magnificent," but what does that mean?
Even in this, God's glory can't be captured or seen.
His attributes I talk of sometimes,
But even that is beyond my mind.

The Holy Spirit in us gives us the gifts,
But even that God's glory lifts.
For God's glory is unspeakable,
If I think I see it all, I'm a fool.

What is God's glory to me?
When I am in heaven, then I'll see.
When pure love found a second in my heart,
Maybe then it was a minuscule part.

But for now, the mystery I must be patient with,
And I know it will be reminiscent
Of just a moment here and there in my life—
Maybe in the moment when I became a wife.

God's glory is such a mystery to me.
It keeps me waiting in captivity.
I am captured to want to be with Him,
But in the next moment I begin to sin.

But I know God made me to desire Him so,
And to God's glory I want to go.
But for now His glory I must seek,
And the thought of it makes me weak.

So the answer to this question I don't have for you.
It is an essence of God; I know that's true.
But what in earthly terms does that mean?
God's glory is beyond me; it can't be seen.

God's glory keeps my heart on fire.
It is what should be my pure desire.
But to you I must tell the truth:
I don't even see God's glory in the book of Ruth.

My mind and spirit are seldom one.
And perfect one day I'll become.
But only then will I truly see
All God's glory is to be.

But until that day I pray I'll ponder more
And allow my heart to be an open door.
God's glory one day will come to me,
But for now I'll pray to see.

And as I go to him in prayer,
Maybe my heart will take me there,
To the place. God's glory I will seek,
But I must then become humble and weak.

For only when I surrender all,
Will God's glory begin to fall?
Upon my spirit with eyes of love,
God's glory I seek on the wings of the dove.

Though this poem was written by me,
In it I hope God's glory you'll see.
For when we search to seek his face,
He does each one of us embrace.

He is magnificent, holy, pure.
I could go on and say much more.
He is all knowing, majestic, beyond belief.
He designed all. Just look at a reef.

He is loving, generous and kind,
Patient, never changing. He healed the blind.
He is self-sacrifice, willing to pay any price,
Always there to answer prayer.

But the glory of God I cannot see.
It keeps me waiting in captivity.
To seek his face may I always look
And read of Him in His book.

But I must remember God's glory. To us be known
If hearts are open and not of stone.
To seek God's glory he wants us to do.
He's asking me, and he is asking you.

"Seek me and you shall find.
Knock and the door shall be answered.
I am with you always.
I came to save the lost."

These words he has brought to me.
Maybe typing them is my destiny.
To seek him and know he's here,
To that my heart will hold near.

To God give the glory, I've heard it said.
I think I have even heard it read.
I hear "glory" used so much.
I pray next time I'll feel his touch.

God's glory is soon to come.
I wait for the day when we are one.
In heaven with him I long to be
No longer waiting in captivity.

This Fourth of July holiday, both of my grandchildren who live here in Canton came over to watch the fireworks with me and sleep over. I have the perfect location to watch fireworks right from my deck because the fireworks appear in the sky straight out in front of me. It is an awesome display each year. I bought fun candy for the kids, which was a big surprise because this grandma doesn't usually give the kids candy. So, it made it special. Our plates were full of junk food and colorful candies, and we sat out on the deck and drank our grape juice, too. It was quite the party with just the three of us, and they kept saying it was the best party they went to *ever*. They are so sweet, and we were laughing and had a great time. We put up the umbrella so we wouldn't get moon burn. Megan and Ryan thought that was so silly. We watched the fireworks that were far off in the distance, and then, around 9:30, when it was really dark, my neighborhood fireworks started. Well, they looked really huge because they were so close. Ryan kept saying, "Oh my!" and "Ooooh!" and Megan said they were so pretty. She liked the ones that looked like Christmas. We had an intellectual discussion about how fireworks were made, and Ryan asked how manufacturers got them to make the different noises that some of them make. I said, "I haven't a clue. I just think its dynamite." Then I made myself laugh.

These times spent with my grandchildren have inspired me to write the last poem I will share with you titled, "A Grandma's Prayer."

A Grandma's Prayer

Thank you, God, for the little ones you've sent to me.
They bring such joy and happiness, you see.
I love to hear them giggle; it's so sweet.
That sound stays with me until again we meet.
To be a grandma is such a treasured gift.
When I am with them, it gives my heart a lift.
Even when they want to jump and play,
I'm so happy to have them with me that day.
I pray I will grow to be the one
They come to when they think of having fun.
I want to be the smile they love to see,
Remind them of the fun we had when they were three.
We played such silly games, it's true,
But we were happy then and never blue.
Our world was innocent and pure.

I want that feeling to last forever more.
To be a grandma is a special gift for me.
There is no price to put on it, you see.
I love to feel that sense of bliss.
Some things in life I never want to miss.
So Lord, please bless me more each day,
And bring my grandchildren here to play.
This is a grandma's prayer I pray.
Forever let our hearts be open and not stray,
And thank you once again I say
For making me a grandma in every way.

MEDICAL ONCOLOGY ASSOCIATES, P.C.

SAMUEL A. JACOBS, M.D.
RONALD G. STOLLER, M.D.
MARTIN F. EARLE, M.D.
JEROME E. SEID, M.D.
J. FRANKLIN VIVERETTE, M.D.

5200 CENTRE AVENUE
PITTSBURGH, PA 15232
TELEPHONE (412) 621-7778
FACSIMILE (412) 621-7359

RENK, ROBERT
10/23/95

PROBLEM #1: Metastatic rectal carcinoma.

Robert underwent a LAR for a rectal carcinoma recently, and at least 3 lesions were noted in the right lobe of the liver. He has recovered from surgery but has not gained weight, and he is here to discuss therapeutic options.

PHYSICAL EXAM: Pleasant male. BP: 130/80.

HEENT:	Benign.
LYMPH NODES:	No evidence of Virchow's adenopathy.
CHEST:	Clear.
CARDIAC:	S1 and S2 are regular.
ABDOMEN:	Longitudinal scar healing well. Liver and spleen are not palpable. No masses are noted.
EXTREMITIES:	No evidence of edema.

IMPRESSION:

Metastatic rectal carcinoma with at least 3 liver lesions in the right lobe of the liver. Postop CEA was elevated at 27.2. CT scan of the abdomen showed a vague lesion in the right lobe of the liver. It wasn't entirely clear whether it was metastatic or not. There was also a defect noted adjacent to the right psoas, but they weren't sure whether or not this was postsurgical.

PLAN:

1. There are multiple options at this time; however, I think my bias would be to:
    1. Repeat CEA.
    2. Do an MRI scan of his liver to see if the liver lesions can be more clearly demonstrated.
    3. Place an infusaport.
    4. Begin Leucovorin/5-FU chemotherapy to see if he responds. If he appears to have a reasonable response with a decreasing CEA, then I think one can consider surgically resecting his liver lesions. If he is indeed resectable, one can consider treating him with further Leucovorin/5-FU and considering radiation therapy to the pelvis; however, that decision will be made down the road.

RENK, ROBERT
10/23/95
PAGE 2

<u>PLAN CONT.</u>

2. I had a lengthy discussion with Robert and his wife for over 40 minutes, and multiple questions were answered. They understand the gravity of the situation and the therapeutic approach and agree to proceed. They do understand that, even if he is resectable, his chances of achieving long-term survival is only in the order of about 25%.

Martin F. Earle, M.D.

MFE:amr

cc: Arnold Fingeret, M.D.
Dr. McCandless - HealthAmerica (Century III)

MEDICAL ONCOLOGY ASSOCIATES, P.C.

SAMUEL A. JACOBS, M.D.
RONALD G. STOLLER, M.D.
MARTIN F. EARLE, M.D.
JEROME E. SEID, M.D.
J. FRANKLIN VIVERETTE, M.D.

5200 CENTRE AVENUE
PITTSBURGH, PA 15232
TELEPHONE (412) 621-7778
FACSIMILE (412) 621-7359

RENK, Robert
2/15/96

Problem #1: Metastatic rectal carcinoma.

Robert underwent a right lobectomy and a left wedge resection of a metastatic nodule involving his liver at West Penn Hospital. Apparently there were 5 metastatic lesions noted and all of the margins of resection were free. The pt had a stormy post-op course w/ bowel obstruction necessitating placement of a stent. He also had pancreatitis and apparently everything is on the mend. He still is jaundiced although his LFTs have improved.

PHYSICAL EXAMINATION: He is a thin, jaundiced male. BP: 120/80. Weight: 142#.

HEENT:	Positive scleral icterus.
LYMPH NODES:	No evidence of peripheral adenopathy.
CHEST:	Clear. Infusaport has been removed.
CARDIAC:	S1 and S2 are regular.
ABDOMEN:	Multiple surgical scars. Liver is not palpable. Minimal tenderness in the RUQ.

LABORATORY DATA: (2/8/96) - GGTP 951, bilirubin 8.8.

IMPRESSION:
1. Successful hepatic resection although stormy post-op course.

PLAN:
1. At this time I certainly would not consider any further chemotherapy or radiation until his LFTs normalize. Note: His CEA is down to 5.9 which is a good sign. If we do do anything, we will consider infusional **5-FU** and RT to the pelvis, however, we will reserve this for a later date. He will be following up w/ Dr. Fingeret and also Dr. Holman in the near future.

M Earle

Martin F. Earle, M.D.

MFE:jll

cc: Arnold Fingeret, M.D.
Bridget McCandless, M.D.

— OTHER OFFICES —

ASPINWALL MONROEVILLE IRTON JEFFERSON

MEDICAL ONCOLOGY ASSOCIATES, P.C.

SAMUEL A. JACOBS, M.D.
RONALD G. STOLLER, M.D.
MARTIN F. EARLE, M.D.
JEROME E. SEID, M.D.
J. FRANKLIN VIVERETTE, M.D.

5200 CENTRE AVENUE
PITTSBURGH, PA 15232
TELEPHONE (412) 621-7778
FACSIMILE (412) 621-7359

RENK, ROBERT
3/25/96

PROBLEM #1: Metastatic rectal carcinoma.

Robert has been feeling a bit better and has had repeat liver function tests and according to the patient they are remarkably improved.

<u>PHYSICAL EXAM:</u> He is a pleasant male. BP: 140/90. Wt. 153# up from 142#.

HEENT: Sclerae have cleared. They are no longer icteric.
LYMPH NODES: No evidence of adenopathy.
CHEST: Clear.
CARDIAC: S1 and S2 are regular.
ABDOMEN: Multiple scars. Liver is not palpable.

<u>IMPRESSION:</u>
1. He appears to be clinically better.

PLAN:

1. Will arrange for an infusiport placement to complete his therapy which will require infusion of **5-FU** and RT to the pelvis followed by **Leucovorin 5-FU**.
2. Recheck liver function tests and once they approach normality will proceed with chemotherapy to complete his planned treatment.

Martin F. Earle, M.D.
MFE/cdl

cc: Dr. Arnold Fingerette
Dr. Bridget McCandless - HealthAmerica (Century III)

— OTHER OFFICES —

ASPINWALL MONROEVILLE WEIRTON JEFFERSON

KEYSTONE DIGESTIVE DISORDER CONSULTANTS, P.C.

SPECIALIZING IN DIGESTIVE DISORDERS - LIVER DISEASE - ENDOSCOPY

ROBERT J. KANIA, M.D.
[illegible]ER J. MOLLOY, M.D.

DAVID H. VAN THIEL, M.D.
SENIOR CONSULTANT
LIVER DISEASE

MRH 16106

August 13, 1996

Michelle Organist, M.D.
2027 Lebanon Church Road
W. Mifflin, PA 15122

RE: ROBERT RENK

Dear Dr. Organist:

I saw Mr. Renk in the office and went over the data available to me.

He looks amazingly well and so far his therapy has been successful. At the present time I don't have an answer for his significant elevation of GGTP and alkaline phosphotase. We usually see such significant elevations, especially in GGTP, with chemical effects on the liver such as drugs and alcohol which is obviously not his case. Whether there is a biliary problem is not too evident at this time. The mild dilitation of his common bile duct in general on his CT scan does not bother me with looking at his partial hepatectomy there may be some compensatory CBD dilitation. The CT failed to show any obvious metastatic lesions and his CEA of 5.4 really does not suggest the presence of metastatic disease. Whether there could be some bild duct reaction such as a cholangiolitic hepatitis is also unknown. I have requested a series of blood results to get an idea of the fluctuations of his liver functions both on and off chemotherapy. We may suggest the possibility of a repeat ERCP and/or liver biopsy pending quick review of these results.

Thank you for having me see Mr. Renk and participate in his care.

With best regards,

Robert J. Kania, M.D.

RJKbk

MED REC
OK TO FILE
MD ______
RN ______
MA ______
UMA ______

4815 Liberty Avenue • Pittsburgh, PA 15224 • (412) 681-1616 • Fax (412) 681-6438
575 Lincoln Avenue • Pittsburgh, PA 15202 • (412) 681-1616 • Fax (412) 681-6438
500 Hospital Way • McKeesport, PA 15132 • (412) 672-1077 • Fax (412) 672-2106

Hematology-Oncology Associates

artin F. Earle, MD
erome E. Seid, MD
75 Coal Valley Road
Lurton, PA 15025
12-469-1926
12-469-7220 (FAX)

RENK, ROBERT
07/14/97

PROBLEM:
Metastatic rectal carcinoma, status post hepatic resection with slowly rising CEA.

Robert feels quite well. His most recent blood work revealed that his liver functions have improved somewhat although his gamma GTP remains elevated at 201. His CEA is up to 8.9.

PHYSICAL EXAM:	He is a pleasant male. Blood pressure: 140/80. Weight: 166 pounds.
HEENT:	Benign.
LYMPH NODES:	No evidence of Virchow's adenopathy or other peripheral adenopathy.
CHEST:	Clear.
CARDIOVASCULAR:	S1 and S2 are regular.
ABDOMEN:	Multiple scars. Liver is not palpable.
EXTREMITIES:	No evidence of edema.

IMPRESSION:

A rising CEA although asymptomatic. He had a colonoscopy last fall and the chances of having local recurrence is quite small. I suspect that he does indeed possess disease in his liver or that his elevated CEA is a manifestation of his diabetes and elevated liver function tests.

ever
eturned
there

PLAN:

He is to move down near Tampa, Florida and we will hold any further evaluation per the patient's request. We will arrange for his blood work to be rechecked in August and we will include a serum ferritin.

Martin F. Earle, M.D.

MFE/mc

cc: Nathan Bennett, M.D.

Hematology-Oncology Associates

artin F. Earle, MD
erome E. Seid, MD
75 Coal Valley Road
lairton, PA 15025
12-469-1926
12-469-7220 (FAX)

RENK, ROBERT
06/12/97

PROBLEM:
Metastatic rectal carcinoma, status post hepatic resection.

Robert remains asymptomatic, however his CEA continues to rise and is now 8.5. His liver function tests have dramatically improved, and the reason for this is not entirely clear. Perhaps this is related to control of his diabetes.

PHYSICAL EXAM:	Pleasant male. Blood pressure 140/80. Weight of 162.
HEENT:	Sclerae clear.
LYMPH NODES:	No evidence of Virchow's adenopathy.
CHEST:	Clear.
CARDIOVASCULAR:	S2 and S2 regular.
ABDOMEN:	Multiple scars. Liver is not palpable. No tenderness noted.
EXTREMITIES:	No evidence of edema.

IMPRESSION:
CEA continues to rise, although no obvious recurrence.

PLAN:
Will CT his chest, and have him return in approximately one month. Prior to return will arrange for CBC, biochemical profile, and CEA. If his CEA goes up further, will proceed with a CEA scan and a colonoscopy.

Martin F. Earle, M.D.

MFE/hkb

NCI CCC. Affiliated with the University of Pittsburgh Cancer Institute, a Comprehensive Cancer Center designated by the National Cancer Institute.

Ambulatory Care Visit

RENK, ROBERT G - 195194

Result Type:	Ambulatory Care Visit
Result Date:	Thursday, April 04, 2002 8:25 PM
Result Status:	Auth (Verified)

*** Final Report ***

Ambulatory Care Visit

DATE OF VISIT: 04/04/2002

REASON FOR EVALUATION: Followup stage IV rectal cancer.

Mr. Renk is doing well without cancer-related symptoms. ECOG performance status is 0. Due to his glycemic control, he may require insulin.

MEDICATIONS:
1. Glucophage 850 mg p.o. t.i.d.
2. Avandia 5 mg p.o. q.d.
3. Prandin 0.05 mg p.o. t.i.d.
4. Multivitamin.
5. Glucotrol Extended Release 10 mg p.o. b.i.d.

Past medical history, family history, social history, and allergies are as per my noted on 08/05/00.

REVIEW OF SYSTEMS: RESPIRATORY: Unremarkable. CARDIAC: Unremarkable. GASTROINTESTINAL: Unremarkable apart from an incisional hernia. ENDOCRINE: Unremarkable. HEME/LYMPH: Unremarkable. MUSCULOSKELETAL: Unremarkable. GENITOURINARY: Unremarkable. PSYCHIATRIC: Unremarkable.

PHYSICAL EXAMINATION:
VITAL SIGNS: Height 175 cm, weight 75.7 kg, blood pressure 154/74, temperature 97.60 F, heart rate 86 beats per minute, respirations 18 breaths per minute.
GENERAL: Healthy-appearing gentleman.

Ambulatory Care Visit

RENK, ROBERT G - 195194

UPPER EXTREMITIES: Normal.
HEENT: Pupils are equal, round, and reactive to light. Oropharynx normal.

LYMPH NODES: There is no cervical or supraclavicular lymphadenopathy.
CHEST: Respiratory clear to auscultation and percussion.
CARDIAC: Regular rate and rhythm without added sounds or murmurs.
ABDOMEN: Postoperative scars. Easily reducible hernia at the lateral aspects of the abdominal scar. Left lower quadrant colostomy.

INVESTIGATIONS: Complete blood count and chemistry group within normal limits apart from elevated glucose at 304 mg/dL. CA has risen slightly to 220.7 ng/mL. CT scan of abdomen and pelvis reveals interval development of a subcentimeter nodule in the right lung base which is likely to be a pulmonary metastasis. In addition, there is a subtle low-attenuation region within the left lobe of the liver in the medial segment which may represent hepatic metastases.

IMPRESSION:

1. Asymptomatic stage IV rectal cancer.
2. Non-insulin-dependent diabetes mellitus.

RECOMMENDATION: I had a complete and in-depth discussion with Mr. Renk regarding the radiology findings. Treatment options include continued observation in view of the asymptomatic nature of this disease, palliative irinotecan chemotherapy, or protocol therapy. He received 6 months of "adjuvant" irinotecan therapy in 1998, following anastomotic recurrence. He has previously had continuous infusion fluorouracil as combined modality therapy, as adjuvant therapy. Discussed in detail with Mr. Renk. He plans to travel to Pittsburgh in the next 2 weeks, and he will review his treatment options with the medical oncologist there.

Dictated by Chris R Garrett,
MD____Chri
s R Garrett, MD

DD: 04/04/2002 8:25 P
DT: 04/08/2002 7:39 A
ID: 000028823.mdq

Printed by: Hensley, Karen E
Printed on: 4/15/2002 10:34 AM